MOMENTS
AND
MEMORIES

MOMENTS AND MEMORIES

REFLECTIONS OF EMERITI FACULTY

Edited by

Victoria R. Gillis, Debra B. Jackson, Kathy N. Headley, and Marty Duckenfield

CLEMSON UNIVERSITY PRESS

CONTENTS

FOREWORD

THE CLEMSON TAPESTRY

Robert H. Jones
Clemson University Executive Vice President
for Academic Affairs and Provost

An insightful way to understand the values and culture of a university is to ask students and employees to share their experiences. We regularly do this at Clemson, and when the results are summarized, we see an institution marked by dramatic change through time, with consistent and admirable core values, a special relationship between faculty and students, and a reputation for excellence that has grown far beyond the borders of our state. This is the gestalt of Clemson, based on the average experience. Yet, human nature being what it is, each individual has a unique and highly variable set of experiences. Some are humorous, some are sad or tragic, some are caught up in the winds of social and technological changes, and some are more random. The individual experiences of Clemson's people are interwoven into our collective fabric, and all are fascinating.

This book provides revealing and thought-provoking examples of real Clemson experiences, collected from faculty who have earned appointments in our nationally acclaimed Emeritus College, now celebrating its twentieth anniversary. Throughout their successful careers, Clemson's emeritus faculty have dedicated themselves to student success, excellent scholarship, and impactful outreach. Their accomplishments and successes were achieved despite economic downturns, multiple administrations, and multiple national or global crises. Our faculty have driven Clemson's emergence as a truly global university through persistence and dedication to their profession.

The stories shared here strike home for me, for I, too, am a product of Clemson, first as a student from 1976 to 1981 and lately as an administrator from 2014 to present. They reveal that life as a faculty member is rewarding and fun, although also challenging and frequently difficult. Some experiences seem to be a happy outcome of serendipity, yet I suspect that most such cases are at least partly predicated on preparation and intellect. Other experiences reveal the challenges of earning promotion and tenure and, sometimes, the struggles to feel fully appreciated.

The rich tapestry of faculty experiences in this book reveal humility and dedication to the land-grant mission and our institution. They make me proud to be a Clemson Tiger.

INTRODUCTION

The Emeritus College is home to more than eight hundred retired Clemson University faculty. The college is their academic home and provides a unique connection to their professional lives, the love of learning, the love of teaching, and the love of questioning. The college provides the intellectual opportunities emeriti enjoyed and, more importantly, a way to remain engaged with their colleagues. The Emeritus College is the place where faculty cross disciplines and connect with other emeriti to have richer retirements. The question at retirement is not what will I do but what all can I do? Faculty develop new areas of expertise, expand their community service, and contribute to Clemson University and the larger Clemson community in a variety of ways.

The idea for *Moments and Memories* grew out of a conversation in our Emeritus College memoir group. Emeritus College interest groups are just one benefit of having survived academe long enough to retire. As we discussed the idea for emeriti faculty to write about their memories of Clemson, one story would inevitably lead to another, all told with humor and an appreciation for academic lives well lived.

This collection of essays is our opportunity to celebrate our contributions to Clemson University. The emeriti played a role in the Clemson of 2022 because of their teaching, research, and service from the past. The stories range from 1961 forward, spanning 61 years. They cover Clemson presidents from R. C. Edwards to James P. Clements and celebrate what seems like countless academic leaders and deans, many reorganizations (small and large), and numerous strategic plans. *Moments and Memories* takes the reader through a series of entertaining vignettes that provide a glimpse into the academic life of faculty members at a land-grant university. These pages show how the interaction of research, teaching, and service enriched the lives of professors and students alike. We sincerely hope that our reflections on the *Moments and Memories* associated with Clemson University give readers a taste of the special place that is Clemson and the warm feeling that is the Clemson University family. For some, the experience of the Clemson family is within the Emeritus College. *Moments and Memories* is our way of celebrating the twentieth anniversary of the Emeritus College, a place where we have found "something to do after breakfast." We know that having an active Emeritus College requires resources and that such resources are often scarce. We are profoundly grateful for the university's continuing support.

We wish to thank the emeriti faculty who contributed to this book by sharing their experiences, photos, memorabilia, and sketches. We are so thankful to Emeritus President James F. Barker for permission to use his sketches of the Clemson campus and to the archives for photos. We thank the Task Force members, Kathy Headley and Marty Duckenfield, for countless hours spent meeting online, providing feedback to contributors, and generally getting this manuscript out the door. A special thank you to Jill Hammond for jumping into the fray with both feet in the middle of this project.

We hope you enjoy the stories. Some are funny, some are not. All make up the history of Clemson University.

Gillis, Jackson, Headley, and Duckenfield

CHAPTER 1

President's Home (1/2/2000) (With permission of artist, Clemson President Emeritus James F. Barker)

PROF. KLUGH'S RECIPE FOR MUSCADINE, SCUPPERNONG, GRAPE, AND BLACKBERRY WINE

The wine was described as "Between Dry and Sweet." It should be noted that Professor Bradbury attributed this recipe to "Prof. Klugh," or Professor Williston Wrightman Klugh, Clemson Class of 1896. He was a long-time professor of drawing and design and known as "Wee Willy." An apparatus for brewing the wine was provided as well. It is thought that the apparatus design was added to the original at a later date.

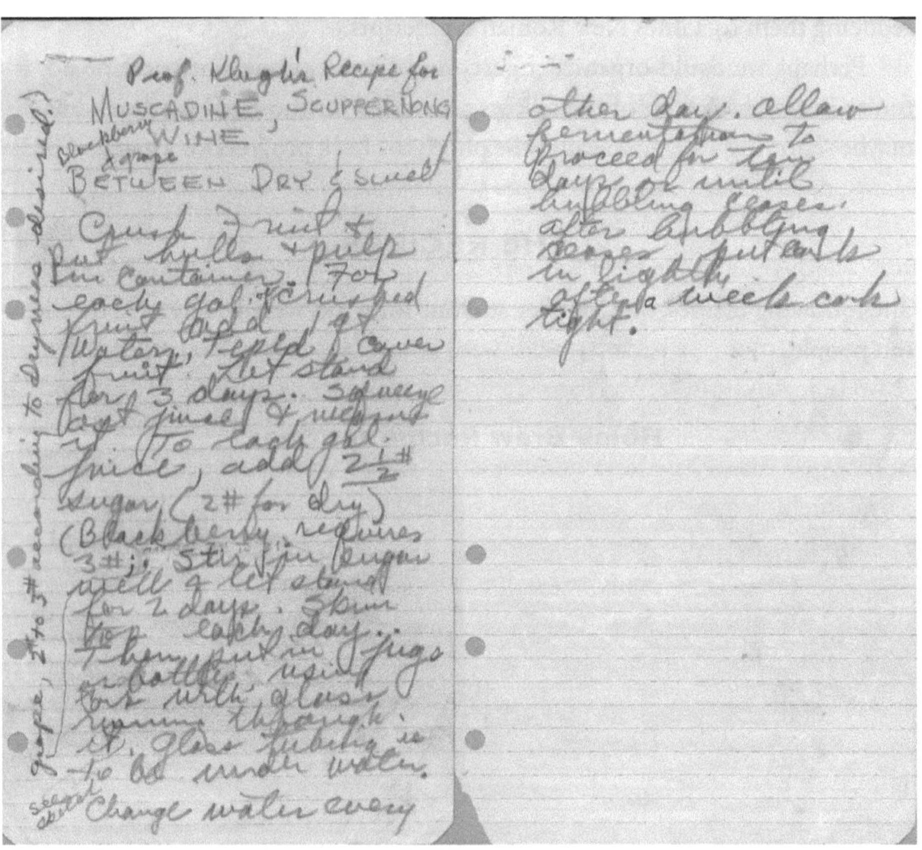

Original copy of Prof. Klugh's Recipe for Muscadine, Scuppernong Wine (With permission of Cecil O. Huey, Jr.)

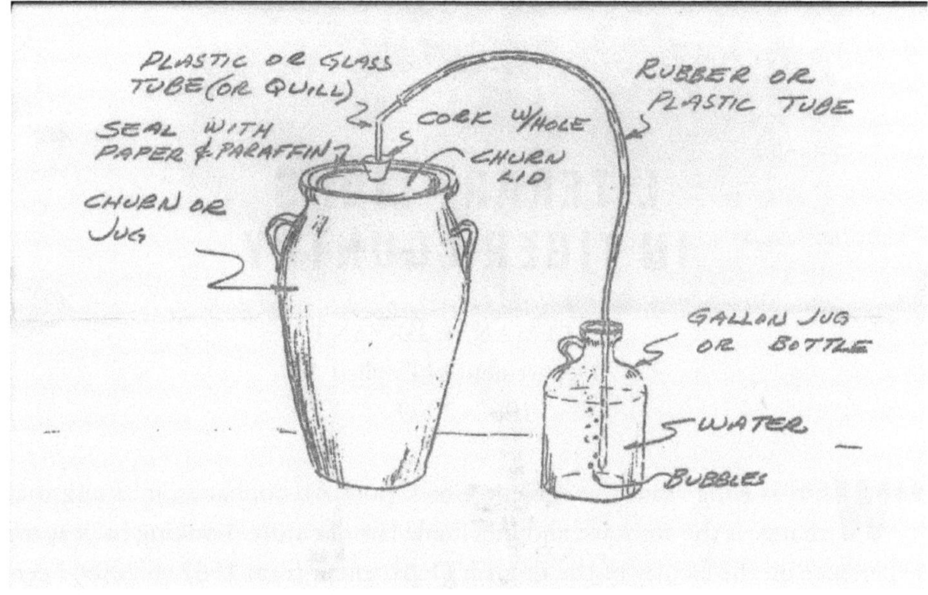

How to build your brewing apparatus for wine. (With permission of Cecil O. Huey, Jr.)

LITERARY LIONS
IN TIGER COUNTRY

HALLMAN B. BRYANT
Department of English
1962–2009

"Whirl is King" said the ancient Greek poet Aristophanes, meaning that change is the constant and inevitable law of nature. Looking back at my experience on the faculty of the English Department from 1962 to 2009, I certainly agree with the poet's observation.

Clemson in the early 1960s was evolving from being an all-male military school and was then named Clemson A&M College. Many of the faculty and administration still retained military titles, and all students were required to participate in ROTC unless they were veterans. On drill days, the cadets filled Bowman Field, a sharp contrast to the meager squads who drill there today.

Other military traditions still prevailed, such as the rat system that encouraged hazing of freshmen as well as rat haircuts and wearing beanies called rat caps until the South Carolina game on Big Thursday.

By today's standards, Clemson undergraduates of that day were rather provincial. Most of them came from small towns in South Carolina, and many were the first in their families to go to college and were culturally unsophisticated. Thus, the English Department sponsored extracurricular literary events to expose our students to writers and speakers and, we hoped, to promote more interest in literature.

During the fall semester of 1962, the writer Truman Capote came to Clemson to give a reading to the students and faculty. All students were required to attend so Capote would be assured of a large (but a captive) audience. Thus, Tillman Hall was filled to capacity for Capote's appearance. At this point in his career, prior to the publication of his sensational book *In Cold Blood*, few people had heard of Capote, so the students did not know what to expect. After an introduction by Professor Dick Calhoun, whose remarks raised the audience's expectations, Capote stepped up to the podium and began speaking, and the students started to laugh. His voice was bizarre to say the least, being prissy, high-pitched, and lispy. It looked like it was going to be an embarrassing evening for everyone, but the students soon got over the strangeness of Capote's voice and began to listen to the story that he was reading—"A Christmas Memory." Its Yuletide setting has made it a seasonal classic. The story is about an odd friendship between a seven-year-old boy, Buddy, and an elderly female cousin called "Sook." It takes place in Alabama during the depths of the Great Depression, and the pair of friends is gathering pecans as well as some whiskey to make fruitcakes for Christmas gifts, one of which they mail to President Franklin Roosevelt. The rest of the plot is about flying kites that they give to each other for Christmas. Afterward, Buddy is sent off to military school, and Sook becomes demented and dies. Soon after getting this news, Buddy looks up and says on that cold December morning, "I kept searching the sky, as if I expected to see rather like hearts a lost pair of kites hurrying toward heaven." After Capote finished reading, there was no more laughter and maybe even a few moist eyes among students moved by the poignant story.

Some years later, another literary lion came to Clemson to speak to the students. The year was 1971, and the speaker was the famous poet and novelist James Dickey, who was riding high on the success of the movie *Deliverance* that had just been made from his novel by the same title. Dickey was also returning to Clemson as a favorite son because he was an alumnus, having played as a freshman on the 1941 football team. He dramatizes the experience in a poem titled "The Bee," which is the only poem about Clemson football to ever appear in a college textbook.

At this point in his career, Dickey's drinking was having a deleterious effect on his behavior. Apparently, the head of the English Department was not aware of this fact, so he assigned Barry Hannah, a young writer who would later become famous, to act as Dickey's cicerone. Unfortunately, Hannah, like Dickey, also had an affinity for strong drink, so the first thing they did was to share a fifth of Jack Daniels. The next day, fearful that Dickey might not be able to perform, Bill Hunter, a local physician who had been his teammate, was called in to sober the poet up, which he did by administering pure oxygen. The effect was only temporary—Dickey slipped off for a six-pack of beer and other beverages, continuing to drink until his evening appearance. At seven o'clock that evening, a large audience was awaiting Dickey in Tillman Auditorium. When Dickey came out on the stage, he looked unsteady, and he was oddly dressed in a buckskin coat and a wide-brimmed black hat with a feather stuck in the brim. He was obviously under the influence, slurring his words. After reading two poems, he stopped and announced that he would not be able to continue, then he bowed and walked off the stage. There was a stunned silence as the audience realized that the event was over after only ten minutes, but because these performances were free of charge, they filed out without protest. As a postscript to this embarrassing moment for the Department of English and the university, the Speakers Bureau was reluctant to pay Dickey his fee of $1,500 for reading only two poems. By this time, Dickey was sober and contrite, and he agreed to return to Clemson at a future date to fulfill his contract, which he did a few years later. Performing before a much smaller audience—because attendance was not compulsory this time around—he gave a brilliant reading of some of his best-known poems.

The last literary lion who came to Clemson was the novelist John Knowles, the author of *A Separate Peace*, a well-known book that is widely read in high school and college English classes today. Knowles was invited to Clemson in 1991 to speak to our students who were studying this novel. I was in charge of his visit because I had recently authored a book on his life and works, which focused on *A Separate Peace*. Unlike the appearances of Capote and Dickey, the public events at which Knowles spoke all went well. He was in his early sixties, dressed in a conventional way, and spoke in a normal voice, slightly refined by an Ivy League accent. Above all, he was sober, having sworn off alcohol. After his speaking appearances the following day, he had been invited to sit in the president's box during the Clemson–North Carolina State game. Knowles was delighted and liked being treated as a VIP. I don't recall much about the game except that the Tigers wore all-purple uniforms for the first time and that not wearing the usual orange and white made them look foreign. When half-time came, the president stood up and announced that he wished to recognize some special people who were his guests that day. I could see Knowles perk up at this news, anticipating being recognized. But the people who were asked to stand when their names were called were all textile executives, including J. P. Stevens and Roger Milliken. Poor Knowles waited in vain for his name to be called, but he obviously had not made the list of notables. He did not say anything, but I could see that his ego had been deflated. It was an egregious omission, and I was deeply chagrined that an important writer who was a guest of the university had not been given due public recognition.

In conclusion, I could have used other events at Clemson as the basis for this *recherche du temps perdu*, such as the day Kennedy was shot, the week of the Cuban missile crisis, or the enrollment of Harvey Gantt as the first Black student, but I will leave those moments for someone else to record.

THE SHALLOW END

Cecil O. Huey Jr.
Department of Mechanical Engineering
1969–2006

Following a late-sixties stint in the offshore oil industry, I returned to Clemson as a graduate student and instructor in engineering graphics. Carl McHugh was head of the engineering graphics faculty and thereby became my teaching mentor and immediate supervisor. He was also the long-time varsity swim coach—in fact, the natatorium in the Fike Recreation facility is named for him. At the time, however, the swim team used an old pool in the Holtzendorf YMCA building that predated the 1920s.

It was tiny by any standard. In fact, it was so small that the entire team could not practice at once, so two training sessions were held each day. Coach McHugh was aware that I had been a member of the track team and asked me to help by handling one of the daily practices. He was my boss, after all, so no real choices there, but I enjoyed it. In fact, I was deemed the assistant coach, earning $200 for the season and traveling with the team. My only relevant qualification was a familiarity with stopwatches, but, before the season ended, I was judging diving right along with the best of them. Normally, the high and low scores awarded to a dive were discarded and the rest were used to determine the official score. I couldn't offer a sound technical evaluation of a dive, but I knew a 4 ½ when I saw one, and my scores were rarely tossed.

At the time, Walt Castro and some others were experimenting with substances that might be added to fluids to lessen flow resistance—stuff most of us would characterize as slimy (think okra juice). Walt wondered whether swimmers who were swabbed down with some of it might swim faster, maybe like fish.

One afternoon, we arranged for him to bring a couple of buckets of his stuff to the pool to try out. It became an interesting experiment.

We opened a can and brushed some of its contents onto two or three volunteers. We weren't careful and dribbled it all around. Instantly, the pool deck

The old YMCA pool (With permission from the University Archives)

became impossible to stand or walk on—try to imagine an icy patch and then multiply its slipperiness by a large number.

We spread a bunch of towels to walk on and managed to roll a couple of good sports into the pool. Their feet were too slippery to stand, even in the water, but they gave it a try. No one had the presence of mind to pay attention to much except the comic elements of the whole thing. Besides, we discovered shortly that the swimmers were sort of marooned in the pool. Their hands and the edge of the pool deck were too slippery to allow them to pull themselves out. Try as they might, they just kept slipping back into the water.

A few others jumped in with some towels and managed to bundle up the guinea pigs and heave them up and over the edge onto some more towels, where they resembled a couple of mummies imitating beached seals. We used a week's supply of towels to pave a way to the showers and sent along a couple of helpers to keep the others from falling. The experiment has yet to make the journals.

INTERVIEWING R. C. (PRESIDENT EDWARDS)

STEPHEN H. WAINSCOTT
Clemson University Honors College
1976–2009

In 1987, I and twelve other Clemson faculty co-authored a book titled *Tradition: A History of the Presidency of Clemson University*. Edited by history professor Don McKale, the book consisted of short biographies of all the presidents from Henry Aubrey Strode through Walter Cox.

Due to my interests in Southern politics in general and the politics of school desegregation in particular, I was asked to contribute the chapter on Robert Cook ("R. C.") Edwards, who presided over the peaceful integration of Clemson in 1963. My task was daunting, for not only was Edwards the university's longest-serving president; his twenty-two years at the helm were arguably the most consequential in the university's history. In addition to the integration episode, Edwards oversaw the saving of the university from being flooded as a result of the creation of Lake Hartwell. His term also witnessed the end of mandatory ROTC, the admission of women students, and the transition of Clemson College to university status.

At the outset of the project, Editor McKale insisted that each of the chapters be typed and no more than twenty-five pages in length. I complied with the first request but failed miserably on the second. Because the Edwards presidency was so lengthy and so fraught with momentous events, I ended up giving McKale a *ninety*-page chapter. That he was able to cut sixty-five pages is a tribute to his considerable editing skill.

My task was daunting in yet another respect: All the other authors' subjects were either deceased or had moved away. My subject, on the other hand, was still alive. And he was HERE! So, although much of my research, like that of the other authors, was spent in the archives, poring through minutes of trustees' meetings and other documents, my chapter also necessitated in-person interviews.

I scheduled three meetings, each at Edwards's Clemson home and each to cover different topics, lasting about two hours at most. When I arrived for the first interview, I was prepared for Edwards to be defensive and short with his responses. After all, I had never met the man, and he didn't know me from Adam. Quite to the contrary, Edwards was completely forthcoming, even chatty and long-winded—and generous with servings of iced tea.

Because of my interest in school desegregation, that topic took up most of our time in the first interview. At length, he explained that his overriding goal was to avoid the violence and political grandstanding that had accompanied integration at other Southern universities. In all my questioning, I got the sense that Edwards did not see integration as a positive thing or as "the right thing to do." Rather, it was clear that he had resigned himself to the inevitable. So determined was Edwards that integration would be peaceful and "dignified" (a word he used frequently), he said that he told faculty he would fire anyone who protested and that "tenure would be no protection."

The Hartwell Dam episode in 1957 was the main topic of our second interview. What most struck me about this exchange was that it was the only time in our conversations that Edwards seemed willing to take credit for something—which was understandable, because at the time the crisis occurred, no one other than Edwards understood the problem, let alone offered leadership in trying to solve it. Otherwise, throughout our conversations, I was impressed with how self-effacing and humble he could be.

I started this second interview by asking Edwards how he came to learn about the threat to the campus caused by the Hartwell project. His response surprised me. While he had become aware of the flooding and what the damage to the campus would be, he said that the root of problem was the obstinacy of the Corps of Engineers. "Back then," he said, "the Corps just loved to build dams. Any excuse to build a dam. You knew there was going to be problems just because they were so dam happy."

I could relate many more accounts of the interviews and Edwards's recollections of specific events, but what impressed me the most were two aspects of his demeanor. One was his steel-trap memory of seemingly insignificant details. For example, in recounting the discussions that took place prior to the university's integration in 1963, he spoke at great length about a meeting in his Sikes Hall office: "Governor Hollings and Senator Brown sat beside each other on the couch. Senator Gressette stood beside them. I let Charlie Daniel sit in my chair. I sat in a chair beside my desk." Then, he recalled verbatim what each said and the order in which they said it.

But what was most impressive to me is what a softie R.C. could be. Here I was in a private home, interviewing a man with a reputation of being a tough, take-charge guy ("a real trash mover," as he was once described). Every once in a while, a fond memory would come up. And the voice would choke. And the tears would flow.

At his memorial service in December 2008, I bumped into Edwards's granddaughter, Sandi Reid, who many years before had been a student of mine. She told me that on several occasions when she was back in Clemson visiting her grandparents, R.C. would recall the interviews twenty-one years earlier. Sandi chuckled: "And he would tell it the same way every time."

THOUGHTS ON R. C. EDWARDS'S THREE "CRISES" AS PRESIDENT OF CLEMSON UNIVERSITY

Donald L. Collins
College of Architecture
1972–2005

My Clemson journey as a faculty member began in 1972. A couple of years after beginning, and a few days before students were to arrive on campus to begin the fall semester, President R. C. Edwards called an "emergency" meeting of the entire faculty in Tilman Hall's Memorial Auditorium. The auditorium was not the reasonably functional space we know today. Instead, it was a dusty old space with uncomfortable, well-worn wooden seats and a creaky stairwell leading to a second-level balcony supported by rather simple cast-iron columns whose second purpose was to obstruct the view from many first-level seats.

After walking uphill in the hot August sun from Lee Hall on the edge of core campus to Tilman Hall for the meeting, I was already damp with perspiration by the time I reached Memorial Auditorium. The only seats still open were on the balcony level. Climbing the stairs into the upper-level heat, I was dismayed to discover in my first venture inside Memorial Auditorium that the only temperature control consisted of opening the large windows as high as possible, hoping to gain some cross ventilation. That had already been done but to little relief.

Naturally, I was hoping the meeting would start on time and be very brief. Neither proved to be the case. Provost Victor Hurst began the meeting. After going through the usual list of mundane greetings and announcements, he turned the podium over to the president. Edwards greeted all in attendance, adding that it was his duty to inform us that he had received news from Columbia that would affect all of us negatively and constitute a new crisis for the university—the "third crisis," he declared, of his presidency.

Instead of elaborating on the crisis at hand, Edwards instead began by speaking of his first crisis as university president. As I remember it, he said that within weeks of assuming the Office of President of Clemson University, he learned that the U.S. Army Corp of Engineers' Lake Harwell would flood the agriculture research fields known as "the Bottoms" (along present-day Perimeter Road). Then, he added that Death Valley's football field would be under eight feet of water, and he could not let that happen.

What? I thought. How could he not have known about Lake Harwell's pending rise to the edge of campus? I had only been on campus a couple of years, but I knew there was a plan drawing showing the future extent of the lake's impingement on the university, including not flooding the stadium by a "holdback" dike just beyond the west end zone. He should have been privy to the plan at some point, for he had been on campus as a vice president before becoming president.

I knew about Lake Hartwell's reach because Robert Eflin had been hired as the university's first "campus planner" the year after I arrived. Prior to Eflin's arrival, campus planning had been the purview of the dean of the College of Architecture, Harland McClure. Eflin's office and planning studio had been carved out of Architecture's Lee Hall gallery space. His first task had been the consolidation of as much data and campus mapping as possible about past, present, and future efforts at campus planning and design. One such document discovered was a commissioned "Clemson University Master Plan" prepared by the Boston firm of architects and landscape architects Perry, Dean, Rogers. The plan was dated 1953! And it clearly showed Lake Hartwell lapping at the edge of the built campus. This was years before Lake Hartwell's dam construction started, and even more years before the lake began to fill in 1961. Although Lee and Lowry Halls had not even been constructed at the time of the 1953 Master Plan, they were clearly proposed to be located at their current locations on the peninsula that would extend into the lake.

Eflin, an architect, and I, a landscape architect, shared a common interest in campus planning and design. We had several discussions about what makes a great campus plan in comparing notes on the campuses we had visited. Several times, he pulled the 1953 Master Plan from the flat file to use in making a point. Imagine, as he did, having Cooper Library not overlooking a valley "dammed" by the Strom Thurman Institute building but instead overlooking an active sailboat marina and a wide stretch of Lake Hartwell beyond. As for a new football stadium, one could have been constructed at any number of places in the university's nearby land holdings. Surely the cost of the dikes that hold back the lake and the "forever" cost of pumping the campus's Hunnicutt Creek watershed runoff up to the level of Lake Hartwell would have been enough to amortize the cost of

The Clemson University 1953 Master Plan (With permission from the University Archives)

a new stadium, not to mention the cost incurred in repairing the middle dike's seepage leaks that developed years after the dikes were constructed.

As I sat there, sweating in the heat and humidity, I concluded that the "first Edwards presidential crisis" ended in a failure in not seeing the pending Hartwell Lake shoreline as an opportunity rather than a problem. How magnificent would it be for Clemson University today to be on the very edge of Lake Harwell!

President Edwards then began to speak about his second crisis as Clemson University's president, snapping me out of my "what-if" daydreams. Edwards was telling the assembly his "second crisis" was the arrival of the first Black student to be enrolled at Clemson. Here, thankfully, President Edwards led the orchestration of the steps leading up to Harvey Gantt's arrival on campus in such a way that Gantt's first day on campus and the days that followed were nonevents, in noted contrast to similar circumstances in Alabama and Mississippi.

But Gantt's enrollment at Clemson makes me wonder about something. I recently came across a letter in the Cooper Library's collection written to President Edwards by a Willie Collins of Bennettsville, South Carolina, a member of the Class of '43. Collins may be distant kin, for the Collins surname is spread all over the areas on both sides of the North Carolina/South Carolina state line between Union County, North Carolina, my father's birthplace, and Bennettsville, South Carolina. Collins begins his letter by saying he wishes "to support the opinion that I have heard expressed by other Clemson alumni and loyal South Carolinians, in regard to school integration." And that opinion is to "do so quietly and without any publicity if possible." Collins also states in his letter to Edwards that he is opposed to the integration of Clemson but nonetheless is pragmatic in his position. Collins was no doubt pleased with the outcome of President Edwards' second crisis.

So, what was President Edwards's "third crisis" of his administration, the reason for our meeting? He had just been informed that Clemson University was only going to be receiving 97 percent of what was known as "Full-Formula Funding" from the state. I am not aware of all that went into the funding formula, but I do know that undergraduate students accounted for one amount per student and that graduate students were funded at a higher amount. (That formula may have had much to do with Clemson College's becoming Clemson University.) At the time, I had no idea what a 3 percent budget cut would mean for me personally. As it turned out, that year, I could not tell the difference from my vantage point as a young faculty member, but as I moved up in rank and responsibility, and as state appropriations continued to decline, that perspective would change. As acting department head in architecture twice and later as department head of planning and landscape architecture, I became acutely aware of repeated funding "crises" as state support dropped repeatedly to today's level, which is below 9 percent.

"I KNOW A GUY. . . ."

Nancy Cassity Dunlap
Eugene T. Moore School of Education
2000–2010

"I know a guy. . . ." Seldom does any good start with these words, but this time it did. The speaker was Bill Hurst, my partner-in-crime through this journey.

The journey began in early summer of 2006 with the unexpected appearance of four eighteen-inch-square tiles in my office. Three were varying shades of bilious beige; the fourth was cyanotic blue; all had speckles that gave them a decidedly trailer-park vibe. "What's this?" I asked of my admin assistant. She allowed that "someone from facilities" had delivered them that morning, and I must decide which to use. "For what?" I inquired. "For the Tillman lobby," she replied. "Oh, h***, no," I opined, or something equally characteristic.

I must digress. I arrived at Clemson in January 2000, and soon thereafter I assumed responsibility for the facility in addition to my primary job of accreditation and assessment. I would daily walk the halls of this august building and feel disturbed by the larger-than-life portrait of the building's namesake (since 1946; prior to that, it was called Main Building or "Old Main"). I found it wildly ironic that the portrait of this rabid segregationist stood opposite a tribute to Harvey Gantt and Clemson's *Integration with Dignity* in 1963.

Tillman Hall (aka "Old Main") has been central to campus life for generations; it is the university's showcase building, and I took my stewardship seriously. The building needed some serious attention, so I began by installing custom shelving and glass cases to display faculty publications and student work; these were artfully constructed, furniture-grade cabinetry and included brass floor railings. By the time these were all installed, there was no wall space large enough to rehang the Tillman portrait. I knew that it must be protected and preserved, so I stashed it in a safe, climate-controlled storeroom where it remained—for ten years.

Back to the summer of 2006: I had the four tile samples propped on chairs in my office. Most faculty were not available during the summer, but I asked those who were on campus to give me their opinions. I asked for input from staff as well, and we were all of one accord: "Oh, please, no!" They were proud of the work we had done, with upgrades to technology, office space, HVAC, and other mechanicals; whiteboards to replace chalkboards; modular and ergonomic office furnishings for faculty and staff; and conversion of all classrooms to Smartrooms. Also, we were the first nonresidential building to install a key-card entry system to increase security.

And that's how I came to partner with Bill Hurst. Bill, as many know, had essentially grown up on the campus; his father was Victor Hurst, vice president for academic affairs and dean of the university at Clemson from 1966 to 1979.

The "guy" he knew lived in Oconee County, and he had recently salvaged a large cache of flooring from Lydia Mill, a cotton mill that was being demolished in Clinton, South Carolina. Bill and I thought, "Hmmm, cotton mill and Clemson—there's a logical connection." And the best part: Bill could purchase it for a favorable price on behalf of Clemson.

How to proceed? The stakes were high, and the time was short; my best (and only) recourse was to appeal to the one person who had earned and conferred stock—a man who was an alumnus, an architect, and the president of Clemson. I drafted my passionate appeal to Jim Barker and sent it on July 19, admitting that although the suggested tile would likely be cost-effective, it had all the panache of a double-wide. While I waited, I had musings of the conversations happening in the executive suite.

A few days later, on a Friday, some workers arrived with equipment. They had been instructed to drill cores through the floor to determine the status of the subfloor. Was it usable? Was it original? Was it safe? What they encountered at the north end (near the doors to the auditorium) was serious scorching from the May 1894 fire. At the south side near the exit doors was another surprise—a sopping-wet floor five layers deep. The nearby cooling unit had been leaking and had soaked the flooring below, but there had been no way to know. We knew then that refinishing the subfloor wouldn't be an option.

When I returned to campus that next Monday morning, I was greeted by two perfectly formed mushroom caps growing from the hole the workers had drilled the Friday before. I realized then that Old Main would have her new floors. Thank you, Jim Barker!

Bill and I went to work. The "guy" came through, as did Clemson's Purchasing Office. We were able to see some of the salvaged flooring installed in a Seneca home; the quality and finish were stunning. The wood had been milled but hadn't lost its patina of age. It had a warm glow that only aged heart pine can evince. We were delighted.

Old Main (also referred to as Tillman Hall): Mushrooms growing in the floor (With permission of photographer Nancy Cassity Dunlap)

By late August, the demolition began, and Bill oversaw the entire process. The old tiles were removed, but not before one was rescued. Our treasured student assistant, Alison Little, seized one of the old tiles and later painted the picture of Old Main that she proudly presented to me for Christmas (*Attachment #3*). It remains one of my treasured mementos.

By late October, the new flooring was being installed. This took several weeks because the workers had to navigate around students, faculty, staff, class changes—all the usual stuff that happens in academic buildings; we couldn't close off the first floor. And there were a few setbacks.

In late November, Marty Duckenfield and I had a pressing commitment at an international conference in the Netherlands as a lead-up to a conference we would be hosting the following year in Brussels. As the time for our departure grew nearer, the project delays became more frequent. Finally, we had to leave, but I had total confidence in Bill, and he came through like the consummate professional that he is. We returned to see final sanding and finishing; we were back on schedule.

The new floor in Old Main (With permission of photographer Nancy Cassity Dunlap)

Bill had arranged for the final coat of polyurethane to be laid during the Christmas break when everyone would be gone. This would give the finish time to dry and cure.

On Sunday, January 1, 2007, as we were returning to campus, I said to my husband that we had to stop at Old Main before we went home. We pulled into Gantt Circle and parked on the yellow line at the top of the circle, and with my key at the ready, I open the front door and stepped inside.

I wept.

And when I retired in January 2010, Pitchfork Ben remained in the storage room, facing the wall.

Old Main (With permission by photographer Delbert L Kimbler)

LOST IN FREEMAN HALL

Delbert "Del" L. Kimbler
Department of Industrial Engineering
1987–2008

It was exciting for me to contemplate moving to Clemson in late 1986, leaving a school where all the engineering programs fit into one building. Don't get me wrong, though—it was also exciting in different ways to be a faculty member in that college and its single building. There was a closeness at South Florida and responsibility given to young faculty members with new doctorates that ranged from satisfying to intoxicating. But there were new opportunities at Clemson, in another young, recently reactivated industrial engineering program. And there were friends, too, whom I knew through my time at Virginia Tech and from professional society meetings.

Industrial engineering (IE) at Clemson had recently moved from its temporary space in the Riggs basement to Freeman Hall, so there was a newness for all of us. My new office, Freeman 102, was a little odd. It was about twenty feet long, with a window at one end and door to the hallway at the other, and about six feet wide. There was a second doorway about four feet inside the hallway door, making it sort of an anteroom. I thought it was a little peculiar, probably a result of renovation that took up space somewhere else. I never figured out a different rationale for that double-door scheme, but that "result of renovation" idea was one that I would see repeatedly in Freeman Hall.

One of my new friends in Clemson IE was the department technician, Tom Harbin. Tom was a treasure in many ways. He could fabricate almost anything mechanical. One of his hobbies was historical reenactment, and he was in a group whose theme was to reenact the clothing, lifestyle, and equipment of two hundred years ago. He loved to show this off to students and was a regular feature of our work-methods laboratory, where he would demonstrate firing and reloading his homemade musket based on the principles of motion economy.

Tom's knowledge of Freeman Hall was encyclopedic. He appeared at my office one day to give me one of his building tours, which covered all floors and historic eras in the building. The central core of the building dated to 1926, where it housed a small foundry and associated crafts and had the sawtooth roof line that you find on factories of that era. That foundry area might be the engineering services machine shop now, but Tom knew which walls housed the foundry and which basements and sub-basements composed it. He would point out the boundaries in existing walls and show how the texture changed from one renovation to the next. This was on display for all to see on the main level, where the different styles of bricks could be seen in an interior wall that was the outside of the building until 1965, when a new façade added a row of offices and other rooms on the first floor and then layered a second floor on top of that.

This was the Freeman Hall that I knew, which would undergo incremental interior renovations every few years. In 1986, most of the central part of the first floor was used by IE or Graphic Communications. By 1995, much of this space had been converted to IE labs and offices. A few years later, the rest of it gave us more classroom space and also provided needed room for Programs for Educational Enrichment and Retention (PEER), Women in Science and Engineering (WISE), and Clemson Computing and Information Technology (CCIT).

Little did we realize back then that with new rooms comes a need for room numbers. And this is when the confusion began. We who lived and worked in Freeman Hall, especially the industrial engineers, knew where our working space was and knew our room numbers. I spent time in 102, then moved to 104A, then to 110 in 1995 (the department office suite by then), and finally to 119. With each renovation, rooms were added, new numbers were needed, and this was not always done with consistency and navigation in mind.

For example, even before renovations, room 120, a small lab, was at one end of the main hall, with 122 at the other. In between, numbering began with 102 and actually increased in numerical order on one side of the hall. But on the other side, we had 101 opposite 110 rather than 102, and 111 was opposite 116. With renovation, things got worse, with a large lab carved up into small offices that ran from 147 to 152 and were adjacent to room 129. And just when you began to grasp the lack of design in these numbers, you found 140 between 138 and 142. How did that happen?

Then, there was the second floor. It had two small offices and a classroom, and at the other end two office suites, and the numbers ran as expected. Room 202 had a staircase of its own, with an access at the other end and a stairwell there for access to the two offices. There was a third stairwell at the far end. But it was impossible to go from 204 to 202 or 201 without going down to the main hall and up a different stairway.

In the 1990s and, in fact, up until the latest renovation, the department office also functioned as sort of a local information center, and our work-study

Freeman Hall (With permission of photographer Delbert L Kimbler)

students quickly learned to serve as guides. We grew to love our building, with all its faults and quirkiness. It was ours, and we learned to function within its constraints. I think it became a sort of home to our students as well.

With the 2015 renovation, the room numbering is rational; the surprises are gone! This is progress; I just wish we had not had to wait so long for it. I fear that I have some responsibility for this. In leading President Deno Curris on a tour through the building, in 1997, I believe, he asked me what the faculty thought of the building. I didn't want to send a message of gloom or take the time to describe our room number shortage problem, so I told him we enjoyed its quirkiness and the IE faculty could do well in any location. Did I move our building down in priority with these off-hand remarks?

If I did, I am glad it finally happened, and that the new number scheme makes sense. But if you go to Freeman Hall today, don't look for my old offices. They are gone, now part of an auditorium, the department office suite, and a conference room. You can find two of those room numbers, scattered throughout the building; rooms 110 and 119 are available as needed. I am glad my room numbers have been put to good use and my old department has been able to expand into this wonderful new space.

CHAPTER 2

The Caden Chapel on Clemson's Campus (With permission of photographer Debra Broadwell Jackson)

REMEMBERING THE CHANGE THAT MADE A FAR DIFFERENT CLEMSON

Donald M. McKale
Department of History
1979–2008

Old historians like myself, it's said, never die—they just fade into the past they have always claimed is so important. That's what's happening in the memory piece shared here.

I arrived at Clemson University in 1979, hired in the History Department at the rank of untenured full professor—school policy at the time prohibited hiring with tenure. The department expected me to teach courses in my academic specialty, modern European history, and, more notably, continue my research and writing on German history.

Previously I'd taught eight years at a small college in Georgia and a year at the University of Nebraska–Lincoln, during which I'd published two books about the Nazi Party, the principal factor that persuaded the History Department to hire me at the senior rank. Always I had found a close relationship between research and teaching; what I learned researching in archives and libraries, I carried often into the classroom to help, I hoped, inform my students.

I believed that Clemson would provide me greater opportunities and resources to expand my research and learning about Europe, Germany, and particularly the world wars. The relatively new History Department, headed since 1974 by talented administrator Alan Schaffer, promoted greater faculty research and publication more than previously and the department's graduate program. Schaffer and other senior department members expanded the department's notoriety beyond Clemson to a greater national academic audience. I benefitted from the new policy.

Soon, I received tenure and eventually university research grants to work in archives in Germany and elsewhere in Europe. In 1988, I received a titled professorship, funded by a gift to the university from the Clemson Class of 1941. My subsequent thirty-year career at Clemson yielded six more books on Germany, the world wars, and the Holocaust and two books on the history of Clemson.

In reflecting on my time at Clemson, I remember how lucky I felt to work there. Nearly every day, between or after classes, I enjoyed going to the History Department lounge in Hardin Hall, sitting at the large round table there, engaging with faculty colleagues in serious and humorous discussions, led often by the quick-minded Schaffer, about major historical and national political issues of the day.

But although the department moved seamlessly in the 1980s and 1990s toward expanding its presence nationally, I recall the turmoil this same issue caused in the broader university. Under university presidents Bill Atchley (1979–1985) and Max Lennon (1986–1994), the school changed dramatically. It moved from the relatively small state-oriented and -supported (financially) undergraduate teaching institution it had always been, with low tuition and other costs, to a larger, national-oriented research university, financed by progressively larger tuition increases and student enrollments, by federal and other research grants recruited by faculty and graduate programs, and by private fundraising.

The huge change created a Clemson far different from the one that hired me. Not surprising, what and how it happened stirred widespread controversy among faculty, students, and others in the Clemson family.

I recall late Friday afternoon encounters of faculty, from engineers and scientists to agriculture and liberal arts people, over beer at the Esso Club, expressing passionately their opposition to or support for the change. Debates on the subject in the Faculty Senate and on pages of the *Tiger*, the student newspaper, centered on the mantra *teaching versus research*. That the faculty and even students had little voice in the issue seemed to intensify the emotions of the moment. Usually, faculty hired many years before mainly to teach and mentor undergraduates resented how their duties now included developing research programs and recruiting grant money.

At least initially, it seems neither I nor many of my colleagues on either side of the policy change realized that Atchley, and much more so Lennon, had received a mandate from the Board of Trustees to build the university into a major research institution that could compete with other nationally known public universities.

The campus controversy grew even more heated. The trustee directive collided with the effects of a major economic recession in the United States that reached into South Carolina. Clemson suffered steady, and overall massive, reductions in funding from the financially strapped state government. Whereas before 1980, the state provided more than 90 percent of the university's funding, by the end of Lennon's presidency in 1994, the university received less than 70 percent. The funding fell even more sharply thereafter. It was little comfort to know that other universities around the nation were experiencing similar financial problems.

I remember how, during those years, faculty and staff morale plummeted. Salary raises were few and far between. Less money existed for academic programs, while others were discontinued altogether. Occasionally, the university implemented reductions in pay by furloughing personnel. Meanwhile, salaries rose for a burgeoning university administration, aggravating many faculty. Unhappiness resulted as well from the university's restructuring and reorganizing of its colleges and other administrative units to attempt to save money.

Yet somehow, the trustees, Lennon, and his successors in Sikes Hall persisted, almost out of necessity for financial reasons, to pursue the university's national ambitions. The school vastly expanded its funding from private giving by alumni and others and from faculty recruitment of external research grants. Little noticed at the time, and still underappreciated today, the university's drive for national academic recognition resulted in no small part from Clemson's 1981 national championship in football.

Athletics, too, divided my faculty colleagues. Some, like myself, loved football and other sports, while others detested them, believing that athletics corrupted the university and took substantial revenue from academic programs. I'll paraphrase what I remember one colleague told me: "This is not the Clemson Football University! It's not Clemson Sports University either. It is Clemson University. An academic institution. Nowhere in Thomas Green Clemson's will do you see the mention of football!" Yet I remember that the more success the football team enjoyed, the more that private fundraising increased for academics as well as for IPTAY, the athletic fundraising arm. After 1981, Atchley, especially the trustees, and most other Clemson people basked in the glory of the championship. The stunning achievement whetted the appetite—indeed, ambition—for further national attention for Clemson, especially on the academic side of campus.

Amid the changes that created a very different Clemson, and often the painful problems they produced, and perhaps because of it all, the university prospered. In 1999, its thirteenth president, James Barker, proclaimed the goal for Clemson to reach the elite club of top twenty national public universities as ranked by the magazine *U.S. News and World Report*. I remember with much gratitude how Clemson helped me grow as a teacher and scholar; I hope that in my own small way, I helped it mature into the nationally prominent institution Clemson emeriti and other Tiger faithful are so proud of today.

CLEMSON MEMORIES:
Adventures as Dean of the College of Liberal Arts

ROBERT A. WALLER
College of Liberal Arts
1981–2000

I began my service as dean of the College of Liberal Arts on my fiftieth birthday, July 1, 1981. Thus began an association that lasted until the year 2000, when I retired to the Villages, a recreational retirement community northwest of Orlando, Florida.

On my first day, I requested an afternoon meeting with the department heads and the business manager to start the process of becoming acquainted. I indicated that I would likely continue such weekly meetings for the remainder of the summer as I became familiar with the personnel, facilities, possibilities, and problems in the college. Long-serving department head Harry Stewart noted the thin file of meeting notes accumulated under the leadership of Dean Morris Cox during the previous decade since the college's founding and in the last year with Acting Dean John Butler. Hopefully, the change was for the better.

During July and August, I made an effort to become acquainted with the buildings assigned to the liberal arts college. The dean's office complex was located atop the seven-story Strode Tower, named for Henry Aubrey Strode, Clemson's first president (1890–1893). It also housed the English, Political Science, and Language Departments. Adjoining Strode Tower and connected to it with a walkway on the second floor was Daniel Hall, a principal classroom building with an auditorium. Named for David Wister Daniels (a long-time professor of English), this facility was the general education center for the campus. Housed across the way beyond the Outdoor Theater was Hardin Hall, among the oldest campus buildings, dating to 1890 and named for an early president, Mark Bernard Hardin. It housed the History and Psychology Departments.

As our first fall semester began, we immersed ourselves in the Tigertown tradition that is Clemson football season. We bought season tickets, watched the parade, and enjoyed the parties. At the first home game, we attended a pre-game brunch at the president's house, watched the game from the president's box at Tiger stadium, socialized at a postgame reception at the Outdoor Lab, and returned to town for yet another party. I am not sure we went to that extreme in scheduling again, but we did accept a faculty member's invitation to drive the eighty-seven miles to Asheville to watch the national championship game as the undefeated Clemson Tigers beat the Nebraska Cornhuskers. As the first fall semester concluded, we decided to hold an open house for faculty and staff members and their spouses so everyone could see where the new dean and his missus lived. A total of 193 invitations was extended on a staggered time basis. To brighten the ice chunks in the two punch bowls we bought for the occasion, Joan added some red berries from the yard. Fortunately, the caterers who were helping us spotted them and removed them, as they were poisonous. At the conclusion of the reception, we noted that the bowl labeled "with" had to be replenished more often than the one designated "without." We had much to learn about Southern culture and taboos.

Our first winter at Clemson, there was an unexpected snowfall of significant proportions. Like most Southern towns, residents want businesses closed early when the first snowflake appears so that they can get "milk and bread" before heading home. In this case, the snow happened overnight. Sturdy Midwesterner that I am, I walked to work as I usually did. It turned out that the university was closed; I was the only one in the office. I spent much of the day on the phone, explaining to faculty and students that classes were not being held. At most Northern universities, there is a fleet of equipment to clear pathways, sidewalks, and roads. At Southern institutions, the sun is the snow-removal machine of choice. Later, the governor gave two days' holiday to all state employees who reported for work despite the adverse weather conditions.

During my tenure, the original college facilities were augmented by the Brooks Center for the Performing Arts, which became a focus on the campus and in the community. A generous gift of $2.5 million from Clemson alumnus Robert Brooks in 1987 kick-started the construction of what became a $12.5 million addition to the campus. As second director of the Brooks Center, Mickey Harder worked tirelessly to contract the performances, including special programming for area elementary students, and to schedule campus groups for their presentations.[1] To that brick-and-mortar venture, a remodeled Brackett Hall named for Richard Newman Brackett (an early professor of chemistry)

---

[1] *Mickey's Memories: Magic and Mayhem* (Clemson University Press, 2021).

became the facility into which the Social Science Departments were collected—political science, psychology, and sociology. With the improved surroundings came master's degrees in each of those fields and a doctorate in human factors psychology. Thanks to a generous and anonymous gift from the Athletic Department, a conference area on the first floor of Strode Tower was remodeled into a spacious complex for the dean and his staff, making the personnel more readily available to faculty and students.

As the college doubled its number of majors and new programs, such as Language and International Trade and Women's Studies, it became possible to establish additional departments to better serve the college's educational mission. Those faculty teaching speech classes in the English Department were gathered into a separate Speech Department. The Brooks Center provided space for a Performing Arts Department. To form it, the Music Department faculty were joined by English Department members teaching theater classes, and a dance instructor was drawn from the Recreation Department in the College of Forestry. Those History Department faculty teaching and researching in philosophy and religion were transferred into a department with that name.

Frequently, public higher-education institutions in the nation were besieged with budgetary reductions. South Carolina was no exception. College deans were encouraged to seek outside funds in terms of gifts, endowments, contracts, and research projects. For liberal arts, a major success was a $1.2 million Challenge Grant from the National Endowment for the Humanities. Alumnus Roy Pearce provided a $1.5 million endowment for a Professional Communications Center. Other funding came from the Kellogg and Rockefeller Foundations. According to Development Office figures, I was party to raising more than $7,000,000 in contracts, gifts, endowments, and grants.

All this activity resulted in the use of an enormous amount of paper. When I was a poor graduate student, I wished I had been able to invest in Xerox stock. I generated so many agendas, memos, minutes, notes, proposals, reminders, and reports that there was a cry of "enough," with the motto "kill the dean and save a tree." One wag sent me a cartoon showing a gigantic tree that the ranger explained, if made into paper, "could supply the federal government for six minutes." My critic attached a note saying, "or Dean Waller for one week!" My favorite cartoon featuring the college is an April Fools issue of the *Tiger* showing Strode Tower leaning significantly to the left, supposedly displaying the faculty's political inclinations.

In the mid-1980s, the nation's higher-education institutions were besmirched with athletic scandals, including points shaving in basketball games, recruiting excesses, and drug enhancements. Clemson was not immune. Twice, I was quoted in the *New York Times* about the classic athletics versus academics clash. Once it concerned the difficulty in recruiting new faculty members and departmental leadership. In the second, I expressed concern about the recruitment of new students and the maintenance of alumni giving at institutions whose priorities are misplaced. At Clemson, the struggle was between university president Bill Atchley and athletic director Bill McClellan. Local cartoonist Kate Salley Palmer had McClellan saying, "Clemson's College of Liberal Arts will be phased out over the next few years. Citing a desire to eliminate waste and duplication of services." A prophet is without honor in his own bailiwick. When the dust settled, both primary protagonists were gone, and the college and I remained.

College deans serve at the pleasure of the provost. Typically, such terms last seven years, ending frequently due to faculty dissatisfaction. I passed a thorough fifth-year review for renewal. At the end of ten years, the faculty proclaimed my title should be "Pontifex Maximus Robert I" as a candidate for beatification and awarded me a plaque listing some of my accomplishments, including inauguration of a sabbatical leave program. Such recognition resulted from a team staff comprising Sandra Burkett (business manager), Shelby Duncan (secretary to the Undeclared Majors Office, directed by Assistant Dean Sixto Torres), Lois Driver (grants manager), Ron Moran (associate dean), Jean Shisler (development officer), Steve Wainscott (assistant dean for honors), and Karen Zauner (dean's secretary).

I continued as dean for three more years, and then the budgetary guillotine fell. To meet an extraordinary shortfall in state funding, the Board of Trustees determined to reduce the number of colleges from nine to four. Eliminated were the colleges of education, forestry, liberal arts, nursing, and sciences. My tenure as dean ended on June 30, 1994. Following a sabbatical leave, I joined the History Department, where I had tenure. My new colleagues had a tradition that the newest active faculty member served as secretary. Thus, I had my first assignment. I taught survey courses in U.S. history and designed and instructed a popular course on twentieth-century American history, serving thirty-six students on first offering. My research interests turned to the activities of the New Deal's Civilian Conservation Corps in the state parks of South Carolina during the 1930s. Ultimately, this effort resulted in the publication of four articles and a book, *Relief, Recreation, Racism*.

I retired in the spring of 1997 as emeritus dean and emeritus professor of history and assumed that my formal affiliation with Clemson had ended. Not so!

On July 17, 1997, Provost J. Charles Jennett announced that he was appointing me as editor of the *Faculty Manual* to bring order to the contract between the Board of Trustees and the Clemson faculty. For an annual retainer, I served three years as liaison between the Faculty Senate and the Board. In late June 2000, I moved to the Villages, a recreational retirement community of three hundred thousand northwest of Orlando, Florida. The experience is sometimes described as "Disney for Seniors."

This brief sketch of my time at Clemson can be augmented with two chapters in my autobiography, *R.A.W.: A Life Well Lived* (Xlibris Press, 2021).

ACADEMICS VERSUS ATHLETICS

DAVID J. SENN
Department of Psychology
1973–2002

As a university professor, my treasured memories most often come from student interactions. However, other unexpected circumstances make a difference not only in the lives of students but also in the direction of a university. For me, numerous nonstudent encounters occurred during the rather tumultuous year I served as Faculty Senate president.

It is well known that an institution's reputation and public image take years of cultivation and nurturing. Unfortunately, both can become quickly tarnished by overzealousness to achieve national prominence and by struggles to attain a power advantage within an institution.

Following an NCAA athletic probation in the early 1980s, President Bill Atchley announced in December 1984 that two track coaches had been suspended and that the State Law Enforcement Division (SLED) would be investigating the alleged use of nonprescribed medications by some athletes. An area newspaper published an interview with Athletic Director Bill McLellan in January 1985. McLellan publicly aired his differences with President Atchley in terms of how the investigation should be conducted. Faculty concerns were expressed immediately. Demands were made that the Faculty Senate address the issue and "do something." During that year, I and other senators became "public figures" as we began a process of defining athletes as students first rather than students as athletes first.

The Senate engaged in a lively debate, resulting in a resolution of "no confidence in the athletic director." Senate resolutions two years earlier, following the football probation announcement, were resisted by the athletic director, with support from some members of the Board of Trustees. The no-confidence resolution was only an expression of faculty sentiment and advisory to the university administration; it did not suggest or demand any specific action or timetable. It simply said that during the previous decade, serious violations of collegiate athletic policy and principle had besmirched the reputation of the university and caused profound embarrassment to its faculty, student body, alumni, and friends.

The Senate believed that this tainted reputation was endangering the recruitment and retention of outstanding faculty members, the evaluation of research grants and contract proposals submitted to funding agencies, the administration's efforts to raise funds for our academic programs, the prestige of the degrees granted to thousands of former students who were Clemson alumni, and, quite possibly, the future recruitment of outstanding high school students for academic and athletic programs in the university. Because of the danger to Clemson's reputation, the Senate no longer had confidence in the person charged with overseeing all intercollegiate athletic events on campus.

Decisions and events progressed rapidly for the next month. Some Clemson athletes admitted to using steroids for body building, the IPTAY Board of Directors supported McLellan, and the Clemson Chapter of the American Association of University Professors endorsed the action of the Senate. The *Tiger* expressed student sentiment. Multiple letters, phone calls, and news interviews converged on campus leaders and senate members. McLellan requested and was granted an indefinite leave of absence. Questions of university priorities (academics versus athletics) and campus leadership were paramount.

In February, a Columbia newspaper reported that several unidentified trustees believed that President Atchley had to be replaced. Events moved at electrifying speed. Small groups of trustees were meeting, telephone calls were being made all over the state—the battle lines were being drawn. At the Faculty Senate's March meeting, a resolution reaffirmed its "commitment to be tireless in asserting that the academic interests of the university take precedence over all other considerations, and in [our] determination to provide all necessary and appropriate support to President Atchley in his defense of those academic interests."

The chairman of the Board of Trustees called a special meeting to discuss "personnel matters." Time had run out. The Board had become polarized in their support of President Atchley, and no reconciliation of their differences appeared possible. No president can be an effective leader without the strong support of the Board to whom they answer. Therefore, Atchley concluded that stepping aside would be in the best interest of the faculty, students, and alumni and would help establish unity within the Board. Athletic Director McLellan simultaneously submitted his resignation.

Academics and athletics clashed at Clemson University. President Atchley challenged the status quo, advocated for higher standards, sought stricter oversight of programs, and remained persistent in his efforts, even though he met with strong resistance. He ultimately was forced to resign his office.

Over the past decades, much has been written regarding the rise of collegiate athletics to the level of professional sports programs and to the equivalent of large business enterprises. Accompanying this rapid rise in prominence are all the problems associated with operating a large business: recruiting the best available talent, offering adequate compensation for services, winning at all costs, and maintaining mammoth stadiums, coliseums, and sports complexes. On some university campuses, it often means a decline in status of other programs, most notably the very academic programs for which the institution was founded.

Any NCAA Division I school with a major sports program is a potential victim of the struggles between academics and athletics. Large athletic budgets, television contracts, politically active booster clubs, win-loss records, national rankings, postseason playoff aspirations, and intense team rivalries all contribute to the pressure to be number one. Influential supporters of athletics become more and more influential, even beyond the playing fields and various athletic programs. These voices can become so strong that even the Office of the University President can be called into question. Trustee members become increasingly involved in the day-to-day operations of the university, particularly in areas related to athletics. Before long, paralysis sets in—a stand-off between the president and members of the Board of Trustees. The university's reputation and public image suffer immeasurable damage as a result.

I now believe that had the Faculty Senate not responded to this issue in 1985, Clemson University might have continued to struggle with the academic-athletic dilemma.

However, almost forty years later, Clemson University has successfully recaptured the essence of a university. Academics is the number-one priority of the institution. The proper role of athletics within the university has been clarified. Board members have gained a better understanding of academics and the educational mission of the university. The faculty are better informed about the authority and responsibility of Board members. It appears that the leadership of the university has been unified. Board members and their president must work in cooperation for the betterment of the entire university community. The 1980s controversies and the role of the Faculty Senate led to the reaffirmation that Clemson University continues to keep the spirit of Thomas Green Clemson's will—that Clemson is first and foremost an academic institution.

CLEMSON UNIVERSITY TURNS ANOTHER CORNER IN ITS AMBITION TO BECOME TOP TWENTY

CLIFTON "CHIP" S. M. EGAN
College of Architecture, Arts, and Humanities
1976–2010

My wife, Diane, and I came to Clemson in July 1976, fresh out of graduate school at Northwestern University. My salary offer as an assistant professor of drama in the Department of English was $12,100 ($500 less than Diane was making as a high school drama teacher in the Chicago suburbs). With only a 5 percent down payment, we bought a 1,100-square-foot spec home in Central for $29,900. I interviewed at Clemson in April 1976, not knowing much of anything about the school. I was enchanted by the rural location, the glorious spring display of azaleas and dogwood blossoms, and the possibilities to help build a theater program. At the interview, Ron Moran, chair of the English Department, told me that four thousand Clemson students had recently signed and submitted a petition to the Board of Trustees, calling for the construction of a performing arts center. The ground was fertile for excitement and growth.

Fast-forward ten years to 1986, and the theater program had grown in size and stature. I was serving as the coordinator of drama in the English Department, and there were three full-time theater faculty and a robust minor. The English Department had been especially supportive of the program and saw it as an important public face. We had achieved national recognition in the Kennedy Center American College Theater Festival (KCACTF), with several consecutive annual invitations for productions to advance to regional competition. Most impressively, in 1983–1984, we had been invited to present Clemson's production of *American Buffalo* by David Mamet and directed by Ray Sawyer as a part of the national theater festival at the Kennedy Center in Washington, D.C. Having won a national championship in football in 1981, Clemson now had a "national championship" in theater!

And yet we were stalled by producing plays in make-do facilities like Daniel Auditorium, a lecture hall. The early excitement generated by students about a possible new performing arts facility had languished, and it seemed like Clemson could not manage to prioritize this badly needed building. The national success of the theater program, in spite of poor facilities, made the situation all the more stark. There had also been turnover in the president's office, and any momentum from the student petition for a performing arts building had been lost.

Feeling frustrated by the situation and believing that Clemson's ambitions to become a truly national university hinged, in part, on building a performing arts center, I wrote a guest editorial for the student newspaper, the *Tiger*. In those days, the weekly print edition of the *Tiger* was widely read by the whole university community, including administrators, faculty, staff, and students. The reaction to the editorial was very favorable and rather took me by surprise. Faculty from disciplines across the campus responded enthusiastically to the argument for a greater emphasis on the performing arts.

I don't really know whether my editorial had an impact on the new president, Max Lennon, but I do know that the climate began to change. Upon the retirement of John Butler, long-time chair of the Music Department Dean Robert Waller decided to combine the disciplines of theater, music, and speech in a single Department of Performing Arts and conduct a national search for a chair. The resulting hire was the prominent national theater educator Richard Nichols. Simultaneously, a program study for a new performing arts center was initiated, using the renowned theater consultant firm Jerit/Boys. Finally, two large gifts were announced: a bequest of $1 million from the Camp family and a nearly $3 million pledge from alumnus Robert Brooks. An international architectural design competition, a first for Clemson, was announced, and the Robert Howell Brooks Center was underway. The building was completed in November 1993.

I kept a copy of the editorial and only recently reread it. The moment seems like part of an inflection point in Clemson University's history and perhaps worthy of reproducing as a part of the Emeritus College memoir project.

RECOLLECTIONS OF THE 1994 UNIVERSITY REORGANIZATION

JERRY E. TRAPNELL
College of Business
1986–2004

After earning my undergraduate and master's degrees at Clemson in 1968 and 1970, respectively, and completing my doctorate at the University of Georgia, I began my academic career at Louisiana State University–Baton Rouge in the Department of Accounting. In 1986, I was contacted to apply for the position of director of Clemson's School of Accountancy. I accepted the position and returned to my alma mater in 1986. After holding this position for seven years, in 1993, I was appointed dean of the College of Commerce and Industry. When I became dean, an academic reorganization study was underway, led by Professor Holley Ulbrich. However, during 1993–1994, no major changes occurred. The Ulbrich Committee and other activities focused on finding economic efficiencies to save money, as enrollments had dropped. In 1994, President Lennon left the university, and University Trustee Phil Prince was appointed interim president. A presidential search was opened. For the most part, the campus saw the change in presidents as an evolution of the university. I do not think that the campus at large expected significant changes during President Prince's interim tenure, but this would clearly not be the case.

In the spring of 1994, the deans were called to a meeting of the Board of Trustees in Greenville. The meeting opened with some routine business, and then the Board went into executive session. The deans were asked to remain to return to the meeting upon completion of the executive session. When we returned, the Board chair announced a reduction in the number of academic colleges from nine to four, which were named and organizationally designed by the Board. The shock of the plan was evident that day: Five deanships would be eliminated, but there was no discussion of the status of any of the academic deans. We left the meeting not knowing our personal status and possessing a high level of anxiety about our future—at least, that's how I felt—as well concern for all our colleague deans. Early the next morning, before the campus opened, Vice President for Academic Affairs and Provost Charles Jennette called me at home to check on me and ask whether I had been informed of my status. My answer was no, making the previous night an anxious one. He indicated that he wanted me to continue as dean to lead the new College of Business, Education, and Nursing (CBEN). Tom Keinath continued as dean of the College of Engineering and Sciences, and Jim Barker continued as dean of the College of Architecture, Arts and Humanities. As the deanship of the College of Agriculture was open, Vice President of Agriculture Jay Gogue assumed the role of dean of the College of Agriculture, Forestry, and Natural Resources.

The academic reorganization of the university was not well received by the faculty and staff. The Faculty Senate and faculty broadly were particularly upset that the faculty committee's submitted reorganization plan had been largely ignored and that few or no campus discussions had occurred regarding the Board's approach prior to its announcement. Importantly, the Board did not eliminate any departments as part of the process. Some departmental reorganization occurred later, but initially the college-level changes were the focus. Of course, some professional staff were moved around, which changed the composition of deans' offices and, in many cases, felt like starting over with a high degree of stress for all, particularly those who were relocated or reassigned to one of the surviving colleges.

Working with Provost Jennette, the deans met almost daily at 5:00 A.M. to discuss implementation issues because the remainder of each day was filled with faculty and staff meetings, continued work with external stakeholders, and all the other responsibilities assigned to a dean's office. During the implementation process in 1994–1995, the presidential search underway brought Deno Curris to Clemson in the summer of 1995.

Clearly, faculty and staff were very upset with the reorganization. Many felt a sense of loss of identity and status as their colleges and departments became part of a much larger organization that, in many cases, had little in common in areas of pedagogy, regulatory, and accreditation requirements (e.g., education and nursing) and lost status in the larger context of Clemson University. Plus, faculty members had concerns for their personal loss of status among their disciplinary colleagues at other universities and in their professional/academic societies. Each new college structure brought together departments and units with little or no familiarity with each other. In my case, my college comprised three major professional programs, Business, Nursing, and Education, each with its own specialized professional accreditation, with two of these reviews in Education and Nursing occurring soon after the reorganization. CBEN comprised more than fifty percent of the university's enrollment and, like all other "new" colleges, was located in numerous buildings spread across the campus. Department chair meetings were initially more formal, given that many faculty members did not know one another. Each department had its own constituency and focus, with little common ground except the normal university policies and processes that applied to everyone.

Although we persevered, I was convinced the CBEN (it was renamed the College of Professional Studies [CPS] early in the following academic year) configuration was not ideal for Clemson. Following his arrival on campus, President Curris agreed that CPS was not workable long term. He agreed to request that the Board split the college into at least two units that had more commonalities. The Board approved the change, and the College of Professional Studies was split into two colleges that would eventually become the College of Business and Behavioral Sciences (CBBS) and the College of Health, Education, and Human Development (CHEHD). This new configuration also included the relocation for a second time of the Departments of Political Science, Psychology, and Sociology into the CBBS organization, another disruption for those departments. The Department of Graphic Communications, which was originally in the College of Education and became a part of CBEN, stayed with the new CBBS organization. I continued as dean of CBBS until retiring in 2004 and, for Clemson's good fortune, I participated in the recruitment of Professor Harold Cheatham to lead the new CHEHD. CBBS offered a more logical combination of academic departments. The business disciplines, for the most part, are applied social sciences based in economics, sociology, psychology, and political science. Graphic Communications was an applied business program focused in a major industry area. The ROTC programs focused on leadership development. Thus, CBBS had some common ground on which it could function. The CBBS structure proved useful as faculty in different departments initiated substantive collaborations of teaching, research, and service.

Although the reorganization process was a period of major change, it must be noted that the five-college model largely survived until 2016, when a new reorganization under the leadership of President Jim Clements created seven colleges. The survival of the five-college model is a reflection of the professionalism of the university's faculty members and staff and their commitment to make things work despite the disruptions the reorganizations and subsequent refinements created.

In hindsight, the impact of the reorganization presented a major challenge and disruption, and adaptation to disruptive changes is often not a strong attribute of any organization. We are attached to our discipline, its traditions, our colleagues at other schools, and our academic home. Disrupting this connection through the reorganization of 1994 was a major shock. Many were irate that the academic faculty had little or no input into the initial reorganization, although the eventual structure was close to what the Ulbrich Committee had recommended during its deliberations. At the time of the 1994 reorganization, many believed that Clemson had made a huge mistake. However, as has been the case for its history, the university survived and thrives today. Even with the current university organization, evidence of the 1994–1995 reorganizational changes remain, maybe because they made sense and all affected faculty and staff committed to making them work. I know that I got to work with many new colleagues; play a small part in recruiting some outstanding leaders, faculty, and staff to Clemson, even in areas outside my business background; and grow in my appreciation of teamwork, collaboration, and cooperation.

PRODUCER STEVE GABRIEL'S TECH REHEARSALS AND PRODUCTIONS AT THE BROOKS CENTER

Lillian "Mickey" Utsey Harder
Department of Music and Brooks Center
1972–2017

One of my favorite experiences of my twenty-one-year tenure as Brooks Center director began in 2005, while I was attending the annual Association of Performing Arts Professionals conference in NYC. While chatting with an agent about an artist I wanted to perform at the Brooks Center, I heard a pleasant voice say, "How nice to hear a Southern accent." I turned around, and Steve Gabriel smiled and introduced himself. We hit it off immediately and began talking about a variety of things: what he did, what I did, and what he wanted to do. Steve told me that he had recently formed a company, IntraMusic Theatricals, so he could tour with children's musicals. He believed that if quality musical theater was not made available to children, there may not be an audience for Broadway musicals in the years to come.

Because renting rehearsal space in NYC is outrageously expensive, Steve told me that he was looking for a free venue to hold tech rehearsals for the children's musical *Broadway Junior on Tour*. If the Brooks Center was interested and agreed to partner in this endeavor, we would also need to provide eight of our best performing arts majors to work alongside his cast and crew. In exchange for our providing the space and the student work crew, Steve's company would present two productions of the musical at no charge. At that very moment, I knew that I was standing in the right place at precisely the right time. Sometimes you just get lucky, and I felt like I had just won the *Jeopardy!* championship!

Our performing arts major, housed in the Brooks Center, was only in its fourth year at the time, and, being a musician and not a theater person, I had no idea whether our students could handle the responsibilities Steve described to me in that chance meeting. But I knew that this could be a once-in-a-lifetime opportunity for some of our most talented students. Should I take a chance and say that I knew our students could rise to the challenge? I knew no such thing, but I said yes anyway. I told Steve that I was confident that our students could and would rise to the occasion.

When I returned to Clemson, I discussed Steve's proposal with Rick Goodstein, chair of the Department of Performing Arts, and he was extremely excited about this potential partnership. Then, I talked to our theater students and told them that I had literally stuck my neck out and did not want to be embarrassed. I explained that, if successful, this partnership could result in job opportunities, and that certainly proved true later, as numerous students became the recipients of wonderful jobs and launched fantastic careers. Many of our majors worked with Steve's company for several years, and several were employed on international tours. It so happened that during the tech rehearsals of *Broadway Junior on Tour*, the professionals had a sound issue they could not solve. One performing arts major, Clemson native Robert Allen, walked behind them at the sound board and quietly suggested that they try something that worked immediately. That made a huge impression on Steve, and, over the years, he loved to tell our students about that incident. Steve laughed and said that here they were, the professionals, trying to solve a problem, and along came this lanky red-haired college student who suggested a fix that worked. He loved it, and so did we.

After holding tech rehearsals for several children's musicals (*Broadway Junior on Tour*, Disney's *The Jungle Book* and *Cinderella Kids*, *A Year with Frog and Toad*, and *The Adventures of Flat Stanley*), Steve asked whether we would be interested in holding tech rehearsals and productions of large musicals, as he was forming a company, Work Light Productions, to tour large productions. Of course, we said yes, and we hosted rehearsals and held performances for *Avenue Q, In the Heights, Mamma Mia!, Nice Work If You Can Get It*, and *Cinderella*. Steve used every available opportunity to share his experiences and expertise with our performing arts majors. He explained how he got started in the business, discussed the process of auditioning, shared the ins and outs of touring, and gave volumes of advice. Steve always stressed the importance of being nice, explaining that when you are on eight-hour bus rides, you don't want to spend time with jerks. He went on to tell our majors that, on occasion, he had to fire people who did not have the necessary work ethic or who lacked the capability of being pleasant. Steve had so much wisdom to share, and our majors listened intently to his advice.

Just imagine how excited our performing arts majors were to have the producer, director, music supervisor, choreographer, lighting designer, costume designer, props designer, sound engineer, and production manager share their talents and expertise with them. The energy level of our students in the Brooks Center was comparable to football players preparing for a national championship, and that is not an exaggeration. None of us could ever have dreamed of a chance like this, and I was thrilled that our students had this extraordinary opportunity to learn from some of the best professionals in the business.

Steve Gabriel wrote these heartfelt words to Rick Goodstein and me after our first collaboration: "While we expected a professional experience, the result was one of the most well-coordinated, accommodating, and enjoyable tech rehearsals that we've ever encountered. My colleagues—some of whom are hardened New York designers—remarked that they wished every production could start out in such an inviting and professional environment. From the graciousness of your staff to the professionalism of your students, you should be congratulated for creating such a wonderful program." Our majors had the opportunity to engage in so many aspects of performances that normally are reserved for professionals, not students.

If you have ever seen the tractor trailers on Bowman Field on ESPN's *Game Day*, then you know how big the production of *Cinderella* was. One by one, six trucks backed into the loading dock and had their contents unloaded and brought into the theater. Every time Work Light Productions teched a show at the Brooks Center, there was a sense of panic that the theater and lobby could not possibly be restored by the time the doors had to open for the show. Truthfully, about an hour before the show was to begin, there were literally dozens of computers, massive amounts of equipment in the theater, and miles of electrical cords running in every direction. Miraculously, all that "stuff" disappeared, and everything came together so the curtain could rise, and we could be transformed.

When I quizzed Steve about the financial commitment of launching a show as grand in scale as *Cinderella*, he said that his company spent in excess of $2 million on *Cinderella* from the beginning of their preparations to getting the show to the Brooks Center. Steve said that when he started his company in 2005 with a production of *Broadway Junior on Tour*, he put a second mortgage on his house; by 2016, he had a $3 million line of credit at the bank. I will always be grateful that the Brooks Center and the Department of Performing Arts had an opportunity to form this incredible partnership with Steve and to have played a significant role in his early success. And to think it all came about because of a chance meeting in the Big Apple when I happened to be standing in the right place at the right time! These tech rehearsals were some of my most memorable Brooks Center experiences because one of the missions of the Brooks Center is to support the educational mission of the Department of Performing Arts. The opportunity to witness the excitement of seeing our students in awe of what they were doing and learning was exhilarating, and a dream come true—especially for those of us who had spent the majority of our careers at Clemson and dreamed of supporting a performing arts major. I can only imagine how proud Robert Howell Brooks would be to see the magic that transpired at the Brooks Center with the production of *Cinderella*.

Even though our students definitely exhibited signs of "wear and tear" by the end of tech rehearsals and the performances, I am confident that they would not have swapped places with anyone in the world. Nevertheless, after the students' exhilarating and around-the-clock work schedule, they could not rest because they had two weeks of classes to make up.

This experience of being immersed in tech rehearsals gave our hand-picked students the opportunity to see firsthand what goes into presenting large-scale performances, to witness the professionalism and commitment that is required, and to experience the satisfaction of working side by side with some of the best professionals in the business. We could not have wished for more!

THE ROAD TO THE RHODES

Stephen H. Wainscott
Clemson University Honors College
1976–2009

Everyone in the Clemson family was ecstatic this year when the news broke that for the first time in the university's history, a Clemson student, Louise Franke, had been selected as a Rhodes Scholar, with another Clemson student, Ronnie Clevenstine, having been named a finalist for the prestigious award. Although the students deserve much praise for their accomplishments and hard work, their success in the rigorous Rhodes competition had much to do with the guidance provided by Robyn Curtis, director of the Office of Major Fellowships.

This essay recounts the history of Clemson's participation in the Rhodes process, but first I want to acquaint readers with the Rhodes Scholarship and why it is considered the most prestigious and selective of postgraduate academic awards. The Rhodes Scholarship, which funds two years of postgraduate study at Oxford University, was established in 1903 by the will of Cecil Rhodes, a British mining magnate and politician in South Africa. A controversial figure, Rhodes was an outspoken and unapologetic defender of British imperialism.

Each year, just thirty-two students attending U.S. colleges and universities are selected as Rhodes Scholars out of a field of more than one thousand applicants. Candidates are first evaluated and nominated by committees on their home campuses. From there, applications are reviewed by Committees of Selection in sixteen districts, with each district selecting two Rhodes Scholars following rounds of intensive and rigorous interviews. First and foremost among the selection criteria is academic excellence. However, scholars are expected to be well rounded in terms of leadership and service. No minimum GPA is specified, but most if not all finalists have a 4.00.

Shortly after I was named director of the Honors College in 1991, I was informed by my superior, Jerry Reel, that he had heard of a Clemson student who wanted to apply for Rhodes. At the time, no university office or employee had the responsibility of guiding students through the Rhodes process. Jerry asked whether I would shoulder this, and I agreed. Shortly thereafter, I received a letter from President Max Lennon naming me as Clemson's Rhodes representative.

I then set about learning about the Rhodes process and figuring out how it could be organized at the campus level. I also began attending national and regional meetings of the National Collegiate Honors Council, where I learned about how other institutions managed the Rhodes process.

Over the next few years, we saw an uptick in interest among students, and we had some modest successes. During that time, students who were endorsed by their campus committees and Rhodes advisors next had their applications reviewed at the state level. For several years, we had at least one student selected to be interviewed by the South Carolina selection committee. In 2001, a breakthrough occurred when Chad Carson, a Clemson football standout, made it past the state level and was named a national finalist. Chad was among eleven students interviewed in Washington, D.C. Unfortunately, Chad was not one of the four finalists named Rhodes Scholars by the Washington committee, but I heard from a member of the D.C. panel that he was "in the conversation" all the way until the final decision. Close!

When Chad returned to campus following his interview, he came to see me about his experience. "I got to my hotel room," he said, "and I sat down on the bed. I put my head in my hands and said to myself, 'I really want this.' And I said to myself that if I got the Rhodes, I was going to tell Coach Bowden that I quit the team, and I wasn't going to play in the bowl game. And I meant it."

About a year later, I got a strange call from Michael Winerip, higher-education editor for the *New York Times*. How he learned about me I do not recall, but he said that he was on campus to write something about athletics and, while he was at it, to talk with me about Rhodes. Over lunch, Winerip said that he had learned about a growing "cottage industry" on college campuses where institutions were increasingly dedicating resources to help students compete for Rhodes and other national awards.

I told Winerip that in his "Ten-Year Plan," President Barker had articulated a goal of two students winning a Rhodes Scholarship (along with the football team winning two national championships). Winerip was astonished. He asked me whether I felt pressured to produce. I responded that if I knew Barker the way I thought I did, he would be understanding if such a lofty goal were not achieved. Nonetheless, when Winerip's article, "Road to the Rhodes," came out, he recounted that conversation and commented, "Just think of the pressure Clemson's Rhodes person must be under."

Over the next several years, Clemson continued to have students selected to compete at the state level. We also had two students, Scott Pearson and Christen

Smith, advance to the district competition. Soon thereafter, the process was changed to eliminate review by state committees. Instead, students who are nominated by their institutions have their applications sent to be reviewed by district committees. There has been some criticism of this change, with some believing that the big leap from campus to district, where the final selections are made, tends to give an advantage to the Ivies and other schools with a long track record of Rhodes success.

My role as Clemson's Rhodes representative and advisor ended in 2006, when I hired Ricki Shine as associate director of the Honors College, with principal responsibility for major fellowships. At that time, I was also Clemson's representative to eight other fellowship boards and foundations. Although I thoroughly enjoyed advising fellowship applicants and considered it to be the most rewarding of my Clemson experiences, the tasks involved had simply become so overwhelming and time-consuming that they were interfering with my primary responsibility, directing and leading the Honors College.

So, what have I learned? For one thing, I have learned that success should be measured not solely in terms of winning but in terms of helping students reach heights they once thought unimaginable. I recall a student who was not chosen for the Marshall Scholarship, and she was upset—I mean *really* mad. Then one day, she found out that she had been chosen for an English teaching position in France. She then realized that if she had gotten the Marshall, she could not have gone to France.

I have also learned that if you do define success as winning, it does not happen by accident. There were times during my Rhodes tenure that I believed that all the university's institutional efforts and resources were for naught and that to win a Rhodes, we just had to wait for a phenomenal student to walk in the door and say, "Here I am! Your Rhodes Scholar!" But as Clemson's recent Rhodes success has shown, we can't think that to win, we just need to sit back and wait our turn.

It has been said in the business world that your most important sale isn't your first one but rather your second. The same could be said about the Rhodes Scholarship. Although Louise Franke's selection represents a milestone for Clemson, when the next one happens, people will start asking, "Is there something in the water there?" Let's hope that happens soon.

CHAPTER 3

Figure Horticulture Faculty Photograph Circa 1988-89 submitted by Mary Taylor Haque. Legend: The original caption was "A Look Back in Thyme: Horticulture faculty at a berry fruitful re*tree*t that wood lettuce grow, pro*grass*, and ex*seed* expectations with our unbe*leaf*able good work.   Partic*plants* are gathered on the Kresge Hall staircase at Clemson Outdoor Lab. **Front Row** (Left to Right): Robert J. DuFault; A. Robert Mazur; Wilton P. Cook; Alta R. Kingman; Ted Whitwell; R. Daniel Lineberger. **Middle Row** (Left to Right): J. Thomas Garrett; David W. Bradshaw; John W. Kelly; John D. Ridley; Jon R. Johnson; James B. Aitkin; Gregory L. Reighard; Donald F. Wagner. **Back Row** (Left to Right): Reginal A. Baumgardner; Judith D. Caldwell; Jere A. Brittain; James W. Rushing; Billy B. Rhodes; Landon C. Miller; Mary Taylor Haque; Dennis R. Decoteau; William H. Courtney, III; R. Gordon Halfacre ; Alton J. Pertuit; G. Ansel King **Missing**: Donald C. Coston (With permission from the University Archives)

RECRUITMENT WHEN CLEMSON WAS STILL A COLLEGE

Rameth Richard Owens
Department of History
1961–2002

In 1961, when our interests first led us to Clemson, the institution was midway through a decade of phenomenal transformation. Until 1955, it had been a military institution with a males-only student body. Suddenly that year, its military identification ended, and its organization shifted to civilian status. At the same time, its doors were opened to women, inaugurating its life as a coeducational institution. Soon more changes of notable consequence would follow. In 1963, Clemson was racially integrated with the successful enrollment of its first African American student. Altogether, these changes brought in their wake seismic transformations of the institution. The curriculum embarked on continuous evolution, interest/emphasis on research emerged, and the student body began its ongoing growth. In recognition of these transformations, the institution underwent successive name changes: from Clemson Agricultural College, to simply Clemson College, and then, in 1964, to the name by which it has been known ever since, Clemson University.

In the 1960s, customary ways of doing things endured, and my husband, Walt Owens, and I, as it turned out, were beneficiaries. In the spring of 1961, Walt was finishing a temporary appointment as a research assistant in the School of Law at the University of Georgia in Athens. We sent out letters of inquiry to perhaps a dozen small- to medium-size colleges in the southeast about teaching spots for the coming year. We had master's degrees in hand, having graduated from Florida State University in December 1960. Walt's specialty was political science, and mine was history. (We thought that we would test the waters of academe before going on to Ph.D. programs.) These letters went out, however, for Walt's benefit only. The idea had been repeatedly expressed in my hearing, especially in the College of Education where I had completed several courses, that appointments for women to college faculties were nonexistent, simply not available. (No women need apply; they were not even welcomed in many high schools, I heard!)

You can imagine how delighted we were when a reply arrived from the acting head of the Department of Social Sciences, Professor Carl L. Epting, inviting Walt to Clemson for an interview. We drove up from Athens for the appointment and parked in front of Hardin Hall, and I waited in the car while Walt went inside to meet Professor Epting. Their conversation went well, and Professor Epting walked with Walt up to Tillman Hall to meet the college dean. With the meetings finished, Professor Epting came out to the car and greeted me. We drove back to Athens with buoyed spirits because Walt had been offered a job as an instructor of political science, beginning with the 1961–1962 academic year.

Several days later, the phone rang with a call from Clemson. It was Professor Epting, calling not for Walt, as we assumed, but for me. Would I be interested, he asked, in teaching five sections of history courses at Clemson, beginning in the fall? To say that I was surprised by his query is an enormous understatement. Never having expected such an offer, I was nearly speechless.

Together, Walt and I came to the campus in the late summer of 1961, taught two full years, and then went on leave to Florida State University for doctoral work. After we returned to Clemson, we were promoted to assistant professors and later granted tenure. We were home, where we remained until we retired, Walt in 1994 and I in 2002, each as emeritus/emerita professors.

Thinking about these events now, more than a half century later, is almost breathtaking. What great fortune we enjoyed arriving on campus when we did! How lucky we were to participate in Clemson University's transformation and be transformed ourselves.

EARLY DAYS

Cecil O. Huey Jr.
Department of Mechanical Engineering
1969–2006

The title of Dwight Eisenhower's autobiography is *At Ease*, and its subtitled *Stories I Tell to Friends*. A subtitle for our Emeritus College volume of memories might well be *Stories We Tell Each Other*. Some of our stories merit long and detailed telling, while others are only anecdotes that often spring to mind in the course of everyday interactions or, maybe, in relaxed moments over drinks. Here, I offer a couple of the latter.

Chance—The short section of sidewalk and steps leading from Fernow Street to the west entry of Riggs Hall can be covered at a stroll in a half minute. I was there as a Clemson senior in 1965, as graduation approached, walking with Professor Douglas Bradbury, who at the time was the chair of the Drawing and Design Department, shortly to be subsumed into Mechanical Engineering as Engineering Graphics. Somehow, he was aware that I had received some nice employment offers, and he inquired about my thoughts and plans. At the time, I didn't know how to approach the looming decision and lacked enthusiasm for my choices, even though a couple of them were coveted opportunities, and I said so, likely with just an "I don't know." There wasn't time for much more. He said, "Well, if you want to go to graduate school, I'll give you a job teaching drawing." I said, "OK," and that was that. I knew little about graduate school and nothing at all about teaching, but right there in thirty seconds max, the die was cast, pretty much for the rest of my life.

I took Professor Bradbury's offer as a flattering compliment, but I believe that he was just desperate, really. At the time, only a small handful of graduate students were in Mechanical Engineering, and only two of us were awarded teaching assistantships in drawing, primarily because no one wanted them, and, in my case, I later learned, someone else had bolted at the last minute. Few wanted those jobs because, depending on the mix of assigned courses, we faced from fourteen to more than twenty contact hours per week and seventy to ninety or so students to manage, all on our own.

My first teaching assignment afforded a mini-epiphany. The course assigned to me included six or seven weeks of descriptive geometry, often a challenge for freshmen that, over the years, had encouraged a good number toward other majors. The prospect of teaching it effectively was a little daunting to me, but once I started through the text, it didn't seem so bad, and, in fact, I found that I loved the subject. My epiphany—maybe I had actually learned something over the previous four years.

Stumbling Ahead—At the time, the entire third floor of Riggs Hall was devoted to Engineering Drawing and Mechanical Engineering. Room 300 was a very large lecture space, half now converted into hallway and an office suite. Then, however, lighting came from tall drafty windows and old-fashioned fluorescent fixtures suspended from a plaster ceiling that had a habit of coming down in chunks. The blackboard seemed miles from the back-row students.

The times required a make-do philosophy, and, for reasons now lost, I was dispatched to a state surplus location to pick up some things designated for Clemson. There, I discovered a wooden box, labeled in WWII military-stencil type "**Chalk Fluorescent**." It was free for the taking, so I added it to the haul. It was a big box—that whole label fit along one side of it.

Back in Riggs Hall, I rounded up a ladder and installed a couple of blacklight fluorescent tubes in the fixtures nearest the blackboard, hoping to stimulate the back-row denizens with my razzle-dazzle chalk. Instead, I discovered why that box might have found its way to surplus stores in the first place.

I bragged a little to the class and started up with the chalk. It worked great, at first, but the folly was obvious in minutes. As the fluorescing chalk dust spread, everything—my hands, my clothes, the erasers, the chalk tray, and, in fact, the entire blackboard—glowed in the most surreal way. Everyone seemed amused, so I just trusted in a measure of pedagogical value somewhere in the combination of tolerant students and a bumbling instructor.

Memories—One lovely memory from the sixties, perhaps oddly, is related to pipe-smoking. All the drawing faculty and a few others smoked pipes, and at least one Mechanical Engineering professor favored cigars in an amber-colored holder. A blend of vapors greeted all who entered Riggs Hall, especially in the closed-up, steam-heated winters of those years. Regardless of the source or mix, the effect was neither unpleasant nor overpowering. Besides, smoking was everywhere back then, and everyone was accustomed to tobacco smoke. In fact, sand-filled ash trays were fixed to the walls throughout the building. Now, tobacco smoke usually irritates and offends me, but, even so, a whiff of pipe smoke redolent of the old third floor of Riggs Hall evokes a sad sense of something lost.

Remembering the wonderful old honest-to-goodness slate blackboards in Riggs Hall evokes a similar sense of loss, particularly the transcendent pleasures of just the right chalk, those blackboards, and things I loved to draw.

My courses usually involved a lot of geometric content, and I depended heavily on the blackboard and figures and diagrams. I believed that it was effective to develop drawings or diagrams and explain them as we went, complemented by the process of students noting them down in the same sequential fashion along with their own notes and comments. For years, in their annual evaluations, students complimented my method and my sketching use of the blackboard.

Then, things changed. We no longer offered instruction in drawing in the introductory classes, and students began to complain of difficulties taking useful notes owing to their weakness in sketching. Of course, I adapted and provided handouts with diagrams included, but because finished drawings, even ones perfect in every detail, masked the logical progression embedded in their evolution, I never believed that they matched the effect of seeing a drawing evolve as we talked. Here, Emerson comes to mind: "For every thing you gain, you lose something [*sic*]" and "In nature nothing can be given, all things are sold."[2]

One of those old blackboards must still be hanging somewhere in the recesses of Riggs Hall, and right now, I am struck by an urge to seek it out and go draw something just for the pleasure of it, maybe something from my first classroom days, maybe the means of establishing the shortest distance between skew lines. I'm sure I can still do it. Finding chalk might be challenging.

-----

[2] Ralph Waldo Emerson, "Compensation," 1841.

CLEMSON MEMORIES:
On Becoming Dean

Robert A. Waller
College of Liberal Arts
1981–2000

The old boy network works. Among my auxiliary roles at the University of Illinois, Urbana, was serving as a consultant with Educational Testing Service, evaluating Advanced Placement examinations in American history at the close of each spring semester. Among my fellow graders was Alan Schaffer, head of the Clemson History Department. At the spring 1980 meeting, he casually mentioned that his college was seeking a new dean. Would I be interested in a nomination? I said yes, for it was time to leave the ivy at Illinois and seek new opportunities. Because Alan was a piranha to some fellow faculty members, he arranged for someone else to make the nomination. I never knew, but I suspect it was Rich Saunders, who also held a Ph.D. in history from Illinois.

By mid-December, the search committee had narrowed the candidate list to six, of which I was one. In mid-November, my wife, Joan, and I were invited to campus for the interview. English professor Richard Calhoun met us at the Greenville-Spartanburg Airport. Being from the flatlands of central Illinois, we were duly impressed in the drive to campus by the low, forested mountains and by the tiger-paw paintings on the highways leading into campus. I was guided through the formalities of the interview process by the chair of the search committee. I plunged into the formal and informal meetings that constituted the maze that candidates must navigate. I also did something unusual, requesting a time slot on my schedule during which I could meet with all the college's secretarial staff because I believed that those individuals were important building blocks on whom the college's future rested. In meeting with Provost David Maxwell, I stressed that he would be getting a "team" by hiring me because Joan would be a most proficient helpmate in doing the extra things necessary to create an attractive learning environment on the campus.

Before coming to campus, I carefully studied the *Faculty Manual* to understand the regulations that guided administrators at Clemson. One practice I challenged was the provision that tenure and promotion were two separate actions. In the environment I knew, promotion to associate professor automatically granted tenure. Maxwell indicated that he preferred the separate tracks with independent decisions, but I was welcome to offer suggestions about other possible changes. That would come years later, when I served as editor of the *Faculty Manual* under Provost J. Charles Jennett. At the same time, the college was drafting new bylaws for its operation, and I was invited to offer suggestions even before coming to campus. Chief among these was the inclusion of an elected Faculty Advisory Council to assist the dean in the management of academic affairs.

Part of the recruiting ritual was an address to the assembled liberal arts faculty about my professional credentials and academic philosophy. I pontificated in a six-page set of remarks that I labeled "Philosophical Perspectives on Higher Education in the 1980s as Viewed from the Role of the Liberal Arts Dean." When it came time for questions from the audience, the first came from my friend Alan, who asked about my views on affirmative action. Fortunately, I had lots of experience in that arena at Illinois and apparently satisfied his and others' curiosity on a pressing question at a Southern institution. The remainder of the visit included various wining and dining opportunities to meet assorted faculty and their spouses. As we returned to Illinois, we were confident that we had placed our best foot forward.

In the ensuing weeks, we heard nothing from Clemson while the interviewing process was conducted for the other aspirants. Then, just before Christmas, Provost Maxwell called to offer the position. What a Christmas present that was! After my oral acceptance, he took the unusual step of asking me to suggest a possible salary. I was taken aback but promised to get back to him with a response. After some research, I learned the salary of the highest-paid full professor in the college. I then suggested a figure slightly below that one, not wishing for the new dean to be paid more than the longest-serving full professor. I did not ask or seek the figures for the previous dean, Morris Cox, or the acting dean, John Butler (head of the Music Department). I was content to have the opportunity for leadership in a new academic environment. At the time, Maxwell was seeking the service of four other college deans, as the new broom had swept the top leadership posts clean. Only the incumbent deans of Agriculture, Architecture, Education, and Forestry remained. Maxwell spoke jokingly of bringing "Clemson into the twentieth century" with all the leadership changes.

COMING TO CLEMSON AND
OUR FIRST CHRISTMAS

Michael F. Kohl
University Libraries
1982–2012

In the late summer of 1981, I was working as project archivist in the basement of the city of Milwaukee's eight-story Flemish Renaissance City Hall Building, with its iconic 350-foot-tall bell tower, when my boss, City Records Manager Bert Hartinger, told me that I had a call from someone at Clemson University inquiring about my interest in a job at the Clemson Libraries. Bert's expression was one of surprise with an element of concern because losing a temporary employee on a limited-time project would cause problems. My own expression mirrored his because I had not applied for a job at Clemson.

I spoke to history professor Alan Schaffer, who explained that my name was on the Society of American Archivists' list of job seekers; it was. I replied that I was gratified by their interest but was committed to finishing the job I was doing and could not start work until next May. Schaffer explained that the search committee would like to do a telephone interview. Once off the phone, I went up to the Milwaukee Public Library's Reference section, which had college catalogs on microcard, and learned that Clemson was in South Carolina, was not a private university but a public land-grant university, and had in its Special Collections the manuscripts of several important people I had never heard of, such as Benjamin Tillman and James F. Byrnes, and one that I certainly recognized, John C. Calhoun. On September 22, I spent several hours on a phone interview, with the outcome that the following month, my spouse, Jane, and I were in Clemson for three days of interviewing and house hunting.

Neither Jane nor I had ever seriously considered living in the South, but at that point in our lives, we needed to resolve whether I had a career as an archivist. I certainly had the credentials, with master's degrees from the University of Wisconsin–Madison in history, library science, and business administration along with work experiences at several institutions. The problem was that at the time, I did not have a secure permanent archival job. We were ready for a move in part because we were commuting forty-five miles (Jane) and sixty miles (me) into work daily during a Wisconsin winter when it snowed 180 inches. We concluded that this move would be a stretch but nothing as bad as some job possibilities that Jane had vetoed applications for, such as archivist for the State of Papua New Guinea or curator of the Polar Exploration Archives in Fairbanks, Alaska.

The interview was successful. After signing the contract with Clemson and purchasing a home with a mortgage interest rate of 15 percent, we moved to Clemson during the spring of 1982. That autumn, Jane began the doctoral program in Clemson's Civil Engineering Department, while I managed a unit with responsibilities for a rare book collection, the university archives, and manuscript collections. That semester was hectic for both of us, and we were sincerely looking forward to putting up a Christmas tree and taking time off to travel.

Much to our dismay, we realized that a storage locker that we had rented for material we did not need in the summer and fall had been burglarized. The boxes of books were still there, but all our Christmas decorations, including some that had been in my family for decades, were gone. On top of that, the director of the Strom Thurmond Institute, Horace Fleming, wanted me to accompany him to Washington, D.C., to meet people and learn more about Senator Thurmond's office operations. With little money to spare, we improvised on Christmas decorations. We had collected aluminum cans during the past months at Clemson. These we took to a recycling center and, with the cash, we went to the Sky City store next to Ingles and purchased a set of lights, tinsel, a tree stand, and several ornament kits that Jane assembled. I cut down a pine sapling on a nearby vacant lot. We decorated our tree and decided to take day trips to Columbia and Greenville. As for going to D.C., I explained to Fleming that my spouse insisted that we have some time together. To this day, we continue to gather aluminum cans to take to a recycling center and, with the cash, go to "Santa Big Lots." This tradition reminds us of the true meaning of the holiday season.

ACS EXAMS INSTITUTE COMES TO CLEMSON

Lucy Pryde Eubanks
Department of Chemistry
1992–2006

It was a warm, sunny day in October 1992, and, after months of preparation, Dwaine and I were moving ourselves and the American Chemical Society's Examinations Institute to Clemson. Our household goods were in a moving van making its way from Stillwater, Oklahoma, to our new home. Being conscious of security as well as the institute's budget, we were driving a large U-Haul truck filled with our entire inventory of paper exams, office records, and shelving. Our staff and some OSU "volunteer" chemistry graduate students had done an impressive job of packing the U-Haul. Little did we realize that we were about to have a genuine U-Haul "Adventure in Moving."

Paying attention to the "All trucks must stop" signs, we pulled into the last weigh station in North Carolina before entering South Carolina. Why did the agent's attitude seem to change as soon as he noticed Dwaine's bright orange Clemson cap? He became convinced we were commercially "hauling paper" without a permit. He issued a hefty fine and insisted that we pay with a check from the Exams Institute account. That meant that we had to *find* the institute's financial records and checkbook in the U-Haul. When we went inside the station office to reluctantly pay the fine, I noticed a poster explaining that the competition to see who could gather the most money in fines ended that very day. I assume that our agent received a nice prize as a result of holding us hostage! I certainly learned that rivalry between the Carolinas had real-world consequences!

I realize that most readers of this volume are not chemists, so some explanation is in order. ACS Exams began as a Committee of the Division of Chemical Education of the American Chemical Society in September 1930. The first national exam in general chemistry was released in 1934. By the end of World War II, the program had expanded to include standardized exams for virtually every high school and undergraduate chemistry course taught in the United

States. As was the case for many years, these exams were all paper and pencil. Remember those Scantron sheets? Remember those very early Apple computers? Yes, we had a couple of those in the truck as well. Don't laugh, but this "high technology" was a step up from the committee's earlier attempt to modernize— the purchase of a Selectric typewriter.

In the mid-1980s, the Exams Committee was changed to an Exams Institute, with a broader mandate to help chemistry educators with their assessment needs. Dwaine was appointed director, and in 1987, the institute moved to Oklahoma State. I was named associate director in 1991. With the help of many volunteers, we significantly expanded the activities of the institute. New authentic assessment practices, such as laboratory practical exams and conceptual exams, were developed. We also prepared study guides for students and extensive test-item banks for teachers. Our Board of Directors encouraged and applauded our ideas, but space at Oklahoma State and their understanding of the national and international significance of the institute were not necessarily in sync with our expanding vision.

One key point for any potential move was finding enough space to house the institute. Enter DeWitt B. Stone Jr., an assistant vice president of Academic Affairs at Clemson at that time. He also was active in the ACS Division of Chemical Education, so he knew of the institute and our leadership in the division. Miracle of miracles, Stone's duties at that time included being in charge of space allocation, and Clemson was embarking on a program of building/remodeling projects! One of these was enclosing the front right corner of Brackett Hall. He enlisted the help of Doris R. Helms, who was the associate dean of sciences at that time. She helped the Chemistry Department understand that they would gain proven teaching faculty who could help expand and focus the fledgling Chemical Education program at Clemson. The Stone/Helms team had the right mix of vision and assigned responsibilities at just the right time, making our move a reality. The situation was a win-win-win for the institute, for the Chemistry Department, and for the reputation of Clemson in science education. Most importantly, it also was a win for chemistry teachers and students everywhere.

We came to Clemson after classes had started that fall. Partly this was because of our need to reliably provide teachers with course placement exams. The bigger issue was time to finish retrofitting the allotted space in Brackett Hall. When we had visited Clemson in the spring of 1992, work was underway to enclose the open corner of Brackett Hall. We were able to go inside and inspect the planned layout for the institute offices. When we pulled up in front of Brackett with our U-Haul, the fully enclosed space was a welcome sight. We were fortunate to have help from several "volunteer" Clemson chemistry graduate students to help unload the U-Haul. I clearly remember one student looking in the back of the truck and loudly exclaiming "Scantron Hell." Under our watchful eyes, everything was quickly moved into the new office space, and the U-Haul was released to await its next adventure.

The adventure continued! We were working to organize everything that first weekend in Brackett Hall when we smelled smoke. The fire alarms were going off but were not yet connected to the Fire Department! We called the Chemistry Department chair, and he summoned the local Fire Department. The firefighters discovered workers down in the basement of Brackett who were being rather nonchalant about how they dealt with oily rags. You might think that was the end of that part of the adventure, but no, the whole episode was repeated about an hour later! At least this time we knew the correct number to immediately call the Fire Department, cutting down on response time and my growing panic.

We soon began to host our working committees again and started teaching during the spring semester. We hosted visitors from many parts of the world, including China, Russia, Puerto Rico, Mexico, South America, The Netherlands, and the U.K. We, in turn, were asked to travel to many places to give talks, hold workshops, and exchange ideas about assessment practices. We participated in several big National Science Foundation curricular projects as authors and helped with the development of authentic assessment practices. All this interaction with the chemical education community led to Clemson's being chosen to host the 1996 Biennial Conference on Chemical Education. The general chair for this important activity was none other than Dewitt B. Stone Jr.! For many years, this conference was the largest nonathletic activity ever held at Clemson, with more than 1,200 registrants from all over the U.S., Canada, and the world. Many Clemson Chemistry Department faculty members took part in conference planning and/or gave presentations. The desired visibility and enhanced reputation of Clemson in chemistry education had more than been achieved.

By 2002, Dwaine had been director of the institute for fifteen years—five at Oklahoma State and ten at Clemson. Rather than accept another five-year term, we believed that it was time for the institute to grow in new directions again. It moved to University of Wisconsin–Milwaukee under the leadership of a new director. The good news was that we had stabilized the financial health of the institute. The new director was able to hire a professional moving company to securely load and transport the still-impressive amount of exam materials. Dwaine retired from teaching at Clemson in 2003, and I followed in 2006. We have repeatedly failed "retirement" and continue to write, travel, and stay engaged with Clemson University in other ways.

COMING TO CLEMSON

Victoria Ridgeway Gillis
Eugene T. Moore School of Education
1991–2010

In the summer of 1991, I was desperately looking for employment, having completed coursework for my doctoral degree and passed comprehensive exams to become what is commonly known in academic circles as "ABD"—all but disillusioned/dissertation. Financial exigencies had precipitated the need for employment, and I had interviewed unsuccessfully with six school districts for jobs as a middle or high school science teacher. I was certified to teach any secondary science course and, in fact, had trained to be a high school biology teacher, the only course I never taught. Unfortunately, I also had twenty years of teaching experience and much of a doctoral degree completed, making me more expensive than the principals at the schools where I interviewed and therefore too expensive. I turned to colleges in the Upstate, writing each one to inquire about the need for adjuncts in literacy. Although I had been a science teacher, my doctoral work was in literacy, with a focus on reading in content areas, what is now known as disciplinary literacy. In August, in complete desperation, I called Clemson and was put through to the coordinator of reading, Lib Galloway. She asked me to send her my curriculum vitae, which I did. I had been a teacher trainer for the Florida Right to Read project and had worked in what was then termed content area reading for more than fifteen years. My doctoral work focused on disciplinary literacy (in science), and I hoped that there might be an adjunct position in either adolescent literacy or content area reading somewhere in the Upstate. Within a few minutes of faxing my curriculum vitae to Galloway, she called to ask me to teach two sections of content area reading in the fall semester, which began in a few short days. It was a dream come true.

I began teaching at Clemson that fall but also taught courses at a local university in Greenwood, South Carolina, where I lived. Parking on the Clemson campus was all but nonexistent in those days, and I often had to abandon my car in questionable areas to get to class on time, as I had only two hours between classes at the two universities, and travel time to Clemson was an hour and a half. Getting ticketed for illegal parking was the price I paid, and I racked up an impressive collection of parking tickets.

Because I had been a secondary science teacher in K–12 schools and had not spent much time in elementary school classrooms, I was more comfortable with the secondary education faculty than with the reading faculty at the time. I began eating lunch with the secondary faculty members on occasion and tried to coordinate my assignments with their methods courses, knowing that doing so would make my assignments more meaningful for my content reading students.

In 1993, Clemson advertised for two reading positions, one in elementary reading and one at the secondary level. I had been teaching as an adjunct for two years at that point and had been on campus only in that capacity. Twenty years' experience in K–12 schools had conditioned me to expect that if I were a tenure-track faculty member, I would be expected to be on campus every day. I lived more than an hour away and had no intentions of driving to campus five days a week. One day, I got on the elevator with Bob Green, who was the chair of the Secondary Reading Search Committee. He said, "I don't have your application for the secondary reading job." I replied that I had not completed my dissertation yet. He said, "Do you intend to finish your degree?" I replied, "Of course, but I also live over an hour away, and I can't come to campus every day." Bob repeated, "I don't have your application." So, smart aleck that I am, I replied, "You mean I don't have to be on campus every day?" Bob turned to me as the elevator doors opened and said, "This is a university, not a high school. I want your application for that position on my desk in the morning." I applied.

When I was invited to campus for an interview, Bob arranged for it to be on one of the days I taught. I dutifully sat in the interview room, where faculty were invited to question me. Dave Barratt was the only faculty member who actually asked questions—everyone else just dropped by for a moment to say hello. Then came the interview with the Search Committee, which included Bob Green; Kathy Headley, who at the time was assistant department chair; and Lib Galloway. Unexpectedly, the interview focused on the upcoming Clemson Reading Conference, a reading conference offered for Upstate teachers at which I had presented. As the conversation turned to faculty responsibilities for a variety of aspects of the conference, Headley looked at Galloway and said that she refused to be the program chair again, as she had departmental responsibilities and was already taking care of exhibits at the conference. Galloway turned to me and said, "Oh, Victoria can be program chair." What was I going to say? My chance at the tenure-track position, something I wanted very much, hinged on my accepting that responsibility. It was not something I wanted to do, or even enjoyed, but for the next fifteen years, I served as program chair for the Clemson Reading Conference, until an administrative decision and greed put an end to the event.

OFFBOARD AND ONBOARD:
Reflections on an Accidental Journey

Dᴀᴠɪᴅ L. Bᴏᴅᴅᴇ
International Center for Automotive Research
2003–2016

The terms *onboarding* and *offboarding* refer to the ways that organizations welcome new associates to the fold and shepherd current associates out. Sometimes the processes are quite formal, at other times *ad hoc*, but they invariably offer an adventure on both sides of the deal.

THE FIRST OFFBOARDING

It all began innocently enough. From 1996 until 2003, I held the Charles N. Kimball Chair in Technology and Innovation at the University of Missouri, Kansas City (UMKC), and I also served on the Board of Directors of two major companies headquartered in Kansas City. In the fall of 2002, I learned through those companies that the chancellor at UMKC had been raising funds for her salary increase by front-running a university development campaign: a clear ethical violation.

I turned the matter over to the Faculty Senate and ensured that my own companies did not support the front-running. It was a risky move, but I thought that my tenured chair had made me bulletproof—it had not. By the summer of 2003, the chancellor found a way to take away the chair but could not remove me from the university—although after that, I had little desire to stay. (The chancellor herself later resigned after a faculty-wide vote of no confidence, but not in time to save me.) That rude offboarding provided the necessary part of any journey: that first step. At the time, it felt more like walking the plank.

CLEMSON: THE ONBOARDING

Shortly before those events, I had met Caron St. John at an entrepreneurship conference in California. She was then director of the Arthur M. Spiro Center for Entrepreneurial Leadership (now an institute) at Clemson. Shortly after those events, in the fall of 2003, Caron sent me a note indicating that the Spiro Center had a newly funded chair available and asking my suggestions for candidates. Disgusted with UMKC, I threw my own hat into the ring, despite knowing little about Clemson.

Amazingly, I was one of two finalists to be interviewed for the job. The other was Bill Gartner, who actually won the chair . . . and deservedly so. The need was for a scholar of entrepreneurship. I had been a practitioner and was also new to the world of academic research. At that point, somebody suggested that Clemson could probably use both of us. To this day, I do not know who raised that possibility, but that was how things came down.

Memories of the onboarding experience stand out. My interviews took place on December 5, 2003, enjoyable conversations with persons of high intellect and goodwill. Here, I name just a few, begging the forgiveness of others equally deserving:

- Caron St. John, who managed the complicated arrangements that enabled my position at Clemson: teaching energy policy in the Political Science Department, teaching technology entrepreneurship in engineering and business from the Spiro Center platform, and so forth.
- John Mittelstaedt, who, alas, succumbed to cancer on December 8, 2020. John launched my interview tour at Clemson. He picked me up at the Martin Inn at 7:00 A.M. for a predawn campus tour after a wakeful night's sleep. Then, over coffee and bagels, he told me about his work in macromarketing, which to my untutored mind sounded a bit like voodoo. John's iridescent smile and spontaneous enthusiasm ignited the launch energy that took me through a day of meeting eleven new people, delivering an energy policy lecture, and attending a late evening dinner. Nothing wakeful about the second night.
- Chris Przirembel, who explained the stunning vision for an International Center for Automotive Research (now CU-ICAR) and later invited me to join that team.
- Debra Jackson, then associate provost, who shared with me the Clemson-wide vision for university building.
- And in a later follow-up, Bill Lasser, then head of the Political Science Department, took me to lunch. He assured me that despite his

department's holding my tenure, I was not a "real" political scientist. (I took that to mean that I would not be required to grow a beard.)

The hiring process began working in its customary, mysterious ways, and in May 2004, I was formally invited to join Clemson University. The opportunity to work with such a group of extraordinary individuals as I met that long ago December simply could not be passed up. We humans are designed to be relational creatures first and rational creatures second . . . perhaps even third or fourth. But the rational part worked also. I accepted immediately.

As the interview and hiring process was unfolding, Clemson's International Center for Automotive Research (now CU-ICAR) was emerging as a reality. Chris Przirembel, Imtiaz Haque, and Bob Geolas were the leaders, each providing complementary talent and vision:

Chris, the visionary leader, built and sustained a coalition of academic, industrial, and political institutions with the resources to launch CU-ICAR.

Imtiaz, as the founding head of the Automotive Engineering Department and co-builder of the CU-ICAR vision.

Bob, architect of the Millennium Campus in Greenville, home to CU-ICAR and now to a growing ecosystem of technology enterprises.

My job was to be steward of the business curriculum and to teach it from an entrepreneurship perspective. (And I couldn't even recall how to change my own oil.) To be sure, there were trials and heartaches along the way, some internally generated, others externally imposed. But those are also among the necessary experiences that attend and shape any enterprise. I counted it all joy to be part of it.

A CONCLUDING THOUGHT

In the title of this story, I use the term *accidental* to describe the journey. But in retrospect, I don't really believe that any of it occurred by chance. The term *unplanned*—by me, anyway—might have been more accurate. It is truly said that "there's a divinity that shapes our ends / Rough-hew them how we will."[3] Or, as an even wiser person once said, "Many are the plans in the mind of a man, but it is the purpose of the Lord that will stand."[4]

(Finally, please forgive the footnotes. I include them to demonstrate my complete conversion to an academic.)

---

[3] *Hamlet*, act V, scene 2, 10–11
[4] The Bible, Proverbs 19:21 (ESV)

THE LONG AND WINDING ROAD
(Or, How a Home Economist Became a Senior Lecturer in Statistics at Clemson)

LAURA SHICK

Department of Mathematical Sciences

2005–2016

Way back in 1968, when guidance counselors suggested careers based on aptitude tests, I was told that I'd become a teacher, no doubt about it. I laughed! No way, I thought. I entered the University of Delaware in 1968 and declared a major in textiles. That was taught in the College of Home Economics and was definitely not an easy program! I carried twenty-one credits a semester and graduated with eight semesters of various chemistry courses, all while working twenty-five-plus hours a week. That was a tumultuous time, with Vietnam and civil rights, but I didn't have time to be out protesting—not that I didn't care. The unstated objective of women in college at that time was to graduate with an MRS. I did, despite my hard-earned textiles degree, but the marriage was short-lived.

Fast-forward to 1974. Although I was not looking for a job, someone told me that Scott Paper Company was looking for a home economist to work in Product Development on their baby diaper project, with a salary of $11,000 yearly. That was almost four times what I was making in graduate school, so I jumped! Little did I know that $11,000 was half the minimum salary for that job level. At my six-month review, my salary was doubled, with the explanation that they hadn't thought I'd stay all that long.

I did stay and was soon supervising a pilot plant operation, making assorted iterations of baby diapers of varying levels and materials, sending the diapers out for consumer testing, and bringing the used ones back to the lab for analysis. Yep, really. That's when the statistics bug first bit. I figured since I was designing product trials by varying levels of different components, I should know some experimental design, so I took my first graduate-level course, Design of Experiments. Then, I took the second semester of Design of Experiments. And then I figured I should better understand how to analyze the data by using multivariate and regression techniques, and those courses followed, all while I was working full-time. Then, I figured it would be a good idea to have a better handle on sampling. About that time, my advisor said, "If you take two more courses and write me a story, you will have a master's in statistics." And so, I did, but it took ten years.

I moved on from making baby diapers at Scott Paper to doing marketing research on the "Red & White" soup brand for Campbell's Soup. During my interview, a senior VP continually ran his hand up and down my thigh (remember, it was skirts and suits only at that time.) What could I say? I needed the job. My alcoholic boss got angry because I wouldn't read the Bible at lunch with him. I learned a lot about marketing research, but it was a terrible place to work.

The next stop was Insurance Company of North America, later CIGNA, doing marketing and market research for the Property Casualty division. Technology was primitive, which made data analysis challenging by today's standards. In 1982, when I was seven months pregnant, my doctor signed me out to await the baby, and I finally wrote that "story" and got the MS before *and* after my name.

That's when my first college teaching opportunity came along, at Delaware County Community College at night. The students were all working full-time during the day and coming to class in the evening, four days a week, and covering a chapter a night. They didn't complain. The college policy was no calculators, so I asked about a slide rule; I got blank stares. Even teaching "old school" without technology, I found that I loved teaching.

Shortly after my second child was born, in 1982, I left the corporate world and started my own marketing research and consulting company. With my network of other former financial services employees, vendors, and clients; a lot of hard work and determination; and a bit of luck, my company was successful. From time to time during that period, I would teach statistics for a semester or two at Widener University, covering for someone on leave or sabbatical.

Fast-way-forward to 1994, when I received an unsolicited surprise offer from Villanova University to join the Economics Department as a full-time statistics instructor. This "home eccy" had truly made the turn to academia. Villanova is a relatively small, private, Augustinian school; it is not a research university. There was not the level of competition for grants as in larger research universities, so there was great collegiality. Faculty were required to place copies of past tests in the department library for students to use as study tools. Still, despite readily available resources, students everywhere are the same. Faculty and students shared the same dining room/study area, and I went to lunch one day and found a group from my class working together on a take-home test! What were they thinking (or not)? I learned so much about the workings of the academic world, and I was very happy and, again, certain that Villanova would be my last career stop. Wrong again.

My husband worked for Scott Paper Company, and in 1996, the company was sold to Kimberly-Clark, with headquarters in Neenah, Wisconsin, and Roswell, Georgia. If he "got" Neenah, I was staying at Villanova; we "got" Roswell and moved south in June 1996. No faculty positions were available, but I was hired by Kimberly-Clark as a part-timer with the title of consulting statistician. By then, technology had advanced so that I could print "pretty" ridge-regression graphs of research analyses! Again, I thought that I had made a final career stop, and again, I was wrong.

My husband planned retirement for 2001, and we moved to Aiken, South Carolina, where I truly had job ADD with four jobs in four years: director of youth ministries at a church, director of community investment for United Way, director of the Social Sciences and Business Research Lab at USC Aiken, and finally adjunct statistics lecturer. My students were typically nontraditional—veterans, first generation, and part-time students working their way through college. All were hard-working and dedicated to their studies. USC Aiken is a very small school where virtually everyone knows everyone. I was happy and, again, thought that I had made my last stop. Again, I was wrong.

In 2005, for some unknown reason, my husband was browsing job opportunities at Clemson and told me, excitedly, that there was an opening for a full-time statistics lecturer in the Math Department. I applied and almost hoped that I wouldn't be invited because I was so happy in Aiken. However, because my husband is a Clemson grad (as are my son, brother-in-law, nephews, and one of their wives), I had little option and so applied. Clemson is SO big, but I interviewed, was hired in July, and in August took the next step down the winding road as a lecturer in statistics at Clemson. There were high highs and low lows, but that's a story for another essay.

And that's how the long and winding road took me from the University of Delaware's Home Economics Department through five universities/colleges, four businesses, two nonprofits, and six years as owner of a successful research consulting firm, culminating as senior lecturer in statistics in the Department of Mathematical Sciences at Clemson. I guess that 1968 aptitude test was correct: ***I am a teacher.***

A SURPRISE PHONE CALL

Lee A. Crandall
Department of Public Health Sciences
2007–2019

It was a late autumn Friday evening in 2006, about 5:30 P.M. I was sitting at my desk on the tenth floor of our shiny new glass-walled building at the University of Miami's Miller School of Medicine, where I was associate chair of the Department of Epidemiology and Public Health and had a large research program that conducted contract research for the state government. It was a job I loved, and at that point I planned to remain at UM until I retired. I was finishing some work and waiting for rush-hour traffic to clear a bit before I made the eighteen-mile trek home to Palmetto Bay in Miami traffic, a trip that could take seventy-five minutes if I left during rush hour. I was surprised when the phone rang but thought that it was probably my wife calling about dinner plans. That no longer meant a spontaneous trip to a restaurant because we had added two new family members in the past three years: our daughters, twenty months and six years of age, had arrived after four trips to Russia to apply for and finalize adoptions.

When I answered, I was surprised to find that the caller was not my wife. (I was glad I didn't say "Hi, Honey"!) My caller was also surprised (and pleased) to find me in the office after 5:00 on a Friday evening. He had been prepared to leave a message and ask me to call back. He introduced himself as Larry Allen, dean of the College of Health, Education, and Human Development at Clemson University, and said that he was looking at my curriculum vitae and was calling to ask whether I had any interest in applying for the position of chair in the Department of Public Health Sciences. Associate Dean Brenda Thames had handed him my curriculum vitae, which she had received from a friend of mine who was working on a midlife doctorate at Clemson. He knew that my wife and I felt challenged by commuting in Miami's traffic and congestion with two young children in kindergarten and preschool, both miles away from our workplaces.

For some fortuitous reason, I listened rather than immediately stating that my current position was one I planned to remain in, as I had done several times with other inquiries in the past two years. At age fifty-nine, having relocated three times, I had declined invitations to interview for several positions, including deanships, for family reasons. My salary at Miami was more than adequate to support the high cost of living there, and I believed that it was unlikely that I would move again. However, I found Dean Allen's vision for the college and his description of the department and the university compelling, and his personality engaging.

After a lengthy conversation, I said that I would discuss it with my wife, fully expecting her to talk me out of it. My wife, Sonya, had been executive director of the Health Council of South Florida for nearly a decade, a job that she loved. But for both of us, balancing great jobs with the needs of two small children was taxing, so to my surprise, she told me to go ahead and apply. Several weeks later, I received a call from the Search Committee chair inviting me for an interview, and I agreed to be on campus in early January. My approach to the interview could best be described as interested but, at the same time, skeptical about the likelihood of leaving my job at "the U."

January weather in Clemson was sunny but cold, a shock to someone who had lived in Miami for the past six years, but far milder than January on the Canadian border where I was raised or during my five years as a department head in Champaign-Urbana, Illinois. As I drove my rental car around on the evening of my arrival, I found the natural beauty of the area with its lakes and mountains immensely attractive.

My interview began with breakfast with the interim chair and proceeded with meetings with many of the faculty, a presentation to the faculty, and something I had not experienced when I was hired as department head at Illinois thirteen years earlier or at Miami—dedicated time to talk informally with a group of the department's students. I discovered the faculty to be very engaged in their teaching and research and highly collegial in their interactions with one another and with their students. As I learned more about the department's curriculum, I realized that it provided a unique and valuable introduction to public health for undergraduates that fit what I had always perceived as a major need for students entering the health professions. Talking with the students reminded me of how much I had missed teaching undergraduates since leaving Illinois six years earlier. I had heard people mention the "Clemson Family," and after two days on campus, the term started to make sense to me.

I discovered that the dean had a very clear vision for the role of the chair and that developing a graduate program and gaining national recognition for the department were at the top of his list. I also spent time with a real estate agent and was pleasantly surprised to discover that we could buy a larger, nicer, new house in Clemson for a little over half of what we had paid in Miami. The only negative was a campus parking ticket on the rental car. (It was because they could not read the date written on the temporary parking permit, and Clemson forgave that ticket.)

I returned to Miami, very interested in the position. But, when you are married, relocation requires the willingness of both partners. In February, we returned so that my wife could see the community and meet people at Clemson. The weather was frigidly cold, but she enjoyed our stay at the Madren Inn, dinner with the dean at Calhoun Corners, and a meal with friends at a cozy upscale Italian restaurant on Main Street in Greenville. I was skeptical about whether a woman who loved Miami would be comfortable in a town that, in 2006, had neither a Publix grocery nor a Starbucks! However, she recognized the advantages for the children in going to school just minutes from a neighborhood where nice homes were available and of replacing my seventy-five-minute commute with a five-minute commute. It certainly also appealed to her to be closer to her sister, who lived in Asheville. The conclusion of our visit was "Let's go for it."

I accepted the position as professor and chair the following week. We arrived in July 2007 to begin twelve wonderful years in Clemson that exceeded our expectations. The staff and faculty of the department were wonderful, as were my colleagues in other departments in the college. The "Clemson Family" was a reality, and, furthermore, it was a functional family. Our department weathered the economic downturn of the Great Recession that began in my second year without losing faculty. The departmental faculty were superb collaborators. Between 2007 and 2012, we added a certificate in public health for nonmajors and a new undergraduate concentration in collaboration with Greenville Health System (now Prisma Health). By the time I stepped down from the chair position in 2014, we had gained approval for an innovative Ph.D. program and had begun recruiting our first cadre of doctoral students. We also had initiated the process that led to our becoming one of the first ten undergraduate programs to achieve accreditation by the Council on Education for Public Health (CEPH).

After stepping down as chair at age 67, I spent five more years at Clemson, finally retiring in 2019. During that time, I authored the accreditation document for CEPH and served one year as graduate coordinator. I also taught special topic classes on drug abuse epidemiology that led to campus-wide symposia in 2017 and 2018. Sonya completed her Ph.D. in policy studies at Clemson in 2018, with a focus on community development, while also serving as the economic development director for the nearby city of Williamston.

We loved Clemson and the Upstate area and hated to say goodbye, but our only grandchildren (both of whom were born after our 2007 move to Clemson) live in Ocala, Florida, so in 2019, we made our retirement home in Ormond Beach, Florida, where we can see the grandkids without an eight-hour drive and we are minutes from the ocean. Thankfully, we get to return to the Upstate several times a year. Our six-year-old child in 2006 is now a young woman of twenty-two and has stayed in the Upstate area, which she loves. We have numerous friends in Clemson and Williamston. And thanks to virtual meetings, I can participate in most Clemson Emeritus College activities seamlessly. I look back on that surprise phone call and think how glad I am that it led to the best move ever!

CHAPTER 4

Woodland Cemetery, (10/26/01) (With permission of artist Clemson President Emeritus James F. Barker)

HINDSIGHT . . . TO A GREAT FUTURE

Bonnie Westbury Stevens
Department of Parks, Recreation, and Tourism Management
1985–2009

As a retiree of Clemson who received all three degrees from the university, and who completed a career here, I'm a rare commodity. My loyalty to the university is understandable, but it started much earlier than my entrance to campus as a freshman or my first day of work for the university. My first real memories of the university date to January 1963.

My dad was a member of a unit of state troopers sent to Clemson to ensure the peaceful enrollment of its first African American student as he came to campus. Having seen the sad and frightening melees at other southern universities, my mom was worried about how things would go and what he would face as a peacekeeper. We watched the news carefully each evening. With my dad away from home and my mom worried, even as a seven-year-old, I paid attention. Things went amazingly well.

President Robert C. Edwards had worked tirelessly, even putting his job as university president on the line, to bring the university to this moment. He had laid the groundwork, along with a cadre of leaders from around the state, to create what would later be called a *conspiracy of peace* meant to accomplish the desegregation of the university with what is routinely referred to as *dignity*. Once the plan for Clemson's desegregation was in place, he met with faculty and students on campus. He also met with law enforcement officers who had been sent to campus to keep the peace.

My father came home from Clemson profoundly impressed by President Edwards and the way he and the university had handled integrating its student body. President Edwards's leadership during this time set an exemplary hallmark for other leaders, Clemson students, and our state as a whole. He led Clemson through one of its greatest periods of growth, not just in the number of buildings and students but in a tumultuous changing societal time.

Early seeds were sown for my brothers and me as to what a wonderful place Clemson University was. Years later, both of my brothers chose to attend Clemson, and I soon followed. President Edwards was still leading the university, and I was able to engage with him on several occasions. He and Mrs. Edwards attended untold numbers of student banquets and events. He stopped to chat with students when crossing campus and regularly invited students to join him on his early-morning walks. Once, I shared my umbrella with him as he crossed from Martin Hall to Sikes Hall when a quick spring shower had cropped up, and he was left unprepared. As we entered Sikes Hall, we ran into a group of Board members. He took the time to introduce me to them before heading off to their meeting. He impressed me, as an undergraduate, with his caring for students and his love for the university as much as he had impressed my father years earlier. He added greatly to the solid foundation Clemson stands on today. For me, it began with a young child's memory of a tense circumstance that showed Clemson in its best light.

CHOOSING CLEMSON:
Civil Rights on My Mind in 1969

GARY L. POWELL
Department of Biochemistry
1969–2006

As a second-year, postdoctoral student in the laboratory of P. Roy Vagelos, I was encouraged to begin looking for a faculty position at a university. A faculty position was the reason that I had worked through my Ph.D. at Purdue University in the Chemistry Department and postdoctoral research at Washington University School of Medicine. I intended to start up a laboratory in biochemistry somewhere and begin training graduate students and teaching within this relatively new discipline.

Roy called me into his office one day in the spring of 1969 and gave me a letter he had received from Clemson University. Faculty in the Department of Chemistry and Geology had written letters to editors of the *Journal of Biological Chemistry*, asking whether they knew students who might be interested in coming to Clemson. I had recently interviewed at Ball State University in Indiana but had turned down the offer. I had not heard of Clemson University, but looking in the dictionary (online resources were not developed like they are now), I learned that Clemson Agricultural College (outdated information even then) was the land-grant university for South Carolina. That was positive. As at Purdue, U.S. Department of Agriculture resources would be available. I was also looking for a position at state-supported institutions because of their comfortable pension and health plans, as many private institutions had watched their endowments dwindle significantly with recent market downturns. I was also told by friends at neighboring North Carolina State that Clemson was lovely. Looking at the map, I could see that it was located on a large lake adjacent to the Blue Ridge Mountains, and not far from the highest peaks in the Appalachian Mountains at Mount Mitchell and Great Smoky Mountains National Park. We had recently enjoyed a backpacking adventure in the park and had experienced wonderful hospitality with friends in the remarkably wild and swampy inland of downstate Georgia.

You may recall that the 1960s were turbulent in the southern states, with civil rights marches and the 1968 assassinations of Martin Luther King and Robert F. Kennedy. An attractive Black graduate student working on her master's in chemistry told me about her visit home to Selma, Alabama, sometime during this time, saying that "nothing ever happens in Selma." I was a bit shocked and did not have the presence of mind to pursue her remarks. But given the difficulties of integrating the University of Alabama in 1963, I had decided that if Clemson University had not integrated, I was not interested in joining the faculty.

Having set up the recruiting visit, I flew into the Greenville-Spartanburg airport in the late spring. Clearly, textile mills had provided resources for the public spaces with lovely carpets. The azaleas and dogwoods had finished blooming, but green farmland was attractive, as were the many large green trees on campus. Garth Spencer was the department head of chemistry, my driver, and host. Not long into the fifty-five-minute drive, I found a way to ask, "Is Clemson University integrated?" He answered, "Yes. And it was done peaceably." After legal battles and a conscious decision by the school administrators to integrate without further incident, Harvey Gantt had been admitted as a student on January 28, 1963. Then, Garth added, "We actually had more trouble integrating women than we did with Black students."

I learned that Clemson College was a military school for much of its history. As in many southern educational institutions, gentlemen were trained as military officers, engineers, farmers, doctors, or clergy. Clemson College trained the first three. Doctors were trained at the Medical College of South Carolina in Charleston, and, because of the separation of church and state, clergy were trained in private denominational colleges, such as Presbyterian College in Clinton, South Carolina. The University of South Carolina carried the traditions of liberal education, with state archives and other resources. History caught up with Clemson College when women were admitted for undergraduate studies in 1955 after a long process starting in 1929.

The faculty and facilities I found in the Department of Chemistry were a pleasant surprise. I was particularly taken by a British Oxford-trained natural products chemist, Reg Pinder, proficient in an area I had delved into at Purdue. Equipment was modern, and space adequate. The faculty was welcoming. Biochemistry was represented by the wife of one faculty member, an inorganic chemist; both held Ph.D.s. I was told that the department wanted to develop biochemistry as a fifth area of chemistry, along with organic, physical, inorganic, and analytical chemistries. On the way back to the airport, I asked, "When can I come?" My answer was in a letter I received a few days later, and I began plans to finish the work I was doing in St. Louis and start the academic year in August 1969. I later learned that Clemson University had hired one hundred new faculty in the academic year 1969–1970.

Connie was surprised by my positive reaction when I got back to St. Louis. She asked whether I had seen a laundromat. I had not. How about a gas station? Nope. Not that they were not there; I just had not seen any. Lying by omission?

In early August, we were on the road to our new home in Clemson, South Carolina. We adventured off the main highway through Maryville, Tennessee, around the east end of Great Smoky Mountains National Park on U.S. Highway 129. Late afternoon, we camped, but it turned out to be too hot and humid in August to sleep in our small tent. So, we found a room in the nearby air-conditioned Nantahala Village. The next morning, fortified by a good breakfast of grits, bacon, eggs, and biscuits, we continued east on Highway NC/SC 28. Highway 28 follows a historic stage route through the heart of the western North Carolina mountains. The road has interminable twists and turns through steep mountains. Poor Connie thought that we were going to live in one of the many houses we saw perched on the mountainside on stilts and that she would undoubtedly have to wash laundry in a creek. Eventually, we asked at a small roadhouse that had a view of Issaquena Falls, how much farther to Clemson? "Just down the road a piece." Driving a few miles farther, we had the view over Six-Mile Mountain, the Piedmont, and the modern campus buildings beside Lake Hartwell.

Our apartment was within walking distance from the campus, so I walked to my office at Brackett Hall, housing chemistry and geology and adjacent to the original chemistry building, Harden Hall. I remember complaining because the window to my office, looking into the interior courtyard and accessible to fresh air, would not open. Garth told me that I could use a rock to open it, but then it might be hard to close again.

Rhodie Sallie, a colleague in the Department of Chemistry, took an interest in my curiosity about the natural beauty in our area. Following his directions, we eventually found Whitewater Falls (the tallest waterfall east of the Mississippi) and Stumphouse Mountain Tunnel, a pre–Civil War effort for a train connection permitting shipping from our area to the Tennessee River. Before 911 emergency services, there were no signs with street names and limited signs with directions. The attitude was "Iffin you ain't from here and don't know where things are, you don't need to know."

One day, I was down on the dirt floor of the basement of Brackett Hall, where an old copper autoclave driven by live steam was located. I routinely used it to autoclave media for growing the bacteria I was culturing for my new research project, and that afternoon the autoclave was warm. That was curious because I was sure that I was the only one in the department who had need of sterile media. I asked around and was told that I should ask Rhodie Sallie. When I did, he looked a little sheepish. "Did you ever eat boiled peanuts?" he asked. Actually, no, I hadn't. "Well, if you put your raw peanuts in salty water and autoclave them for ten minutes, they come out just about right."

We learned quickly that a house on Lake Hartwell cost a $10,000 premium. I bought a new bicycle at Sloans (where Clemson Boulevard begins) for $50, so I could ride from our new house on Skyview Drive to my office and keep the $10,000 in the bank. In a landmark telephone call to my parents in California in April, we announced that Connie was pregnant and that we had bought a house in Clemson. Clearly, we were not "coming home" to California any time soon.

I asked Garth that spring whether I was reappointed and needed to sign a renewal contract or anything. He just smiled and said, "Don't worry about it."

I had learned that my draft board in Los Angeles had classified me as 1A after deferring my studies in chemistry as a critical industry. I called the draft board and asked how likely it was that I, at age twenty-eight and a new professor, was going to be sent off to Vietnam. She told me to wait a moment. She got back on the phone after a couple of minutes and said, "There are plenty of eighteen-year-olds in your pool. Don't worry about it." I was relieved. I would have gone if ordered to, but that war was a good one to miss.

THE CLEMSON FAMILY: Vignettes

DEBRA BROADWELL JACKSON
College of Nursing and Department of Public Health Sciences
1991–2017

Arriving at Clemson University, I immediately heard that it was a special place and that I would be part of the Clemson Family. I had been at a large research university and medical center. The Emory School of Nursing was a small community, but I would not have described it as a family—or perhaps it was a family. All families are happy and get along, right? Families have disagreements about who was the favorite child, who had more gifts than the others, and other typical arguments in which siblings engage. So, I wondered about the family I would find at Clemson. In some ways, Clemson is no different. The same rivalries exist over limited resources. Like children, departments disagree about space and money or money and space. It is always limited. The dean is the parent who tries to keep the family together and moving toward a common family goal. Department chairs are older siblings, fighting for every inch and dollar. I have a few stories to tell.

RESTRUCTURING THE UNIVERSITY (1995)

Others may write in more detail about the restructuring of the university, but I would like to focus on the Clemson Family I found during the process of restructuring. I served on a university task force on restructuring, whose recommendations soon went into a black hole. I did meet numerous people I did not know, including University President Phil Prince. Keep in mind, I was a department head until June 1995, when I was allowed to apply for the position of department chair. Prior to 1995, department heads served at the pleasure of the dean and had budgetary control and hiring control, while department chairs served at the pleasure of the faculty—or so we were told during the restructuring. Both positions, chair and head, should have the faculty and students as their primarily focus. In one quick trustee meeting, nine colleges were reduced to four.

My college was eliminated, along with a non-family-like demotion of my dean. Other deans suffered the same sharp change in their jobs. The departments in colleges were reassigned. My department became part of a "world-class peculiar academic configuration," the College of Professional Studies, under the leadership of Jerry Trapnell. He was understanding and helpful to all of us during this major upheaval. Under his leadership, we began discussions to see how we might make a cohesive college of these diverse majors (such as marketing, economics, finance, education with its five departments, political science, psychology, sociology, nursing, health science, and graphic communications). Meetings to help the College of Professional Studies be successful and function collaboratively were held. The department chairs in social sciences, nursing, and health started exploring collaboration opportunities. Was there a way we could form a unit within the new college? We were doing well, developing a plan, when suddenly it was announced that a new college would be structured: the College of Health, Education, and Human Development. The search for a dean began.

Dean Harold Cheatham joined Clemson as the founding dean of the College of Health, Education, and Human Development. We were lucky. Dean Cheatham approached his new role with enthusiasm, hope, and a commitment to the combination of disciplines he inherited. His goal was to help us become colleagues and more. What I did not know about was the mixed reception Dean Cheatham received from the "Clemson Family." I consider Harold to be my former dean, my colleague on the Provost Council of Academic Deans, and, finally, my friend. He shared this thought with me when I wrote to ask him to consider a contribution for this book: "Could I be true to myself, as my happiest memories and triumphs are pervaded by disquieting ones? Could I write beneficially about the time a doctoral graduate and professional practitioner was caught flatfooted in the commission of the ultimate academic sin (plagiarized dissertation) but managed to wriggle out, blaming me and the university for appointing Blacks, holding deceits, and wielding axes to high administrative posts?" I discovered that a Trustee Emeritus asked for forgiveness for having been opposed to hiring Dean Cheatham solely because of his race. Or that a few faculty members were not supportive and actively worked against him. The latter was the only one that was not a surprise. I have known faculty whose work seems to be to undermine deans; the goals and interests of the college are not important. I have experienced "administrator" as a negative title. I am sure many have heard this statement: Deans (or provosts, or presidents) come and go, but faculty stay.

Dean Cheatham needs to celebrate his many achievements at Clemson and in higher education. He deserves praise and thanks for his caring leadership;

his worthiness should never be diminished by the word *but* in any thought or sentence. I am thankful he continues to collaborate with me for the Emeritus College, for his time and care for our graduate students in our Conversations with International Students (CIS) program, and just because he a great person.

THE GRADUATE SCHOOL (1997)

Within all of the typical university environments at Clemson, I did find a family. I want to tell you about my "sister," Frankie Felder. I did not know Frankie well when I went to the Graduate School. She was an associate dean, one of the few women in administration, and, perhaps, the only female African American academic leader on campus. Provost Stef Rogers had assigned me to be the acting dean of the Graduate School (July 1997–July 1998). Frankie and I found that we had much in common. We showed up at work almost every day in the same colors, if not the same style. We loved our offices warm and often blew a fuse in Martin Hall because we turned on our "heaters" at the same time. Thankfully, Teresa Henry fixed that trivial problem by having the wiring in Martin redone.

I remember one evening when Frankie was at our home for dinner. As we went through the house, we got to our bedroom, and Frankie started laughing. It turned out we had the same bedspread! I was stunned. I had picked the material from a fabric store in Anderson and had the spread custom-made. How was it even possible? Frankie, as a good sister, had me and my girls (Katie and Stacey) over for dinner before Katie headed off to college. I will never forget the amount of time she took to offer Katie advice for college. I remember the details she provided about note taking, listening to faculty, asking questions, and studying to learn, not to memorize. My daughter would never have listened to me; I'm her mom. It was a great family evening. Frankie and Sam's wedding was another special evening, although not a small affair. It included numerous colleagues from across the campus. I am so thankful to have Frankie as a friend.

ASSESSMENT AND INSTITUTIONAL
RESEARCH (1998)

The staff in the two separate offices of Assessment and Institutional Research also became a family. Teresa Henry found me and asked whether she might collaborate with me to set up the Southern Association of Colleges and Schools (SACS) Office in 1998. I was now responsible for the regional accreditation of Clemson University. How did I get so lucky? This was at a time when Georgia Tech was put on public warning by SACS for its lack of assessment. When we showed up in the basement of Hardin Hall, we found Eleanor Nault, a doctoral candidate working as the de facto assessment director (the director had taken a job and left her in charge). It is not easy to transition from coworkers to family. It takes time and commitment to each other's well-being. The Institutional Research (IR) staff was stable and had worked together for years before being assigned as a unit under my supervision in 2008, so it took time for their acceptance of Teresa and me. Assessment and IR have commonalities, but they are uniquely different in methodologies. But by my retirement in 2017, they were all part of my Clemson Family. Teresa and I were relocated to the attic of Sikes Hall, with no windows and a maze design of the space, while assessment was in Martin Hall, with lots of windows and light. I learned to use a slow cooker, make pudding shots, and do pivot tables. I watched my children and theirs grow up.

TAKING CARE OF FAMILY (2010)

One final story. Our daughter, Stacey, died by suicide on December 5, 2010. This is truly when I experienced how the Clemson Family cares for its members. Stacey died on a Sunday, and I was in Lexington, Kentucky, at a Southern Association of Colleges and Schools Commission on Colleges (SACSCOC) annual meeting. I was enjoying a wonderful presentation on critical thinking when I noticed that I had missed a call from Stacey. I tried to call her back, and it went to voicemail. I sent a text message. I had spoken to Stacey at 3:00 A.M. and had talked to my husband Vince that morning. I knew that she was home with Vince, so I kept trying to call her and trying to call him. When I was on the bus back to the hotel, Vince finally reached me. The news was horrible. I don't know how I would have managed to get home if not for David Knox, who was also in Lexington, and Doris Helms, vice president and provost, in Clemson. It was exam week at Mercer University, where our daughter Katie was. Dori went the extra mile, as she always does, and managed to browbeat the provost at Mercer until he allowed Katie to skip her final exams, taking her current grades as final for the semester, which enabled her to graduate without returning to campus. The night before Stacey's funeral, Vince had a heart attack and had emergency surgery. Gail DeSabatino, the vice president for student affairs, showed up at our home to drive Katie and me to the funeral. I had no idea she was coming. She was just there, taking care of us. Providing support. She stayed until Dori arrived. Dori brought us home. Guess who was in our kitchen with stories of Stacey when we arrived home? All the wonderful family I had made, whose names appear throughout these stories: Frankie Felder, Brenda Goodman, Dori Helms, Teresa Henry, David Knox, Ronnie Chrestman. Who fed us? The faculty (Bill Surver) and staff (Rose Ellen Davis-Gross) senate presidents showed up with enough food for an army. It was a tough time, but the Clemson Family showed up, stayed engaged, and helped us move forward.

THE EMERITUS COLLEGE (2022)

The Emeritus College feels like a complete Clemson Family. Perhaps we are still siblings in that we come from all academic disciplines, with decades of experiences in both work and life, but we are grown-ups who no longer complete for attention or for money or for space. We have moved into the next phase of our academic careers and our lives. The emeritus faculty share their knowledge and skills. The gatherings of emeritus faculty, whether for seminars or bird walks or parties, is absolutely wonderful. Every time we have a group gather, I am amazed at the faculty expertise, their research and scholarship, their new adventures, and their willingness to share and give back to each other and to the university and community. It is a joy to be involved with this wonderfully diverse set of colleagues.

MY CLEMSON:
It's the Same, but It's Different[1]

Harold E. Cheatham
College of Health, Education, and Human Development
1996–2001

I begin these reflections with a full disclosure, a warning of my awareness that some among prospective readers will find them unwelcome, even insulting. I tried to convince my entreating colleagues, while providing them exemplars of my *total* Clemson experience, that my story is not the stuff of Clemson Family legend. I failed, however, as each story I told, arguing that its inclusion would be necessary for honoring my unimpeachable personal value of being true to myself, served only to undermine my argument. So, here I sit, mere days before the submission deadline date, penning reflections in honor of the twentieth anniversary of the Emeritus College, a deeply treasured professional affiliation.

A curiosity to me is the events and decisions that preceded my appointment at Clemson. We had planned and prepared for full retirement at the end of academic year 1995–1996. Then, suddenly, our life became cluttered as I succumbed to pressures from a "headhunter," and from one university's alumnus of NFL notoriety, who prevailed upon me to accept a nomination for dean searches in a state where I prefer not to visit—even for a conference or vacation. Belatedly, realizing my dilemma, I decided to search for a desirable appointment, having unconsciously decided to possibly delay retirement. Clemson's December posting for a dean of its newly organized College of Health, Education, and Human Development totally captured my imagination. I applied and in early January received confirmation of receipt of my application along with a promise of immediate follow-up correspondence. In March, colleagues composing an unofficial delegation from Clemson contacted me at our profession's national convention (I was the national president that year), inviting me to join them for coffee and discussion of their Clemson. After two quickly arranged official visits for interviews and consequent discussions, the dance was over. A contract was offered, and, recalling how I had been drawn away from our planned future into the job market, I hurriedly inquired regarding the status of my candidacy at each of the other two universities, only to discover that despite their official correspondence to me, at one, my credentials had been misfiled internally. The search chair confessed to having no idea why I was inquiring about the status of their search.

My Clemson experience capped the final five years of my forty at the schoolhouse. And it was both like and unlike the preceding years, excepting, perhaps, that at the U.S. Coast Guard Academy, Clemson was an affiliation in which I was to become convinced that sometimes brand loyalty is paramount even to personal integration and professional competence. As recorded in my Story Corps interview, my experience here is that one can hardly praise Clemson sufficiently to be allowed to utter a "But." And child that I am of the 1940s and student, beneficiary, and emergent professional of the 1960s academic revolution, I have a lot of "buts." So, I'm aware of being regarded in some quarters within these climes of pervasive, unswerving piety as being a negative person.

My Me also is part of the sensitivities born of those four decades of functioning professionally in spaces where I was one of the few, but most often being the only person, of African American descent, and of being the most senior or go-to person, especially in matters of race, ethnicity, and gender. My Clemson stint capped and burnished My Me. My highs here have been abundant and gratifying. They are bookended, however, by some lows of peculiar composition. And they're unshakable.

During the first spring following my appointment, I was a guest at a Charleston alumni event where an aged trustee emeritus greeted me with ebullience and then sent me into disequilibrium, as his demeanor changed entirely. He was now speaking in quavering, sad tones. Eventually, I realized that he was apologizing to me for his previous allegiance to "pitchfork principles" that dictate that no Black person shall be admitted to Clemson, nor other high place. He said that he had been wrong and, having now changed his mind, hoped that he'd be forgiven. He welcomed me to Clemson and wished me well. The bookend: That first fall, Arlene and I were guests in the Trustees Box, where one of the sitting trustees went out of his way to offend me by expressing his disapproval of my attire. We had scarcely hung our jackets and moved to settle in when said trustee approached me and said, "I see you wore your wife's coat today." I've concluded that sometimes one is such a hopeless blob of humanity that their mere presence arouses others' hostilities. And sometimes. . . .

Clemson students have been a source of endless joy—most all of those whom I've encountered. One, Gwynn Powell, I share about especially because she has returned as a faculty member and achieved the rank of tenured associate professor. When Gwynn and I met (I've no idea where or why), the chemistry was such that she offered to "*teach* me the ropes." Amused and fascinated, I accepted her offer of tutelage. And weekly, she sent the published university dining halls menu to my office with a request that I inform her of my choice of dinners (day/s), after which she faithfully arrived at my office, with PRTM (Park, Recreation and Tourism Management) classmates in tow, to escort me to Schilletter, where we regaled one another, and I learned the ropes. Bookend that engagement with the student who without provocation *showed* me the ropes.

It happened that I, among others, had been invited by the student affairs dean, Joy Smith, and the housing director, Verna Howell, to a consultation and team-building discussion in Tillman to address a matter that these days is termed *diversity*, *equity*, *inclusion*, and *belonging*. As I approached the Tillman circle (Gannt, now), I observed a gaggle of young men straggling from Bowman Field toward a parked, open-cap Jeep. I double-parked about two vehicles' distance behind the spot they would eventually vacate. Upon exiting the circle turn and coming parallel with my vehicle now positioned to park, one of the Jeep vehicle's occupants, with the unlikely given name Christian, showered me with the N-word, amplified by the now ubiquitous f-bomb. I noted the vehicle license plate and its fraternity markings and, still shaking with great anger and dismay, reported the incident upon arriving inside Tillman. Campus police were summoned, arrived, and recorded my reporting of the episode. The identity of the miscreant and his problem fraternity was easily achieved. Charges were filed, and ultimately the student judiciary assessed the appropriate punishment, which I was later to learn was "on appeal," set aside by the reviewing authority.

I came to learn that the restructuring of the academic colleges immediately preceding my appointment had left many casualties in its wake. Although some faculty behaved reservedly, others spoke fulsomely of their sense of broken trust and behaved with attendant suspicion and caution. Turf issues abounded. Indeed, in what had been the public-lecture phase of my on-campus interview with the faculty, during the Q&A portion, dear, dear, senior professor Madelyn Oglesby, acting, I'm confident, as she perceived appropriately in behalf of and in defense of her collegiate colleagues, addressed her observation to me in a sentence that began: "Since you don't know anything about nursing. . . ." In as calm and respectful tone as I could muster, I assured her that I had once been a patient, and that my curriculum vitae shows that I've served as a senior U.S. Naval hospital corpsman and as a certificated neuropsychiatric technician. Within HEHD, I was indeed fortunate to have a few self-appointed "guides" who early on steered me from the traps and invested generously in the prospects of my success. Upon her retirement, Dr. Ogleby presented me with a gift, which has ever since rested atop my desk, and a note proclaiming me "The best friend the School of Nursing has had." Some time after my own retirement, I had the occasion to notice Professor Janie Hodge, upon making eye contact with me at the rec center, leave her workout station and walk directly toward me. When she reached me, she began explaining that she was in the gym at 10:00 A.M. because she was teaching a night course that semester. I thanked her for the intended courtesy in sharing that information with me and added that she need not explain her presence there to me, "Since I'm not your dean." Her cherished retort was "You'll *always* be my dean!"

And finally, there was May 9, 2002, the day that 2001 faculty retirees had their "LOYAL AND FAITHFUL SERVICE" cited with inscription as Emeritus in the COMMEMORATIVE SCROLL OF HONOR CLEMSON UNIVERSITY. We were seated on the stage of the Brooks Center and Provost Helms was officiating, enunciating the tradition for the occasion when a late arriving honoree appeared offstage peering in at those seated. His assigned seat, the only vacant chair onstage was to the right of mine. After some apparent cognitive mapping he ambled to the vacant chair and stood further studying it, seeming to await arrival of some assistance. When no assistance materialized he leaned over to me and asked: "Are you sure you're at the right place."

My brief stint at the university enriched our lives, adding some esteemed colleagues to match those dating from our first professional appointments. I'm happy to not need to name those colleagues, as all know who they are, and many of them are contributors to these chronicles. Alas, I salute Deno Curtis for his confidence in me and for his leadership, and continuing friendship, as I know that had he not been here, I would not have been.

---

[1] *"It's the Same . . ."* has been borrowed from the work of Pulitzer Prize–winning Harvard child psychiatrist Robert Coles, who studied and wrote expansively of adolescent moral, political, and psychosocial development, with a focus on their response to the trauma of dislocation or relocation. *"It's the Same . . ."* is a recorded utterance of Sally, a Black child from New Orleans, regarding her sense of self and place as she was ". . . confronted with the hate and violence of mobs and the forced, pointless loneliness brought on by the boycott of 'her' desegregated school." (*Daedalus*, 1965, 94(4), p. 1107).

FIRST-SEMESTER TEACHING AND LEARNING

Frankie O. Felder
The Graduate School
1987–2017

It never occurred to me to question what reaction I would get when I walked into the classroom in 1993. It took about eight steps to reach the front center of the room, place my textbook and class roll on the table, and slide my purse under the desk. Facial expressions told an entire story. A few heads slightly cocked to the side, a couple of brows furrowed, and some blank stares that I could not quite interpret were evident. Mind you, this all occurred in just about ten seconds.

These young people sitting in my classroom hoped to soon be heading out into the world to assume their places in their chosen profession, the most critical job in the world in my mind—one that touches virtually every human being on the planet. They would become teachers. And from the initial reaction to their discovery that I, indeed, would be *their* teacher, I realized immediately that I would be teaching much more than the subject matter outlined in the syllabus.

I don't remember during exactly which week this conversation ensued (unfortunately, in hindsight, I did not keep a journal), but it was early in the semester—perhaps by the end of the second week. The young man with curly red hair in the front of the room seemed to assume the role of self-appointed class spokesperson. They were interested in knowing all about me: "How did you get to Clemson?" "You went to Harvard, right? That's what we heard." *From whom?* I wondered. That was not on my syllabus. He asked, "What do you think of us?" I could have asked him, "What do you think of me?" but I did not. I am a Southerner. I already knew. Instead, I asked, "What do you think I think of you?" And, in the class discussion that ensued, they learned a lot about me, and I learned a lot about them.

What they learned about me was that I expected excellence—especially from them—because they would be influencers, exposing the world of possibilities to thousands of young people over the course of their teaching careers: shaping minds, forging thinking, narratives, and attitudes for the future. They learned that I would not "round up" their grades, that they would receive on their transcripts exactly the grade they had earned. An 89.5 would be an 89—a "B" in my class. They informed me that I had "the highest grading scale in the College of Education." "No one," they said, "had a 10-point grading scale!" I learned that from them, but I never did check the accuracy of that statement. They learned from me that I would be the parent who would be in their classrooms observing their methods if they sent home poorly marked papers, suggesting to me that they had not paid sufficient attention to the work that my child had turned in, or, worse yet, if I sensed that as teachers they really did not care about the quality of my daughter's progress in school. I had already had this experience when I arrived in Clemson in 1987. Following many conversations with the my daughter's teacher, counselor, and principal, as well as with parents of kids in the school who were faculty and administrators at Clemson, particularly with Black faculty at the university who had experienced the local school system ahead of my arrival, I knew precisely what to do: I removed my daughter from the public school system and began to question how long I would stay in the area.

What else I learned from these young people is that they had been honors students in high school—nearly *all* of them! I was impressed and expected great conversation in class and enthusiastic students! After the first couple of assignments, however, I learned that most of them would need to be taught how to use Cooper Library to enable them to research deeply into topics and write papers of substance. I learned that many of them, despite having been honors students, really did not know how to take effective notes in class or how to dissect a page in their textbooks to cull the essential knowledge from each chapter. But I was willing to teach them. They learned that I was always upstairs in my office and had an open-door policy: "Just bring your class notes, your textbook, and let's talk. I will help you." Only a couple did.

They learned that I cried after the first exam I gave them. It was an essay exam. They could not articulate what I thought I had taught. They had difficulty applying the content to real-life education issues. The majority of these undergraduates were planning on teaching right in the area—in the Upstate, in Clemson, if possible. They loved Clemson! But they did not know that there were "education issues" in the Upstate! What this taught me was to modify my approach to the content of the course and to the types of tests I gave in class. I required students to read the newspapers and to watch the news and come to class prepared to discuss local education issues as they related to course content.

I adjusted my exams to use the Scantron that other faculty were using, to develop multiple-choice, fill-in-the-blank, and true-false tests.

The dean who hired me, Arnie Schwartz, invited me to South Carolina to consider working in the Graduate School or as the executive director of the Greenville Higher Education Consortium. When we met over dinner at the Ramada Hotel in Clemson, I was surprised that several other South Carolina University administrators were there whom Arnie had invited to meet with me as well. Dean Schwartz was so welcoming and interested in my considering Clemson that I immediately decided I wanted to work with him, and, despite the multiple offers with higher salaries that I received from some of the others to work elsewhere in the state, I accepted the offer to come to Clemson.

By the time I assumed my first semester teaching assignment, however, I had been at Clemson six years and had engaged in many conversations with the president and other senior administrators about where I had come—to an up-and-coming university in the Upstate of South Carolina that had, unfortunately, a national reputation regarding race and cultural diversity, particularly of African Americans, as did the state in which it was located. I had not done my homework. I was not aware that I would be teaching in a building named for one of the university's first trustee members (Benjamin Tillman), quite the avowed racist; that I would be walking across a campus that was the former plantation home of U.S. Vice President John C. Calhoun that told *HIS*tory (his-story) of the university in a manner that failed to acknowledge the names and contributions of the African Americans who were once the overwhelming majority population on the property in the 1800s; and that I would be conducting research in the archives on the history of graduate and international education at Clemson in the Strom Thurmond Institute, named for the internationally known Southern alumnus who never publicly acknowledged paternity of his Black daughter, Essie Mae Washington Williams. By the time I had walked in the classroom that day, I knew that I had been hired as the eighteenth or nineteenth Black faculty member on campus in a tenure-track position. So, I was not surprised to sense some unease in the classroom on that first day of teaching.

I intentionally did not make eye contact with the student whose body jerked so noticeably that I saw it in my peripheral vision as I settled myself in front of the room. She never said a word about her reaction, nor did I. Actually, no one said anything directly the entire semester, but on the last day of class, after I had dismissed my dear undergraduate students for the final time, two students asked to speak with me. The first shared shock to see me walk into the classroom on that first day and claim the "teacher's desk." In her four years as an undergraduate education major at Clemson, that had never happened for her. She acknowledged it had really thrown her off—so much so that she had physically reacted. I told her that I was aware—that I had noticed her reaction on that first day. We talked a minute, laughed, and then hugged each other. It made her proud, she said, finally to have just one Black faculty member; finally, to see someone representing herself; proud to meet me. I was proud to meet her and happy that she would soon be an influencer in the schools. I wished her well, and she did the same for me.

The second student explained that he was an older returning adult, excited to be coming back to school after having served in the military. He was looking forward to completing his education and training to become a teacher. An ardent student, he shared that he had always been an A student but that he had never had to "work too hard" for those As. Then, he provided a plausible explanation for some of the blank stares I had noticed on day one. He said that he had never had an African American teacher before, and when I walked into the classroom and put my books on the "teacher's desk," he said to himself, "*Hmph!* What can *she* teach *me*?!" He didn't expect much of the class. He continued: "I owe you an apology, Dr. Felder. You really challenged me this semester. I got an A in this class, too, but I had to *really work hard* to earn it. Like you said on the first day, we could all get As, but we would be earning them. I EARNED this A!" He then said, "This is the best class, and you are the best professor, that I have ever had." I thanked him for his openness and willingness to share his experience about race with me. I wished him well. He wished me well.

That semester I taught the College of Education's first diversity class as well, Multicultural Counseling. It was a graduate course, so I elevated my expectations from those I imposed on the undergraduates. The experience was priceless. We listened intently to each other. Overall, the students learned that they knew very little about race and their own feelings, attitudes, and narratives they carried around with them from wherever they had acquired them. I learned that I could still effectively teach content related to race in the South. In the final analysis, the first semester teaching at Clemson taught me, particularly, that I was better suited to teach graduate-level courses. It also taught me a lot about the environment I had joined and the lessons I needed to teach as well as some I needed to learn. It taught my students a lot about the environment they had always experienced—and that which they had not. I would say that we learned together, aptly reflective of the intent of the course: Principles of American Education.

CLEMSON'S CREATING A SENSE OF COMMUNITY:
Vignettes of My Faculty Experiences

Dolores A. Stegelin
Department of Teaching and Learning
2001–2017

Following are personal vignettes that reflect Clemson's deep commitment to creating a sense of community at local, state, and global levels.

PART I: BEGINNING THE JOURNEY

My first day at Clemson was September 11, 2001. I was hired for a unique role: to provide leadership for a large state-funded early childhood grant with the National Dropout Prevention Center (NDPC) and to assume a faculty role to build an expanded early childhood teacher education program in the School of Education. My interview with Dr. Jay Smink, director of the NDPC, was cordial, informative, and inviting. Jay explained the new grant and the emergence of an emphasis on early childhood education in the South Carolina. Governor James Hodges and the South Carolina legislature were providing competitive, state-funded grants to develop a new initiative in the state: The Office of First Steps. Through this new office, South Carolina's county-based programs were established to provide coordination and expansion of early learning opportunities. The NDPC received one of the largest of the state grants, and I was brought into the Clemson community to provide leadership on this grant. As the details emerged, my start date would be September 11, 2001, and Governor Hodges would come to the Madren Center to recognize the NDPC and Clemson for this important new early childhood initiative.

On the morning of September 11, 2001, I drove to campus to meet Governor Hodges and the NDPC leadership team to become part of this hardworking group of professionals. I was excited and nervous—so much was about to happen—and my journey with Clemson and the NDPC seemed full of promise. As I drove through the winding, tree-lined, quiet streets of the Clemson campus, I got closer to the golf course and the Madren Center. Suddenly, my car's radio began to blast news alerts about a plane flying into one of the Twin Towers in New York City. Even over the radio, I sensed the broadcaster's anxiousness and unease at this emerging situation. With apprehension, I arrived at the Madren Center and found parking close to the front door of the Martin Inn. When I entered, I noticed scurrying individuals exchanging confused glances but mostly focusing on the large-screen television in the front foyer of the Martin Inn. There was a general feeling of uncertainty, and all eyes were riveted to the television. No one seemed to understand what was happening. I noticed a flurry of activity among the Madren staff, guests, and Clemson professionals organized for this major event. And then, unexpectedly, another plane appeared on the TV screen and flew into the second tower in New York City. The tension then erupted, and there was a clear state of disbelief and fear. I learned that the momentous announcement by Governor Hodges had been canceled and that his entourage abruptly returned to the governor's office in Columbia under heavy security.

The atmosphere at the Madren Center was one of disbelief and concern for others' welfare. Dr. Smink and the NDPC staff—including Marilyn, Linda, Susie, and John—decided to return to NDPC's home on the edge of the campus to digest what had just happened. I took note of how Jay and the NDPC staff reached out to one another in a caring and supportive way—the NDPC was feeling a little like home, but in an unexpected way. We were asked what we wanted to do: stay at the NDPC office or go home. Given that choice, several retreated to their homes to provide care for themselves and their families. But I wanted to stay at the NDPC house—I felt comforted there, and it was my first day at Clemson, and I recognized that this was a very special group of professionals.

In the upstairs of the two-story NDPC house, I shared office space with Linda and Susie; Jay and the administrative team were on the first floor. Everywhere, there seemed to be emotional outreach and support. After such a shocking and harrowing day, and, despite a completely disrupted first day at Clemson, I felt a quiet sense of belonging. My first day at Clemson University left an indelible impression on me—people cared about each other. Land-grant universities are community-focused, and my 9/11 experience reinforced my impression that Clemson was all about creating a sense of community.

PART II: CREATING A SENSE OF COMMUNITY
IN BARNWELL, SOUTH CAROLINA

As part of my role at the NDPC, I traveled to many rural counties in South Carolina, and I was drawn to the town of Barnwell. A grass-roots citizen group had formed to study, improve, and expand programs for its youngest citizens—children from infancy through third grade. I was asked to join this group and to provide research and instructional support for its early childhood settings, including childcare, Head Start, and public-school classrooms. This group of citizens included a local attorney and Clemson alum who provided leadership as well as facility and financial support, along with parents, merchants, teachers, and other citizens of Barnwell County who were interested in the education and overall health and well-being of young children and parents.

This experience taught me the value of grass-roots leadership and the character of a small city with a great deal of determination and resolve. My experiences included attending meetings of the grass-roots group, conducting professional development workshops for teachers, researching the quality of each classroom setting, and even helping with the painting of classrooms in a private childcare center! This effort was collaborative; we (teachers, director, parents, and community volunteers) all met at the center on a Saturday morning and painted all day long. The pride in the center was apparent, and the shared effort was very meaningful. Lunch was served by a volunteer who wanted to facilitate this important event. Again, finding this level of collaboration and shared citizen activism in a small, rural town in the Lowcountry was a very special professional and personal experience. Once again, I experienced a sense of community, collaboration, and shared vision, all supported and encouraged by Clemson.

PART III: FINDING AND CREATING A SENSE
OF COMMUNITY IN REGGIO EMILIA, ITALY

As a faculty member in the School of Education, we were encouraged to work beyond our comfort zones and to be creative in our work. Before coming to Clemson, I was engaged in a study of an Italian early childhood methodology, known as the Reggio Emilia Approach, originating in the northern city of Reggio Emilia, Italy. With support from the global engagement and study-abroad staff, I developed a three-week study abroad to Reggio Emilia specifically for students in education, social studies, psychology, health sciences, and others interested in child and family development. As part of this process, I reached out to faculty members whom I knew at the University of South Carolina and the College of Charleston who were also engaged in early childhood education. Together, we formed a collaborative study-abroad experience for thirty students each spring.

Little did I know that the destination city of Reggio Emilia, Italy, would be a great fit for Clemson University! Our study-abroad experiences included living with Italian host families, forming relationships with teachers and students in preschool and elementary schools, learning the Italian language and currency, and traveling to the nearby cities of Parma, Bologna, and Modena, in addition to Milan, Florence, and Venice. I quickly learned that the Italian culture very much values collaboration, a sense of community, and a focus on families and relationships. This study-abroad experience endured for many years and still exists today. Once again, I experienced Clemson's support in creating a sense of community, this time in a faraway city that also values a sense of community. Today, relationships that developed between students, students and faculty, students and host families, and faculty across the universities still thrive!

Reflecting on my professional journey at Clemson University, I came to realize that the most enduring memory I have is the *constant commitment to creating a sense of community*. Clemson's mission as a land-grant university was apparent to me from the beginning. Over time, this mission has evolved into a more global outreach model, but the land-grant mission remains visible to all who become part of the Clemson community.

THE INTERNATIONAL FESTIVAL

Frankie O. Felder
The Graduate School
1987–2017

My initial assignment at Clemson, as associate dean for International Programs and Services, was to develop the infrastructure for "internationalizing" the university, a trend of the late 1980s and early 1990s in U.S. institutions. As such, when Clemson was planning to celebrate its one-hundredth anniversary, I was asked to create an activity or program that could include the international population. I gathered my few staff members and drove in a state van to UNC–Greensboro to observe their international celebration. What creativity was evident, and what an opportunity for international students to teach about their cultures, countries, values, and more.

I returned to campus and designed what we called the International Food Festival. The suggestion to focus on foods came from CAIF (Clemson Area International Friendship). Having no idea how the community would actually respond to such an activity, I instructed the international students who agreed to participate to prepare foods from their countries for no more than seventy-five to one hundred people. They would be able to sell samples of these food items for no more than $1. There would be no American cuisine. This was a time for us to learn about them. This was an opportunity, also, for them to earn some money for their organizations or for themselves if they happened to be the only student from their country.

The Food Festival was advertised to be held on the first Sunday in April at the base of Cooper Library. There would be a "Parade of Fashions," an international emcee (Dr. Hassan Behery), international students dressed in their native attire, and foods from the seventeen represented countries. At that time, we had about 450 international students on campus, with the majority being from India and China. "Doors" (actually police tape) were to open at noon, and festivities would continue for a few hours . . . or so we thought. However, by 11:30 A.M., hundreds of people were lined up to attend this event!!! I was pleasantly mortified! Attendance was estimated at one thousand! Food, of course, ran out in no time, but we had so much fun watching the International Parade of Fashions, getting to know members of the community, and meeting international students, faculty, and staff who had come out to join us.

As my staff cleared the debris at the conclusion of this very quickly concluded Food Festival, I announced, "This is an activity that we will develop and hold each year." And we did. For twenty-five years now, the International Festival, which became the signature event of International Awareness Week, which my staff created, has been an anticipated activity of the university's spring events. I'm so proud to have been the creator of this event and all the many programs and activities that have been a part of our celebration of the international students, faculty, and staff who help make Clemson the university it is.

MANY FIRSTS FOR ME

Almeda Rogers Jacks
Division of Student Affairs
1975–2020

I never thought that I would come to Clemson as a freshman in 1970 and stay until my retirement as the vice president for Student Affairs in June 2020! Throughout my career, I was able to experience many wonderful learning opportunities and, I hope, through my work in the positions I held, positively influence the lives of Clemson students and those faculty and staff with whom I worked.

Perhaps the most significant highlight of my career was being selected as the vice president for Student Affairs at Clemson in 1992. When then-president Max Lennon let me know of my selection, I was thrilled beyond words. I was the first female to hold this position at Clemson—at that time, senior administrative positions were primarily a "man's world," with the glass ceiling being broken far too late. However, I didn't often think of myself as a "first," but as someone who had been selected in a highly competitive search process due to a solid record of achievement and many noted accomplishments in the world of higher education over seventeen years in previous positions. Initially, being the only female at trustee and executive leadership retreats was a bit strange (Patti McAbee was elected as Clemson's first female trustee a year after my appointment), but I never felt uncomfortable or as if I were wearing the banner for women. Over the years, I worked with spectacular leaders, many of whom were women, and was able to help advance and develop the careers of those who earned it through their work, just as I believed that I had done.

When I began my work at Clemson in 1975, I never aspired to become a vice president, much less the first female vice president. However, when I was growing up, my parents encouraged me and my three siblings to believe that we could be and do anything we worked to achieve if we did our best. I always tried to do just that and benefitted from the guidance of great mentors along the way. In my first job, I reported to Nick Lomax, the director of housing. Nick was a great mentor, and I would continue to learn from him as our careers followed similar paths.

As I grew in the profession and advanced to higher-level positions, various university presidents became mentors as well. I was blessed to have learned so much from so many, and although I have never seen myself as a pioneer at Clemson or within the student affairs profession, many do. To that end, I still have men and women reach out asking for counsel. As I did while working, I always try to do my best to advise them on their careers or other matters we discuss. Many of those have written or called to let me know how much they appreciate and value the example I set for them. Without a doubt, this is the most rewarding aspect of my career and makes me very proud of my forty-four years in higher education.

Another first was assisting in establishing the Bridge Program in 2006. While I was serving as vice president, Clemson began a partnership with Tri-County Technical College that allowed students who did not qualify for regular admission to Clemson to attend Tri-County for classes and, after meeting certain criteria, "cross the bridge" to become a Clemson student. Those criteria still exist today, with students having to earn a 2.5 grade point average (GPA) after having completed thirty hours at Tri-County Technical College. Bridge students have access to all Tri-County and Clemson academic success resources. Students may participate in ROTC, band and choral groups, and most student organizations. They are not allowed to participate on an NCAA athletic team nor join a Greek organization. When I first retired in 2006 after thirty-one years, I had the opportunity to assist in putting a team together to get the Bridge Program up and running during its first three years. We were able to successfully launch a program with some 240 students. Students at the time were housed in off-campus properties in the area. Today, the Bridge program has grown to nearly one thousand students who live on Clemson's main campus, enjoying the opportunity to engage in a more robust first-year campus experience. About 75 percent of bridge students cross over to Clemson for their sophomore year, and, interestingly enough, 90 percent of students who participate in the program go on to graduate from Clemson, which is about the same rate as regularly admitted freshmen. It has been a very successful program, with many institutions inquiring about it and starting similar programs.

In December 2014, Jim Clements (the fifteenth president) asked me to return to Clemson to assume the position I had retired from in 2006, vice president for Student Affairs. I was surprised and excited, having worked with various presidents since 1975. I had the pleasure of working in the administrations of Presidents Edwards, Atchley, Cox, Lennon, Prince, Curris, and Barker. I reported directly to four of these presidents in my first seven years as a vice president. In working with their various leadership styles, I learned a great deal. I have always said you can learn from the good, the bad, and the ugly, and I experienced them all—enough said!

In the fall of 1974, I was a graduate student working as the graduate resident assistant in Housing the first year that the Clemson House was used as a residence hall. I would supervise the resident assistants on the six floors of the building. The Clemson House was built in 1950 as one of the grandest hotels, with 250 private rooms with a bath and air-conditioning throughout. It was open to the public all year long. The first year as a residence hall (called dorms back then) was a challenge, but also a blessing. Seven family units were termed "permanent residents" who were allowed to remain in their unit after the Clemson House became a residence hall. Most of these residents were older, and we discussed for hours how to mesh the two groups. They loved the students, and we lived harmoniously with each other when most thought we could not. When the Clemson House was torn down in 2017, memories of that year flooded my thoughts.

In 1988, I held the position of associate vice president for Student Affairs and dean of Students. I was asked to teach in the College of Education (later to become the Eugene T. Moore School of Education) while serving in these roles No previous vice president of Student Affairs had been in the classroom on a regular basis. I taught several graduate courses in counseling (personnel services) for the secondary level and later the introduction of student affairs, working closely with the director, Dr. Tony Cawthon. I learned a great deal from him and my students. One case in point was a student who was always late and had done hardly any work on assignments. After three classes, I asked her to stay late so we could discuss any issues that may be affecting her work. With many tears flowing, she explained that she was working two jobs while raising three children, living with her parents, and being the caregiver for one. My heart sank, and we worked out a different schedule for her assignments This most important lesson taught me to consider that things are not always what they seem and to respond with empathy whenever appropriate and possible. This approach guided my work style as much as anything else throughout my career.

SURVIVING THE FIRST YEAR OF ADMINISTRATION: MY LESSON

Kathy Neal Headley
Department of Elementary and Secondary Education
1987–2021

1989: The College of Education's faculty filed into the small auditorium. The dean, hands in pocket, walked forward to the podium. The college began its last faculty meeting before the holidays with the standard business. At last, new business on the agenda was addressed. With the College of Education's plan for reorganization in the final approval stage, faculty members were curious as to who would fill the newly created positions, but the dean declined to reveal specific names. "The new assistant department head for Elementary and Secondary will be a woman," the dean briefly hinted. A slight murmur erupted as the faculty discussed possible nominees for the job. I knew who the person would be but permitted myself only to squirm anxiously in my seat. A faculty member from within the department would fill the position of assistant department head—me. The department buzzed with the news: a young, untenured, female assistant professor with no previous administrative background. Suppressing my tensions, I anticipated the future.

Spring semester began. The grapevine was in full blossom, but I was too busy with classes, advisees, and committee work to stop and sniff. What I lacked in experience would certainly be rectified with on-the-job training and my compulsive perfectionism to get the job done. With avid interest, I set about the task of serving on the search committee for a new department head. I would work closely with this person, so the selection would be important. Tenured faculty members, the *Old Guard*, provided me with moral support for the coming term. By the time the new fiscal year was in progress, much of the buzz had ceased. With trepidation and excitement, I started my new position in an office with a new department head next door. The feeling was similar to that of a first grader starting school with brand-spanking-new shoes.

The beginning weeks were especially hectic. Teaching full-time with the Writing Project and preparing to train for an at-risk reading program were more than enough to take care of the half-time academic responsibilities. Administrative duties pressed the remaining half-time into overtime. Scheduling classes for the department was my first administrative task. Computer printouts with names and numbers arrived in bulk on my desk. Due dates blared at me. Okay. Now what? The former schedule coordinator came to the rescue. Headed in the right direction, I met with program personnel and organized course offerings. Then, the next surprise arrived: the Southern Association of Colleges and Schools (SACS). I was elated to chair the departmental committee until I realized that I was also second in line to head the college committee. Administration was becoming a lesson in irony for the road not taken. As chairperson, I took pride in the fact that SACS committee meetings were conducted with efficiency, but I feared that *the blind leading the blind* was an apt description. As I simmered in the process of evaluation, my other hand was preparing lessons for an inaugural telecampus course, teaching two sections of secondary education majors, chairing a state reading committee, and assisting with a local reading conference. Perfectionism was increasingly hard to achieve. The expertise of committee members established a strong basis as we struggled together with goals, objectives, assessment, and utilization. Directives blended together as we worded key phrases and debated central issues. The first draft turned into the second, then into the third, and so on. The date of completion coincided with final exams, research presentations, and more SACS meetings. With the deadline's arrival, I breathed an exhausted sigh of relief. Next time, I would employ the skill of delegating.

The holidays were greeted with the reminder that as a new twelve-month employee, I would have two days' annual leave for Christmas. As a long-term student, teacher, and faculty member, my entire being rebelled at the notion that I would remain at my desk while others scurried home to mix eggnog and bake cookies. Well, at least I could salvage time of my own for scholarly writing. Ha! Administrative duties seem to cloud normal vision at such times. Other more pressing projects filled the presumably quiet days between semesters. Scholarly writing rested on the backburner. Oh, well, I'll be better prepared to use the time wisely at the next semester break, I told myself.

January. Registration, in-services, writing meetings, tenure materials to submit. When would I ever pick up the dry-cleaning? Classes started, and I felt the wind on my back. By February, I had the hope that somehow, I would be able to manage teaching, administration, and a personal existence in addition to single parenting. Then, March and April came. Conference presentations, writing retreats, SACS assessment reports, public school and college evaluation visits, state education committee assignments, Writing Project startup tasks. The end of spring semester found me recuperating at a low-cost motel during a national reading conference. How could a simple accident such as breaking the heel of one shoe cause an outburst of tears? Slow down, I reminded myself, but the opportunity to collaborate on a grant with another college was too good to miss.

The first six weeks of summer brought a much-needed reprieve. No teaching responsibilities, just state reports to file and the Clemson Writing Project to organize. As I filed away stacks of mounting papers, I asked myself, "What did I learn during this first year as an administrator?" Lots. I learned to listen and interpret words spoken not as personal daggers but as concerns and frustrations. I grew a tougher skin. I wrestled with personal growth and professional development issues and discovered that administration can be isolated when compared with classroom teaching. No longer was I just one of the gang when it came to faculty matters, but I wasn't one of the big boys either. I learned that projects can be accomplished with collaboration even though paperwork multiplies, regardless of diligent efforts to subdue the beast.

What advice would I pass on to other young professionals eager to climb the administrative ladder? Well, the most important point is actually very simple: Stay in touch with the classroom because teaching makes a good administrator better. Only through interaction with students can one avoid self-defined goals, keep focused on what is worthwhile for students, and render paperwork as a necessary ingredient in achieving realistic academic objectives. For me, teaching is a constant reminder that students are the center of what education is all about, especially at the administrative level.

CHAPTER 5

Hardin Hall (4/16/2002) (With permission of artist Clemson President Emeritus James F. Barker)

BIOCHEMISTRY AT CLEMSON:
The Beginning of a New Department

GARY L. POWELL
Department of Biochemistry
1969–2006

The strength of biochemistry as interdisciplinary led to a problem. If you needed chemical or physical tools to solve a biological problem, or vice versa, great. Administrators, however, with all those different subject areas in their organizational chart, like neat demarcations and lines of responsibility. Dean Clayton Aucoin called me into his office one day and asked me whether I would like to be chair of the Department of Biochemistry. At the time, I was still untenured; I had just recently received funding for one of my research projects; and I was content with my associations in the Department of Chemistry. I told him that I did not think so. He may have warned me that if I did not take the position, I may find myself answering to someone else. And that is what happened. A new department was formed in the School of Agriculture, where the Department of Food Science and Biochemistry was housed. Dean Aucoin did insist that the new department be separate from food science and be moved to the College of Sciences, a move that cost him his position, as I recall. The new dean brought in a department head, J. M. Shively, and the resources to hire one faculty member in biochemistry, Jim Zimmerman. They were charged with creating the programs for undergraduate, master's, and doctorate degrees in biochemistry. Although my appointment remained in chemistry, I was expected to help. They created the programs and then fought to get them approved to award the first biochemistry degrees in South Carolina. We prevailed sometime in 1972. Then came the campaign to let others in the state know about Clemson University's new programs. Using a map of the surrounding states, we divided up the undergraduate schools and began writing letters, asking for them to invite us to lecture to their students about our research and tell them about our new programs. I remember visiting such schools as Berry College, Claflin College, and Belmont Abbey, with very limited resources in their science laboratories. When the graduate programs were approved, we were in a position to choose faculty and earned enmity when no one was chosen from the program in agriculture to pursue our new graduate degree programs. As I remember, we had enough students admitted to begin the undergraduate program around 1974.

About that time, now Dean of Sciences Henry Vogel called me into his office:

"Gary, we would like you to move to the Biochemistry Department."

"But I am happy in Chemistry."

"Well, I cannot make you move, if you are happy, but we are going to move the core courses in Biochemistry that you teach in Chemistry to Biochemistry."

I did not have to think about that very long. I had helped with the organic chemistry laboratories the previous summer in a poorly ventilated space filled with the smoke of amateurly run reactions. I had worked hard to give interesting lectures about structure, function, and metabolism, some for general students, some for chemistry majors. I could not see myself giving up the biochemistry courses to teach organic chemistry courses. Of course, I was a young, naïve faculty member. It never occurred to me to go back to the chemistry faculty and the department head, share what the dean had told me, and then ask them what they thought that I should do. It may have meant a fight, but I might have been able to retain the courses I had created for chemists and stay in the Department of Chemistry—although that may not have been the best option for the university. Unlike some universities, Clemson University has only one department called Biochemistry (now Genetics and Biochemistry). Again, there was some enmity from my Chemistry colleagues when they learned I had moved to the new Department of Biochemistry, costing them their fifth area of chemistry.

Another problem was that I was teaching too many courses: five, with a pair of laboratory experiences. Although I enjoyed instructing chemistry and biochemistry students, preparation time came from time that could be spent in the laboratory doing research, working with graduate students, and writing the grants and publications required to support that work. I wrote up my accomplishments and began circulating my curriculum vita to seek other jobs. I did hear from Purdue University. The offer from them was interesting and somewhat satisfying, but did Connie and I want to live and work back in West Lafayette? No, not really. The physical environment in South Carolina, with mountains and lakes to the west and north; green, rolling hills to the east; and the Atlantic Ocean only four hours away was far superior to the glaciated flats of corn and soybeans in the northern half of Indiana. I had also been promoted to associate professor with tenure in 1973, and Purdue was not prepared to hire me as a tenured associate professor.

At Clemson, I had recruited two smart young graduate students. One was as Southern as one gets, from the local area. She simply wanted to earn a master's degree in chemistry and get on with her life with the new avenues an advanced degree would open to her. The other was from Turkey. She was married to an engineer, also Turkish, working toward his doctorate. I had some good ideas that came from my postdoctoral work and set them working on those two separate ideas. I recall a Chinese student with limited English asking whether Oya's husband "was a Turkey, too?" Recently, we were privileged to visit this couple and their son in their home across the Bosphorus Strait from Istanbul and at their beach house near Sile. We celebrated Oya's retirement while we were there in 2013.

When I was ready to present the results of this research at the annual meeting of the American Association of Biological Chemists, I needed a sponsor from that society. I learned that only five members resided in the state of South Carolina. One, retired downstate, agreed to sponsor my paper. I also remember having to spell the name of Clemson University when ordering biochemicals by phone from Sigma Chemical Company in St. Louis. I did have an advocate at North Carolina State University. Sam Tove was also a lipid biochemist and had taken an interest in this new arrival in the Carolinas, and he invited me to the Annual Southeastern Lipid Conference, which moved its meetings between various universities in the southeastern United States. John Coniglio from Vanderbilt University was the host of the first meeting I attended, and Fred Snyder at Oak Ridge National Laboratories was the other best-known member of the group. Having a group of people to share your interests and look out for you is vital, and even more important when you are attempting to start something new. I participated in the Annual Lipid Conference for many years. In retrospect, I suspect that Sam let the department head know that I was starting to look at employment at other universities. Perhaps that helped my situation and figured in my quick promotion.

The biochemistry program grew rapidly, as we were the only undergraduate program in that discipline in South Carolina. My colleagues also had recruited graduate students, and we began teaching our graduate courses as well. The university scheduled the construction of Jordan Hall in support of the biological sciences, within the College of Sciences. Although we had some input, most of the burden of the planning of the second floor for biochemistry fell to the department head, Dr. Shively.

Sabbatical leaves are a privilege of tenured faculty. They are an opportunity to leave one's settled position, make new associations, and learn new techniques. When I returned in 1976 from a wonderful year's experience at the Molecular Biology Institute of the University of Oregon, I had a new laboratory in Jordan Hall. My colleagues Jim Zimmerman and Jess Shively had moved me from my laboratory in Brackett Hall to Jordan Hall, a generous boon I have fully appreciated only in my later years.

I also recruited my first doctoral student, Mickey Cable, funded by a grant from the National Institutes of Health obtained largely on the strength of my experiences at the University of Oregon. I set Mickey working on the preparation of spin-labeled cardiolipin, a four-tailed lipid found exclusively within mitochondria. I had learned the value of a spin label at the University of Oregon and thought that this would be a useful addition for the family of labeled lipids for specialists. Fortunately, the National Science Foundation agreed, and I was able to pay Mickey a reasonable salary to work on this project. This led to his doctorate in a reasonable time and to multiple years of support for my laboratory.

CREATING THE UNIVERSITY ARCHIVES AND RECORDS MANAGEMENT PROGRAM AT CLEMSON

MICHAEL F. KOHL
University Libraries
1982–2012

My wife, Jane, and I moved to Clemson during the spring of 1982. The major reason that I was hired was to oversee the management of the papers of Senator Strom Thurmond, which were a key element in then–University President Bill Atchley's plans for fund-raising and meeting critical needs, such as a performing arts center. Within six months of my coming aboard, a young, competent archivist was hired specifically to handle the Thurmond papers, with the result that I was no longer needed to supervise the daily operations of this key undertaking.

Special Collections had a wide range of responsibilities, including some truly fabulous rare books, such as first editions by Galileo and Darwin, and the university's own records documenting its history. Unfortunately, the University Archives barely existed, with a few boxes of material cataloged like manuscript collections and about a dozen wooden filing cabinets that were organized by subject rather than by who had created the material. The origin of the material was often unknown, and contents varied wildly from early correspondence of university faculty and presidents to newspaper clippings and items filed there as a last resort. Some files had a memo attached stating that the staff in the President's Office had "striped the files" and that this folder or folders were deemed worth sending to the Archives.

During the autumn of 1982, I did a bit of exploring of storage areas on campus, including an old cattle barn, where I found what proved to be some of the earliest records of the university. The materials were mainly routine financial records, but they were the only detailed records that existed from that period. Fortunately , the materials also included the original minutes of the Executive

Committee of the Board of Trustees, beginning in 1889. In May 1983, these records were transferred to the Special Collections Unit in the Cooper Library. The associate director of the libraries was dismayed when he saw about three hundred cubic feet of material, some covered with pigeon droppings, in Special Collections. At the time, the Thurmond papers consisted of about 1,500 cubic feet of material, and now more.

Something needed to be done to retain records documenting the university's history, and I had the good fortune to find supporters of this opinion. One came from an unusual part of the university administration: the internal auditor, Michael Hughey. Michael was a Clemson graduate who was deeply concerned about preserving the assets of the university, including those that were of historical value. He also was responsible for records management at Clemson University. Records management is more than filing and maintaining space for keeping old records; it is grounded upon legal requirements for how long records must be kept and when they can be disposed of as well as which records are of permanent historical value. As the internal auditor, Hughey had more pressing concerns than these mundane matters unless auditing issues arose.

South Carolina was, and is, blessed with one of the best state archives in the nation, and I contacted their personnel regarding what could be done to improve the situation at Clemson. They recommended that I apply for a grant from the National Historical Publications and Records Commission (NHPRC). I was familiar with the NHPRC's operations and personnel, having received a grant from them while serving as the archivist at Rhode Island College. In these efforts, it was helpful to have Clemson's director of the libraries on South Carolina's NHPRC Board. The grant I prepared asked for federal funding of a records manager and university archivist for one year, with the university having the positions become permanent, as well as funds for student assistants and archival supplies.

The university's provost needed to agree to these new positions. When the director of libraries and I met with him, he mentioned the need for records management and agreed that at least he could tell Mike Hughey that something was being done. He explained that agreeing to allocate positions as part of grant proposals was always a risk if all the grants were funded, but for better or worse, in the case of Clemson, that never happened. In this case, the grant was awarded in 1984, and the first records manager, Kerry Strong, was hired in 1985. The following year, the first university archivist, Dennis Taylor, was hired. Several colleges and deans, such as Liberal Arts under Dr. Bob Waller, enthusiastically embraced records management for its opportunities to transfer or rid themselves of old files.

I continued to explore the storage areas and material kept there. In the unfinished basement of Lehotsky Hall, several storage areas were separated by walls framed by two by fours and chicken wire, holding all sort of unused equipment, old furniture, and files. Among them were records of the Cooperative Extension Service from the 1910s to the 1970s, including thousands of photographs documenting its operations. These needed to be transferred to the University Archives. After negotiations, this space was reallocated to the University Libraries for the Records Center, and the Extension records were transferred to the Cooper Library for proper care and cataloging.

In the late summer of 1985, the Records Management program and Special Collections found themselves in an unhappy administrative feud regarding whether the Purchasing Department could convert thousands of invoices dating back decades to microfilm. State law required that the records coordinator for an agency (in this case, me, the head of special collections) sign off on requests for new microfilm equipment. I had examined some of the invoices located in the cattle barn when retrieving the early university records several years before and knew that they were of little value and should be trashed. The issue for the Archives and Records Management program was not just one of saving the university thousands of dollars but whether the South Carolina Department of Archives and History's records retention schedules would be followed at Clemson. However, the purchasing administrator was adamant and threatened to go to his vice president for Business and Finance. In 1985, Clemson was in the midst of administrative upheaval following the resignation of President Bill Atchley, Athletic Director Bill McLellan, and Vice President for Administration Melvin Barnette. The provost, Dr. David Maxwell, became the acting vice president for Business and Finance, including the Purchasing Department. When confronted by the assertion that I would report to his vice president, I pointed out that his vice president was now my vice president, the provost who strongly supported the Records Management program. There was silence on the phone, and no new microfilm cameras were purchased.

With competent staff to manage the development of the Records Management and University Archives programs, Special Collections no longer solely depended on political collections. When reviewing my day-timers for these years, I realized that I spent a great amount of time at meetings of which I have no remembrance of their consequence, if any. Nevertheless, the foundation for the permanent improvement in preserving Clemson's history did occur during those first years, and I eventually was awarded tenure.

BOOKENDS—CLEMSON UNIVERSITY'S LANDSCAPE ARCHITECTURE PROGRAM

Donald L. Collins
College of Architecture
1972–2005

Clemson did not recruit me—I recruited Clemson. After six years of northern winters, including military duty in Illinois, graduate school in Massachusetts, and a faculty position at Indiana's College of Architecture and Planning at Ball State University (BSU), my wife and I had had enough. It was time to head south. After sending letters of inquiry to Virginia, North Carolina State University, University of North Carolina at Charlotte, Clemson, and Georgia, asking about a position for a landscape architect who could also possibly teach architecture, I received positive responses from Virginia, Clemson, and Georgia. The Clemson response was a surprise, for, unlike Virginia and Georgia, it did not offer a landscape architecture degree. The invitation made me curious.

I set about scheduling interview trips. Virginia was scheduled first, only to be canceled by a blinding late-February blizzard closing the airport in Muncie. Next came Georgia. Everything went well, but after the visit, I was not really interested in Georgia, having not been impressed with the student work I saw. By the time I was able to get to Clemson, it was mid-April. I had already received an offer letter from Georgia, and time was running out. I soon discovered that the fastest way to get to Clemson and back to Muncie by air was to charter a flight. Thanks to my farming neighbor who worked a thousand acres using a small plane occasionally to see from the air how his crops looked, I was able to contact another pilot who had a twin-engine Piper Apache. He agreed to fly me to Oconee "International" Airport, located across Lake Hartwell from the university, and he would do it for only $100 more than the commercial flight was going to cost me to bring my wife and young son along.

The morning we were to arrive at Oconee, the airfield was closed due to low visibility. We landed at Anderson instead. Luckily for me, there was a rental car agency at the airfield. Driving to Clemson, I could not help but notice that it was spring. I had just left winter a few hours ago. The pressure was on to make a good impression, but landing at a different airport had already made me late for my scheduled meeting with Harland McClure, the dean of what was then the College of Architecture. In my naïveté, I assumed that my tardiness would be a strike against me, but that was not the case. Dean McClure was a busy man, so he simply rearranged his tasks for the morning. I also wondered whether he would remember and hold against me that I had left Clemson after one year in Architecture for NCSU and Landscape Architecture after he had gone to bat to get me approved for in-state tuition and arranged for my wife to have a job on campus.

After I was shown into Dean McClure's office, with the customary handshake, he offered me a seat. He began my interview by asking to see my portfolio. Portfolios are customarily in book format, but all I had was a tray of slides. He called for a projector. Nervously, I began showing my work and the work of my BSU students. I began to relax a bit, seeing that he was engaged in my examples and my approach to design and teaching. When I finished, he summoned Gayland Witherspoon, the head of the Department of Architectural Studies, to his office and asked me to show my slides again. Professor Witherspoon had no idea I was a candidate for a position in his department. Deans ruled back then!

After I ended my second presentation, McClure began telling me that he had had landscape architects on the faculty in the College of Architecture since becoming the college's dean because he believed that landscape architects could and should play a role in shaping buildings as well as being "architects of the land." He said that my timing was fortuitous, for Ed Pinckney, a landscape architect, had just resigned his professorship to practice full-time on Hilton Head Island. (Pinckney later was inducted into the College of Architecture, Arts, and Humanities Hall of Fame for his professional work.) McClure then pulled a document from his bookshelf, saying, "This is a copy of the 1971 *Academic Master Plan for the College of Architecture*, produced in response to a Commission on Higher Education (CHE) mandate that all state-supported institutions had to state where they stood and where they would like to go in the future with respect to programs of study offered." He continued, "This document calls for the establishment of a Master of Landscape Architecture (MLA) degree program at Clemson. You could be a vital part of this realization." At that moment, I was sure that I wanted to come to Clemson and that Clemson surely wanted me to come.

Georgia had made an offer. Clemson made an offer. Georgia's offer was better than Clemson's offer. I contacted McClure. He matched Georgia's offer but stated that he would go no higher. I accepted. I arrived at Clemson in July

1972. I expected to be quickly called to McClure's office to be given the charge to begin work on the MLA degree program, but that didn't happen. Budget cuts, a building addition, establishment of an overseas program, and other issues kept the MLA degree off the college's agenda. Each delay hardened my belief that Clemson would have a Landscape Architecture Program because the institution was ready to support it appropriately and not because I fiercely advocated for it.

It was eight years before I was called to McClure's office and told that it was time to move forward with getting the university's approval for the MLA program. I devised a two-year program clearly focused on land design with a strong technical competency within a traditional professional practice framework. It would require an undergraduate background in design. The anticipated program's course requirements, credits, course descriptions, and evaluations sailed easily through the university's approval process. It was signed off by the provost and sent to the president for approval. The new Clemson university president, Bill Atchley, an engineer by education, rejected the MLA program, writing that it largely duplicated the program in civil engineering. There was some truth to his statement, for there are similarities in what civil engineers do and what landscape architects do. The former work from an engineering bias, while the later work from a design aesthetics bias.

Years later, and shortly after Jim Barker became Dean of the College of Architecture, I met with him to discuss the college's 1971 Commission on Higher Education (CHE) Master Plan, apprising him of the MLA program being rejected by Atchley. Barker was simpatico but not then in a position to do much about it—or so he thought. Enter Max Lennon as president of Clemson University. One muggy September afternoon, Barker was paying a visit to President Lennon's office, when Lennon asked, "Jim, why do you not have a landscape architecture program in your college?" It was a natural question. Lennon had come to the presidency at Clemson after being a vice president at The Ohio State University (OSU), which boasted a very large and "visible" landscape architecture degree program. Jot Carpenter, the head of the OSU program, had just finished a term as the elected president of the American Society of Landscape Architects (ASLA). Barker rushed down the hill to my office in Lee Hall and burst into my office, sweat on his forehead, saying, "Do you still have that document you did on establishing a landscape architecture program at Clemson?" When I said yes, he said, "Dust it off and go see Jerry Reel, assistant provost for undergraduate affairs, right away."

Barker was savvy and knew that under the CHE, "Full Funding Formular" undergraduate students were funded less than graduate students. The undergraduate degree, he reasoned, would be easier to "sell" to the CHE. After I met with Reel and discussed the program possibilities, including accreditation by the Landscape Architecture Accreditation Board (LAAB), Reel greenlighted advancing a five-year professional undergraduate Bachelor of Landscape Architecture (BLA) degree. Full of tips from Reel, I set about once again devising a curriculum, writing course descriptions, determining course credits and faculty needs, and identifying possible instructional spaces.

The BLA proposal was received favorably by the Curriculum Committee but then hit a snag: Horticulture objected. Reel called a meeting in his office of those concerned and simply announced, "This is a design-focused degree, not a horticulture-related degree. It will be managed by the College of Architecture."

Within two weeks, the BLA program proposal had passed through all university channels, been signed by President Lennon, and forwarded to the CHE in Columbia. There, it hit another snag: The CHE staff academic affairs director reviewing the proposal recommended that it be denied, writing, "I do not see why Clemson needs five years to do what the tech school can do in two years." It was obvious the reviewer was equating the proposed degree to tech school offerings in "landscaping." I invited the reviewer to come to Clemson to discuss the concerns, which he accepted. Contacting every landscape architect in South Carolina, I asked them to send me slide images from some of their best projects, with an emphasis on projects to which the public had access. I got an amazing response from which to make a presentation. At the appointed hour for the meeting with the CHE's staff advisor, following the usual meet and greet with involved Clemson players, I dimmed the lights and made a thirty-minute presentation on landscape architecture in South Carolina. When the lights came back up, the CHE person stood up, turned around to face the audience, and said, "I think I need to rewrite my report to be in the affirmative. I had no idea the projects shown to me today were by landscape architects. I have visited many of them. I thought they were the work of architects."

With that, the BLA proposal was placed on the agenda for the CHE Board's May 1987 meeting. Dean Barker and I went to Columbia. Expecting the worst, we were completely surprised when the only comment was from a Board member who stated that it was "about time South Carolina had a landscape architecture program, for the Board has too long been sending landscape architecture–seeking students out of state under the Southeast Educational Compact. Many don't return to South Carolina to practice." Three months later, the first four majors arrived unexpectedly on campus for the fall semester. The degree was "on the record" but not yet even in the university's *Announcements*, a catalog of fields of study. By 2005, the program had grown to 140 students, twice the statically based "flesh-out" number predicted in the BLA degree proposal.

Lolly Tai was the first new hire for the program, followed by Frances Chamberlain the next year and Umit Yilmaz the following year. Cecile Martin, an artist and extraordinary teacher of design fundamentals, was soon "captured" by the program and moved over from Architecture to teach the program's first-year students. The first LAAB accreditation visit came in 1994, and the second in 1997. The findings of the third LAAB visit in 2002 were a stunning but pleasant reveal for all five of us associated with the program: "no recommendation for program improvement." Clemson's BLA 2002 LAAB review marked the first program to ever be accredited for a six-year term. The program soon rose to rank twelfth in the nation by *Design Intelligence Magazine* out of seventy accredited degree programs. Not bad at all for a relatively new start-up!

Jot Carpenter, mentioned earlier, died at an early age. He was giving testimony at the Ohio State Capitol on a piece of legislation when he was stricken. To honor his achievements and legacy, his family established the ASLA's Jot Carpenter Medal for "sustained excellence and contribution in Landscape Architecture education." In 2006, with a nomination from the ASLA's South Carolina chapter, I became the sixth recipient of this award. Former faculty member Lolly Tai, who left Clemson after ten years to become the program head at Temple University, received the metal in 2022.

OSU's Landscape Architecture Program's reputation without a doubt helped trigger the establishment of a Landscape Architecture Program at Clemson. OSU's Jot Carpenter and the ASLA medal given annually in his memory has been awarded to two individuals associated with building Clemson's Landscape Architecture Program, quite a bookend set for the program.

COMING TO CLEMSON UNIVERSITY

Debra Broadwell Jackson
College of Nursing and Department of Public Health Sciences
1991–2017

My move from Emory University's Nell Hodgson Woodruff School of Nursing to Clemson University might at first seem like the career paths that many of you have followed; however, after you read what happened over my first twelve months, you might disagree. I had a completely unanticipated problem. Two weeks before the scheduled interview, Vince and I received the unexpected but great news that I was pregnant. We had an eight-month-old who was still breastfeeding, and now I was pregnant and had interviews scheduled. My cousin told me that she would rather be forty than pregnant. I was both!

I knew of Clemson in very general terms. My family moved to Anderson, South Carolina, when I was five, and Clemson was seventeen miles away, but it just as easily could have been five hundred miles. As a teenager, I attended one Clemson football game and a couple of basketball games but knew nothing about the academic programs. None of my friends was headed to Clemson for college. The only high school graduates that I knew who would go to Clemson were in agriculture programs or football. Against the advice of the "guidance" counselor at T. L. Hanna High, I applied and was accepted to the Medical University of South Carolina (MUSC), which had just started a baccalaureate program in nursing. I did not tell my parents of that particular counseling advice, as I knew that they would have wanted me to follow it. My dad had to cosign loans for me to go to MUSC.

My four years in a medical research environment was a phenomenal experience, and upon graduation, I accepted a staff nursing position at Emory Hospital. For nineteen years, I worked there as a staff nurse, head nurse, director of a nondegree nursing program, and, finally, a tenured associate professor. I had worked for Emory Hospital, the Department of General Surgery, and the School of Nursing. I was forty, had a new baby, and had a fantastic job. Why would I leave? My dean suggested that I take a professional leave of absence because I had no professional experience other than at Emory, and although I was on track for full professor, I would never be considered for a deanship without additional experiences. He recommended a public university. With my husband Vince's encouragement, I started the application process.

One of my interviews was at Clemson, where I met Dr. Robbie Hughes, department head. The interview process was as expected., but the opportunity for my research was going to be difficult. I had always had access to a medical research center, for the Emory system was large and inclusive. I believed that I could find a way to conduct my NIH (National Institutes of Health) Area Grant, but it would be harder at Clemson.

When do you tell your potential boss you are pregnant, and does it affect your hiring? I thought it best to wait until I was offered and had accepted the position. Unfortunately, the department had arranged for a local real estate agent to take Vince and me on a little tour of Clemson. She drove fast, up and down hills, and around curves. Finally, she had to stop so that I could be sick on the side of the road in a prestigious residential neighborhood. Obviously, my secret would not remain a secret in this small town. The position was offered, and I negotiated a start date for January 1991. During our house hunting, the real estate agent turned us over to someone else in her office; I assumed that she wanted no repeat of the earlier morning sickness or perhaps the emotional need for nesting during pregnancy. I remember hiding in a closet in one home, crying because it was my dream home and the real estate agent wanted us to have it.

On November 25, 1990, Vince and I left Piedmont Hospital in Atlanta with our two-day old daughter Stacey and our seventeenth-month-old daughter Katie and drove to Clemson. We had been married for three years and eleven days. Our lives had been turned upside down, with marriage, two babies, a new home, one new job, and Vince starting to look for his own. My family in Anderson was thrilled we would be close.

Within a week of arriving, I received a phone call from Dr. Paul Adams with Clemson University's Telecampus Office. I was going to be teaching a tele-campus graduate nursing theory course starting the first week of January, and I needed telecampus training before he left for the holidays. So, off Stacey and I went to the second floor of Edwards Hall (then called the School of Nursing Building) to learn all we needed to know about the technology. It was not good. Unfortunately, the thousand educational slides I had would be of no use, nor would the hundreds of overhead transparencies. In fact, the camera was directly overhead and could pick up whatever I printed on white paper. I liked slides and overheads. They helped me organize my class content and helped students organize their notes. I learned that my students were to be in three locations: the Clemson studio, Greenville, and the Low Country. I would not be able to see those students in distance locations, but they could see me. Questions came through a telephone line. The class met one night each week for three hours, starting on a Monday. The first Monday of the semester was Martin Luther King Day. I had thought that it would be a holiday, but at that time in South Carolina, it was not, and so I had to be ready. Thankfully, we found a sitter. She did not last long, but at least she was available that first Monday.

I had a second class as well, a general health wellness course for which I was provided the textbook. I had sixty undergraduate students, another challenge. I had only taught nursing students, and usually graduate nursing students. I had no class notes, tests, or other materials related to general wellness topics. I had materials for pediatric oncology, wound and ostomy care, nursing theory, and nursing education courses, not general wellness. The second week of classes, I was called to the Dean's Office. Dr. Opal Hipps had a proposal: She needed someone to take on a special project, and if I agreed, she would reassign my undergraduate course to another faculty member, and I would focus my efforts on the approval of an undergraduate degree in health sciences and continue my telecampus nursing theory course. This was not an easy decision: I was breastfeeding, and traveling to and from Columbia would require a breast pump and cooler.

The South Carolina Commission on Higher Education (SC CHE) staff had rejected the first proposal submitted by the School of Nursing for a proposed undergraduate degree. I needed to meet with the SC CHE staff and determine what needed to be done, do it, and have the program approved as soon as possible. My decision to take on this special project started a career trajectory at Clemson that I could never have anticipated.

I headed to Columbia for my first of several meetings. I met with the staff member who had rejected the curriculum plan, the projected enrollment, interest in the program, potential job market, and faculty qualifications. I started by trying to have a better understanding of his concerns while introducing myself and providing my qualifications for being assigned this particular task. It turned out that we had common interests. I had taught a nurse who had cared for him during a recent surgery. He had seen copies of my patient education book. His approach changed from blocking efforts to approve the program to helping me address the concerns the staff had about the curriculum. I headed back to Clemson with a plan. We communicated often throughout the spring semester.

While I continued to teach my class, I needed to obtain human subject approvals across a number of hospital systems in the Upstate, continue my work on a scheduled textbook, and care for my family. I had the challenge to meet Dean Hipps's plans for the program. Collaborating with a team of nursing faculty, we made significant changes in the curriculum (seeking all of those approvals on campus), conducted a formal needs assessment of students and potential employers, and met with campus leaders. I had meetings with Provost William David Maxwell, Dean of Undergraduate Studies Dr. Jerry Reel, and Dr. Dee Stone (SC CHE contact for academic affairs). A revised proposal was submitted to SC CHE for their final approval cycle for the year. I went to Columbia for three formal SC CHE meetings, networking with higher-education faculty and administrators across the state. The program was approved by the full CHE in December 1991, a record time for a new degree program.

The Board of Trustees approved a new Department for Health Sciences, and I was selected as department head in August 1991, whereupon I started the faculty hiring process. We enrolled our first Clemson change-of-major students in January 1992, exceeding enrollment expectations. In May 1994, twenty-six students were in our first graduating class.

Not a bad first year at Clemson University! I met my personal goal, becoming an academic department chair. A new degree program had been approved and implemented. My research was going well. The textbook was with the editor. The change of jobs had been good. I loved being near family. Vince had started his business. The girls were healthy.

In closing, several of the individuals with whom I worked during those first years have died. I miss them and remember their contributions to the health science program, department, and students. Carol Schwartz, Joyce Klein, and David Phoenix were special friends.

A MID-LIFE VISION COMES TRUE

J. Terry Farris
Department of City Planning and Real Estate Development
1994–2017

I came to Clemson for my first academic job interview at the age of forty-four on April 1, 1994, with azaleas in full bloom after leaving the Detroit airport with twenty inches of snow, and said, "This looks pretty good, and they play great sports!" I didn't know where Clemson was or anything about it, but I wanted to be in the Midwest or South; I knew after the first day that I wanted to be here. I had accidentally met Professors Jose Caban and Barry Nocks at a national planning conference in Philadelphia earlier, when I was just completing my doctorate from Michigan State (MSU), and the Master of City and Regional Planning Program (MCRP) was looking for an applied-oriented planner—that's me!

A New Beginning: Prior to pursuing my doctorate as an instructor at MSU in 1991, I had had a seventeen-year development planning career in St. Louis. I packaged public-private partnership real estate developments in more than forty cities in ten states as a consultant and was director of development for the St. Louis Development Agencies. I followed in my father's footsteps, who was nationally known in urban redevelopment, including working on Busch Stadium for the St. Louis Cardinals.

I had a mid-life crisis at age forty-one. I had enjoyed adjunct teaching on community development policy since the age of twenty-five at Washington University. I always enjoyed working with students and various neighborhood and professional groups. I *never* thought that I would pursue a doctorate at forty-one and go into teaching. Frankly, I wasn't married with a family, after a long-term engagement had failed earlier, so any decisions only affected myself; I would never have entered the academy otherwise. So, I left for the ivy-covered halls, and Clemson was a perfect fit for me. I will never forget waiting for that phone call at the end of April, anxious to hear whether I was hired, when James Taylor's "Carolina on My Mind" came on the radio. I kind of teared up—and then got the call about fifteen minutes later and was totally thrilled.

A Vision Comes True: At my first interview with then-Dean Jim Barker, I told him that the disciplines were here to set up an applied, professional Master of Real Estate Development (MRED) degree. His eyes lit up, and he said that he had been thinking about what he called a "Master Builder" program. He encouraged me to pursue its formulation. So, I set up an interdisciplinary "Development Process" class for forty graduate students and had Charles Fraser, developer of Sea Pines at Hilton Head, as my first guest. MCRP established a "Development Specialization." That first summer, I secured a new faculty grant to tour the SC coast for a month and meet planners and developers. I broached the subject about an MRED program and received very positive reactions.

In the fall of 2000, an alumnus approached Business Dean Jerry Trapnell with a desire to fund an interdisciplinary real estate program. President Jim Barker and Dean Trapnell came together to support a joint-college program and paid me in the summers to formulate the MRED program.

My 18 Years of Paid Summer Vacation: In 2001, I thought that a short version of my summer coastal trip would be great and initiated the twelve-day Maymester SC Coastal Tour seminar class for twenty interdisciplinary students. We visited forty developments and met with the professionals, eventually adding Savannah. I taught that class for eighteen years, my pride and joy. I called it my "paid vacation" with graduate students, and it has been a key aspect of the program compared to others nationally! And I ran a tight ship that ran on time for the whole day—students knew that they'd better be on time and on good behavior! Ahhh, the smell of jasmine every May!

A New Program Is Born: I received tenure/promotion to associate professor in 2001, was appointed MCRP director (until 2005) that summer, and became immediately responsible for the preparation of a yearlong, seven-year national accreditation review by the Planning Accreditation Board. Lucky me!

Coordinating with faculty and professionals, I prepared an interdisciplinary fifty-six-credit MRED proposal in 2003, including classes in business administration and finance, law, construction science, architecture, planning, and new real estate development classes—eleven new courses. I shepherded the proposal through six departments, two colleges, and the administration, including the Board of Trustees and the SC CHE. It was approved in the summer of 2004; fortunately, we had seven prospective students ready to go (typically, around twenty are admitted now). I was MRED's founding director from 2004 to 2010.

Located in downtown Greenville, our nationally known program has 280 alumni working in fifty-five metro areas in twenty-nine states and ten countries. Our differential tuition allows us to tour approximately thirty days in Atlanta,

Charlotte, Nashville, the Coastal Tour, and the Fall Urban Land Institute (ULI) Conferences.

Great Memories: I have been known by a couple of nicknames (I'm sure I don't know them all—and don't want to know!), but in MRED, I have been known as "Big Tuna," from Georgetown SC's waterfront restaurant/bar. Many planners know me as "Dr. Disco"—we won't go there! Perhaps the greatest memories have been on the Coastal trips and the ULI Fall Conference (seven thousand attendees), with all thirty to forty of our students for five days in major cities—Chicago, Denver, LA, San Francisco, NYC, DC, Dallas—even Miami Beach and Las Vegas—my, oh my! And whatever happened in [city] stays there! Never had a major problem on a trip—that I know of?!?

I have become well-known for lifting my wallet up and saying, "If this don't work [i.e., money], it ain't gonna happen!" I tell students that their spiritual life comes first, then family, then friends, and then the job. I tell them to be pleasant and respect those "above and below" you—even the janitor and the hotel maid—and the homeless and those with no voice. I raise my wallet and say, "Don't let this run your life. You will have plenty to live on—but don't lose your soul over business and personal greed." I tell them about people whom I have known going to jail or committing suicide—primarily over money and power. Nothing is that important. I am very aware that I affect these students positively, and we have a mutual love that is very fulfilling.

I was extremely fortunate throughout my life with a great family and education. I had nuns in grade school and Jesuits in high school and undergraduate—they were exceptional. I tell our students how lucky they are to have had family, friends, and mentors who gave them a leg up to get where they are—and that they should have real empathy for those who are less fortunate—it's the luck of the draw who their parents were. What if you were born to drug users in poverty? I know that I am spreading the "Good News" of all faith traditions in the classroom in various ways. We are called to serve others.

I am honored to have been a part of two great professional graduate degree programs, teaching more than six hundred students. I came into academia primarily to teach, work with the professional community, and perform some applied research—my main desire was to work closely with students and see them become successful in their careers, making great places.

So, I was sitting on the floor in the Gunnin Library, rummaging through the stacks many years ago with a planning student, when he asked me why I had quit a well-paid professional job advancing in my career to enter academia as a "lowly" assistant professor in my forties. I looked at him and said, "So I could be here with you right now!" I do believe that God has a plan for us!

LEARNING THAT MATTERS:
The Service-Learning Collaborative

MARTY DUCKENFIELD

National Dropout Prevention Center

1988–2018

The weather was perfect for filming on that early spring afternoon on the Clemson campus, the sun shining with no threat of rain. Veteran Clemson videographer Tom Shockley, always solidly reliable and ceaselessly patient, and Tom Neal, our outgoing and lively director, were poised to begin filming the action. Carol Collins, a creative master of improv from the Performing Arts Department who coached our performers, had made sure that they had rehearsed this scene multiple times so our stars would feel comfortable. As the novice producer, I had leaned on all three of them to make the decision that it was now time to get it on film. Although the segment had been carefully planned with our desired content and Carol's guidance, it was, after all, unscripted.

Seated on a white concrete bench, perusing a catalog of Clemson University courses, was Thomas Quisenberry, a former Daniel High School student who now attended Clemson and had been a leader in the high school's Interact Club, focusing on service in the community. I gave an encouraging smile to our gifted performers before I paused briefly to take a deep breath. They were ready to go, and so, at a nod from me, Tom Neal held up three fingers and counted down, "three, two, one!" and pointed at Thomas.

And with that, this improvised yet perfectly executed scene played out. Thomas, portraying the Clemson student he now was, mimed searching the course catalog. Up walked Dr. Jerry Waldvogel, a dynamic biology professor who was always open and friendly with students. It appeared completely natural for Jerry to stop by to say hello and ask Thomas what he was up to. In response, Thomas pointed to the catalog, explaining that he was looking for a course like he'd had in high school—one that included service learning, A brief conversation followed, during which Jerry mentioned his own curiosity about service learning and suggested that the two of them go to the library and look online to answer their questions. After all, the year was 1999, and that was the place to do more research. And so began the filming of *Learning That Matters*, a video that the Service-Learning Collaborative produced so more Clemson faculty could learn about a teaching strategy that also incorporated service and research.

Two years earlier, Jerry had become one of several Clemson faculty who joined the newly established Service-Learning Collaborative, attracted by the offer of a mini-grant to support improvements to their teaching. The collaborative, along with its mini-grant program, had been created in 1996, when the National Dropout Prevention Center (NDPC) received the first of five years of Innovation Funds from the Provost's Office. The goal was to foster the development and expansion of service learning at Clemson.

In the first year of the establishment of the collaborative, mini-grant recipients were given the basics of the teaching methodology, an area of expertise I had acquired through my involvement with service learning in the K–12 world. They took that framework and experimented with small projects to implement the style in their classes. Their success was trumpeted at the end of the spring semester, particularly by the students' presentations.

In our second year, experienced faculty began their roles as peer mentors, helping those who received the new mini-grants. We had also begun working in partnership with the Pearce Center and the Office of Teaching Effectiveness and Innovation. Together, we sponsored multiple workshops led by experienced collaborative members to introduce the practice more broadly to other faculty, and a small but interested group of people would attend. These were major steps, but collaborative members saw that it was extremely difficult to find a time when more faculty were free so we could attract a larger audience. We soon realized that it was necessary to find a more innovative strategy to reach out.

Our collaborative members' meetings were always well attended. I was never sure whether it was because of the faculty's genuine interest in our mission or because the collaborative's Parks, Recreation, and Tourism Management (PRTM) graduate student, a great Louisiana chef from Baton Rouge, prepared tasty little treats for our group. At one of these meetings, perhaps inspired by her delicious refreshments, collaborative member Cheryl Dye, a professor in health sciences, came up with a novel suggestion: "Why don't we do a video to meet this need?"

It didn't take long to sell all of us on this idea. The faculty members of the collaborative were more than willing to lend a hand. Participation in service learning and the collaborative had already brought a freshness and vitality to their teaching lives. Now they had another opportunity to do something different, first in the planning stage and then with starring roles in the video. Here was a new venue where they and their students could talk about their projects, the teaching and learning benefits, the research enhancements, and the value of serving the community for the students and Clemson University. Other faculty and several students also joined us in making the film, enthusiastically sharing their service-learning experiences.

This would be only my second opportunity to go behind the camera. Temporarily leaving behind the publications and training that took up many of my National Dropout Prevention Center (NDPC) days, I also had an opportunity to provide some freshness and vitality to my own job as well as have a lot of fun with our entire production team. My only prior experience had been working on a video the year before with some local middle-school students, again as the producer and content manager. Then as now, we had benefitted greatly from the assistance of Carol Collins and the two Toms (Shockley and Neal).

And so, with this new project begun, the joys of our collective creativity were in abundance. What a delightful change from other job activities, and I noticed that the faculty felt that way, too. With the university's Communications Department providing their expertise for us at no cost plus our Innovation Funds, we could afford to produce a video *and* make multiple copies of it for every university department in all five colleges.

After weeks of filming and recording the narration by Steve Madden, of speech and communication studies, we turned over the results to David White in the Communications Department, located in the basement of the Poole Agricultural Center (P & A Building). We had to wait a few weeks while he worked his magic, but the results were worth waiting for. The world premiere was held that spring in one of the Madren Center's meeting rooms, and the audience included our cast in addition to many other interested parties. It was a thrilling moment to see the finished product on the big screen. And after that, with our copies delivered to all the college's departments, we thought we had it covered. And yet, there was more to come!

Awareness of the benefits of service learning had gradually moved up the chain of command. Many faculty and college administrators had been coming to the end-of-spring-semester sessions to watch the students report about their service-learning projects, with an emphasis on the learning. Their interest was indeed piqued by the enthusiasm expressed so openly by the students. Soon, the vice presidents and the dean who would soon become president, Jim Barker, all became aware of the benefits service learning could generate across the university. Their advocacy for this grassroots initiative led to *Learning That Matters* being adopted by Dr. Jerry Reel as a regular feature of new faculty orientation in the fall of 1999, with Provost Steffen Rogers providing his early endorsement at the conclusion of the video.

Without a doubt, the making of *Learning That Matters* was one of the most enjoyable and fun experiences I had at Clemson University. As a bonus, I found it particularly rewarding to be in partnership with so many outstanding faculty to help catapult service learning into becoming an integral part of a Clemson education. By the time of the completion of *Learning That Matters* in 1999, the Service-Learning Collaborative had already laid the groundwork with this cadre of highly regarded faculty peer mentors and the availability of substantial resources, including a library of guidebooks and a website. As awareness and practice grew over the next few years, along with new partnerships across campus, our collective efforts carried our goals even farther, expanded our vision, and witnessed major changes in teaching, research, and learning throughout the university.

NOTE: The cast of *Learning That Matters* included these faculty and staff: Jerry Waldvogel, biology; Steve Madden, speech and communication studies; Mary Haque, horticulture; John Mumford, construction science and management; David Hartmann, performing arts; Lolly Tai, planning and landscape architecture; Patricia Connor-Greene, psychology; Carol Collins, performing arts; Cheryl Dye, health science; Carol Weatherford, educational foundations and special education; Brenda Vander Mey, sociology; Doreen Geddes, speech and communication studies; John Wagner, geology; Erik Caldwell, geology; Laurie Haughey, academic learning center; and Steffen H. Rogers, provost.

SERVICE LEARNING AS A BRIDGE TO LANGUAGES AND CULTURES

Clementina Adams
Department of Languages
1989–2014

Service has always been a focus of my life. From an early age, my parents impressed upon me the importance of helping those in need. As a child, I provided help to a middle-aged man who was deaf and mute. To communicate with him, my brothers and I used all kinds of made-up signs and gestures, and it truly paid off. I realized then that serving others yielded good outcomes and personal satisfaction. This discussion presents a brief description of a variety of services that I have provided at various stages of my life, especially during my time at Clemson University.

While in high school, I began to serve others when our class participated in a project to assist the residents of a nearby rural community by teaching them reading, writing, and math skills. Initially, we were frustrated because those in the community were reluctant to participate. However, one afternoon, on the way back to school, I saw an older man sitting at his doorstep, holding a small stick in his hands. As he drew a vertical line, I approached him and asked for his name. He replied, "Tito." Then, I asked whether he knew how to print his name, to which he said, "No." I told him it was going to be easy because he had already made the first part of the first letter of his name. That was the beginning; eventually, other people approached us, and we were able to assist many families.

In my junior year of high school, we worked in teams to provide help to the community. We gathered used clothing, utensils, books, and toys to give to poor families. Initially, we were not successful, and we wondered why. I suggested that because everything was free, the families might have felt humiliated. I recommended that we put a price on things, set as low as possible, and then see what happened. That change helped, and we continued the campaign until the end of our graduation year. That initiative has continued over the years and is still active.

As a graduate research assistant and student at Florida State University, I worked on projects dealing with best practices and resources for teaching. I was also part of a team funded by the U.S. Agency for International Development (USAID), responsible for the assessment and improvement of Colombia's National Radio Literacy Program for rural populations. A model of that program was available to local communities as well as nationwide and to other countries.

In 1980, I became an assistant professor at Gallaudet University, a school for the deaf, in Washington, D.C. I wanted to work there for two reasons: First, my husband was a faculty member there, and second, because on the occasions when I stopped by the college, I was impressed with the way the students communicated with each other, even at long distances of separation, using signs and gestures. I decided that I needed to learn that language. After an intensive period of training, I taught Spanish to deaf students, using American Sign Language (ASL). Those were students for whom ASL was their first language, English their second, and Spanish their third language. It was particularly challenging, but it worked out so well that in the summer of 1985, I took a group of the students for a summer workshop in Cuernavaca, Mexico. They did so well there that when we visited arts and crafts fairs as well as open markets, I would ask them to buy things for me because they were much better than I at *regateo* (negotiating with vendors) for a better price.

When I came to Clemson University in August 1989 as a visiting assistant professor of Spanish, I implemented a great service assignment. I was responsible for the coordination of the program Foreign Languages for Elementary School Children (FLES), which offered free foreign language classes, such as Spanish, French, German, and Italian, to school children in the Upstate. The Department of Languages provided this service as an after-school class activity, and children came to Clemson University on buses from their respective schools. I implemented the initiative with the assistance of professors and advanced language students from the Department of Languages, to whom I provided on-the-job training. It was a rewarding yet time-consuming activity, and I coordinated it for more than three years. Over the years, I continued to work with students in projects to aid the Hispanic community and elementary and high schools in the Upstate.

During my tenure-track years, through the university's Service-Learning Initiative, I prepared teams of students to provide interpreting and Spanish-teaching services to Upstate Hispanic communities at schools, police stations, Mexican restaurants, and churches that offered community services. Another service that I provided during my time at Clemson University, and that I continued to do even after my retirement in 2014, was assistance to the Sullivan Center. There, I have served as a certified medical interpreter for Hispanics at the Walhalla Clinic as well as at hospitals and health centers in Clemson, Anderson, Easley, Greenville, Simpsonville, and Marietta, Georgia.

On one occasion, Dr. Sandy King, the Department of Languages chair at the time, asked me about my experience with ASL and whether I thought that it would be possible to teach in our department. I loved the idea, and in 1999, I designed a plan to present to the entire department. I must confess that it was not as easy as I thought; some did not consider sign language to be a regular language. I had to convince them that ASL is a full language with its own history, culture, and grammatical structure. I also presented research that accounted for the characteristics and properties of this silent language. It helped that some universities had added ASL to their curricula. Three institutions—Gallaudet University, Rochester Institute of Technology, and Boston University—had well-established programs. Finally, after many meetings and discussions, the Department of Languages was ready to accept and include ASL as one of our language offerings. At that point, I went through the process of planning, preparing, documenting, and attending college and university curriculum committee meetings and discussions before receiving all final approvals. Once it was approved in the spring of 1999, I designed the curriculum and the first four basic semesters of sign language (ASL 101,102, 201 and 202); in addition, I volunteered to teach the labs until an experienced and well-known ASL professor, Dr. Alton Brant, started working as coordinator of the new Sign Languages Section. Today, ASL classes are offered on campus and at the University Center of Greenville. In the last twenty years, the ASL program has grown by more than 600 percent to now include a major in modern languages, a minor in ASL educational interpreting, and a minor in ASL studies. Today, Clemson University is the only institution in the state to offer a four-year degree in ASL.

In 1991, I began coordinating the annual Hispanic Month program and continued to do so for more than five years. During those years, Mexican and Colombian ambassadors, among others, came to Clemson University as guest speakers. Folkloric groups, artists, poets, and authors as well as Hispanic movies and concerts were also parts of the Hispanic Month program. Those activities were excellent and feasible ways to reach out to the Upstate community.

I participated in the Faculty Outside the Classroom with Undergraduate Students (FOCUS) program, for which I received a certificate of appreciation for contributing to the program's success during the 1997–1998 academic years. Another important service was my training and participation on behalf of

Clemson University's affiliation with the National Coalition Building Institute, 1999–2010. The purpose was to help students understand racial, religious, and other discriminations and to clear up related misconceptions. In 2009, I received a certificate of service in recognition and appreciation of more than twenty years of loyal and faithful service to the citizens of the state of South Carolina. One of my contributions was the coordination of a team responsible for the assessment of the existing Spanish Exit Exam for South Carolina secondary schools and the design and field testing of an updated version of it.

In 2010, and until my retirement in 2014, the Creative Inquiry Initiative allowed me the opportunity to work with my language and international health (L&IH) classes on a variety of projects that included research activities focused on the Hispanic community's culture, history, myths, and traditions. Other projects included teaching English to the Hispanic community in schools and teaching English to workers in Mexican restaurants, police departments, and community/church centers. Students demonstrated a prominent level of motivation and satisfaction for the services they provided.

One of the last creative inquiry projects that I coordinated with my advanced L&IH students was the study of North Americans' perception of Hispanics living in the United States. That project took more than a year and resulted in the design of surveys for Hispanics and North Americans about their concerns and fears when interacting with one another. Based on the data, we designed a survey for North American students at Clemson University. The project is now ready for refining, with a duplication of the study to larger population samples from other universities and colleges in South Carolina, and abroad, if possible.

Each one of the types of service that I have described could have easily resulted in an individual discussion; however, through this writing, it has been my intention to show the variety of opportunities that faculty members, whatever their discipline might be, have to become involved in services and service-learning projects at Clemson University.

CU-ICAR AND THE DEEP ORANGE PROGRAM

Imtiaz Haque
Department of Automotive Engineering
1982–2019

BMW's decision in 1992 to locate a manufacturing facility in South Carolina was a great boon to the state in terms of job creation and in upgrading the state's image as low-tech. BMW, arguably the world's most technically sophisticated automaker, was now building cars for the world market in South Carolina that would be ambassadors testifying to the quality of South Carolina's workforce the world over. By the early 2000s, BMW, along with other car manufacturers, was grappling with the reality of rapidly changing technology and the transition of vehicles from predominantly mechanical platforms to those with immense product complexity due to the confluence of mechanical, electrical, and software disciplines and the progress in advanced materials. Consumer demands and the rate of market change had also increased dramatically, challenging product development speed and innovation cycles, making it increasingly difficult to forecast and integrate future product requirements into new products and services. By the turn of the twenty-first century, it was increasingly clear to BMW that the automotive industry was in dire need of a workforce that could master/lead this process, and it was willing to put significant money behind its creation. Because of its proximity to the BMW plant in Greer, Clemson University took on the challenge of producing this desired workforce, specifically through the creation of new master's of science and doctorate programs in automotive engineering.

Having spent a sabbatical year (1996–1997) at the BMW Research Center in Munich, Germany, I had a firsthand opportunity to observe the challenges BMW was facing. As a newly appointed department chair in 2003, I led a department that had previous experience in motorsports engineering—albeit in the NASCAR domain, where the technology used was still mostly mechanical and cars were not produced en masse. None of the faculty had any experience with the kinds of challenges that BMW laid at our doorstep, and there was no program anywhere inside or outside the United States for us to emulate. Creating a program from scratch that would break new ground in engineering education and that had the support of a can-do university administration, a prestigious automotive manufacturer, and the state of South Carolina was a heady proposition, albeit daunting. Failure was not an option. It was truly the most exciting and fulfilling time of my academic career. Creating an innovative curriculum, hiring new faculty and staff, and shepherding the construction and outfitting of a building that screamed innovation meant many long hours at the wheel and lots of interesting interactions with industry stakeholders, Clemson administration, and faculty.

One of the most refreshing things about the project was how the Department of Mechanical Engineering, with support from BMW and other industry partners, came together as one to deliver a rigorous graduate program, maintain its innovative nature, and shepherd it through the academic channels and the Commission of Higher Education in record time. Hiring faculty who could teach the curriculum and conduct research in the areas outlined by BMW was another story. After much thrashing around in academic circles with little luck, I made the decision to follow the German model and look for outstanding individuals who would have industry experience and academic credentials good enough to be appointed in the department. This decision led to the hiring of an individual who was unconstrained by traditional academic norms and whose unlimited creativity and boldness in going where no one had gone before put the academic program on the map as one of the most innovative programs in the world for training the new breed of automotive engineers. We had started out with BMW, Michelin, and Timken supporting the vision for the program. Pretty soon, General Motors, Ford, Mazda, Toyota, and Honda all signed up to support the program and give preferential treatment for hiring to the graduates of the program.

The doctoral program opened in 2006, and the MS program followed soon after in 2007. Dr. Paul Venhovens was hired as the BMW chair in Systems Integration in 2008. He had worked at the BMW Research Center in Munich and had excellent academic and industry credentials for the job. I remember the day that Paul proposed the Deep Orange Program to me in January 2009. The proposal was for students to build a car from scratch as part of their MS program—not just any car but one that started from a futuristic big-picture question posed by an auto manufacturer. The car, featuring next-generation innovation, was to be delivered, start to finish, in two years. It was to be displayed at premier automotive trade shows, such as SEMA in Las Vegas and MBS in Travers City,

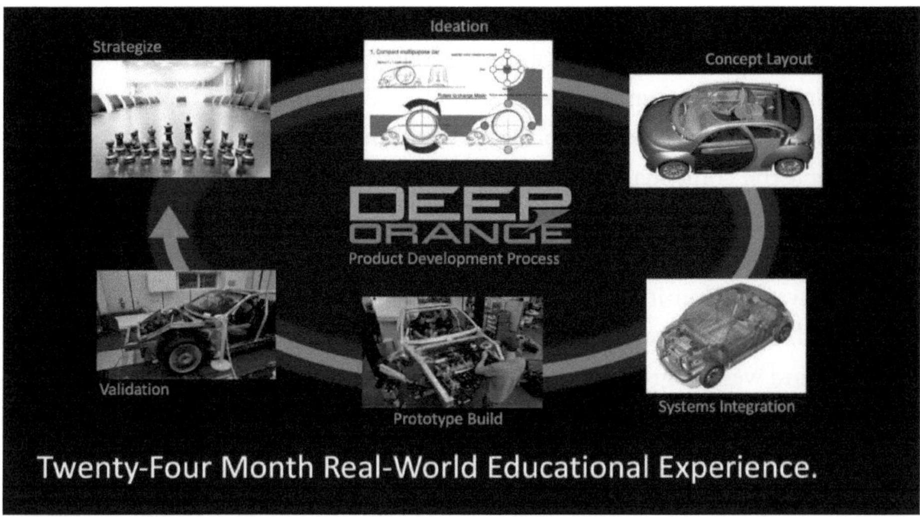

Figure Deep Orange--Twenty-Four Month Real-World Educational Experience, submitted by Imtiaz Haque

Michigan, thereby bringing a different level of realism to the project. Its development and manufacture were to be funded by the sponsoring auto manufacturer and suppliers to the auto industry. Not every MS student was required to participate in this project, but for those that did, this effort would be in lieu of the internship requirement that had been built into the MS program. The scientific rigor of the academic program was not to be compromised. The proposal was audacious and scary, yet exciting if it could be pulled off.

The design and production of an automobile requires people from many different disciplines to come together. Engineers, artists/designers, human factors experts, psychologists, and businesspeople all work together to produce the final product. There is lots of give and take and lots of compromises to be made, which is especially challenging for engineers, whose training typically does not include dealing with uncertainty and promotes the idea that every problem has only one right answer. Paul's and the department's goal was to create the type of environment that would challenge the students' established notions of engineering. The Department of Automotive Engineering hired faculty in the disciplines of psychology and business to augment the engineering faculty who were to form the core of the program. We created a partnership with the Arts Center in Pasadena, California, which had the reputation of being the top school for producing car designers, and put a framework together that enabled constant interaction between these diverse disciplines. We invited Arts Center faculty to come to CU-ICAR (Clemson University International Center for Automotive Research) and deliver workshops to our students on creativity and design, and we invited Arts Center students to interact with the engineering students during the design phase of the project. Watching the interaction between these groups and the continual growth that was taking place in the students and faculty involved is one of the highlights of my career as a teacher and administrator. Traditional engineering students were being asked to work with students whose thinking was predominantly right-brained; some of them could not handle it and bailed. Those that stuck it through became the face of CU-ICAR to the auto industry and were in great demand. It was very exciting to watch.

The program has been successful beyond belief. As of today, students are working on the thirteenth iteration of Deep Orange, with the U.S. Army Ground Vehicle Systems Center (GVSC) as a sponsor. The program has been written up in newspapers in seventeen different countries and in such prestigious publications as *TIME Magazine*, the *Wall Street Journal*, *Automotive News*, and *Autoweek*. The automotive companies continue to line up to hire our students. The program that I once thought was undoable turned out to be the most memorable experience of my career at Clemson and continues to this day to affect student lives and bring honor and attention to the university.

CHAPTER 6

Tillman Hall from the Clemson House (4/16/02) (With permission of artist Clemson President Emeritus James F. Barker)

ADVICE FOR AN ASPIRING TEACHER

Sterling "Skip" K. Eisiminger
Department of English
1968–2007

A damp sponge absorbs far more than one dry,
so travel, and read, and ask the world why.

Before the light appears, chop a cord of wood.
The need for cutting will be understood.

Barbers apprentice on lathered balloons,
so that in practice, the face is immune.

Look close to see the grit in the pearl—
teach students to know all of the world.

The sword's in a book, not buried in stone.
Until it is freed, none takes the throne.

If colts led to water just stand and blink,
some salt in their oats may help them to think.

When no one is watching, seize the poor dears
and bite the shrink-wrap that covers their ears.

Just as hikers who wish may leave the trail,
your students too have the right to fail.

Students deserve the unvarnished truth—
if Sherlock's a failure, don't call him *sleuth*.

Most sources of knowledge lie under a roof.
Add lamps, and love, and learning is rainproof.

Mother Nature, of course, needs no shelter,
but students will need a guide through her welter.

When unprepared, fall back on your genius—
often, you'll find something ingenious.

Be patient with every student project—
the lower the score, the greater the prospect.

Apollo's rebus is drawn with a sun,
a pen, a lyre, and the future outspun.

Unlace the girdle and scatter the stays—
you gathered yourself to give it away.

THE WAKE-UP CALL

Robert L. "Larry" LaForge
Department of Management
1981–2011

I felt my new-fangled Nokia mobile phone vibrate in my pocket but didn't think anything of it. I had turned the ringer off immediately after entering the classroom and arranging my papers and things at the podium. Moments later, the class session that changed everything began.

It seemed like business as usual in Management 402, Operations Planning and Control. My fourth-floor classroom/laboratory in Sirrine Hall was a little musty, but that was normal in the early mornings of the spring semester. The students seemed ready to begin. Each student was seated at a computer terminal providing access to the latest business management software. This put Clemson students in the same decision-making situations, with the same information systems support, as real operations managers in real companies. In the mid-1990s, this technology was big stuff.

Life was good. This was my kingdom. I spent most of my career trying to create active learning opportunities for business students by integrating real-world management information systems technology into operations management courses. The Manufacturing Management Laboratory was the result of incredible support from Clemson colleagues, administrators, computer staff, fund raisers, and donors.

The class session went as expected. If asked, I would have answered that the class went well. Some students were into it more than others, but that's the way it goes. The class ended without incident, and the students hurried out of the room. Most of them had to navigate at least two flights of the stairwell in Sirrine to get to their next class, a logjam just waiting to happen. I gathered my things and pulled my phone out of my pocket, remembering that it had buzzed just before class started. Sure enough, a voice mail awaited.

The next thing I knew, I was listening to myself talking. *What in the world?* It only took a few seconds to realize that the voice mail was a recording of the class session I had just completed. I stopped the playback immediately and looked around sheepishly. To my relief, none of the remaining students seemed to be aware of my bewilderment and distress. Wasting no time, I headed straight to my office, closed the door behind me, and listened to the entire recording.

It took several minutes to figure out what had happened. I must have accidentally depressed the call button on the phone in my front pocket when I bent over to check the power cord on my workstation before class. This had somehow initiated a call to my number, which had gone to my voice mail. The recorded "message" lasted nearly five minutes before it timed out—but that was enough.

I was horrified at what I heard. I played it over and over, feeling worse each time. It was like a button had been pushed in a silent room and a robot started talking. Everything the robot said was technically correct, but there was little voice inflection, animation, or passion. The robot asked several questions, but few students responded. They apparently knew that if they waited long enough, the robot would answer his own question. Simply put, I was talking *at* students instead of talking *to* them.

After much reflection, I started thinking about how I began my class sessions and how that might affect the tone and atmosphere in the room. I would typically make the "professor's grand entrance," arriving after most students were in their seats, just before the scheduled start time. I would then hurriedly silence my phone, sign in at my terminal, and get right into the business at hand. This process allowed no time for casual conversation with students and sometimes led to a somewhat rigid or abrupt start to the class session. It was equivalent to turning on the ignition of an automobile on a very frigid morning, flooring the gas pedal immediately, and driving off with no engine warm-up at all. I felt the need to "warm the engine" before starting my classes, and I developed a pretty good idea of how to go about it.

From that point forward, for nearly twenty years until my retirement in 2011, I made a concerted effort to show up at least ten minutes early before every class session I taught, ready to greet and chat with students as they trickled in. This time allowed me to interact with students on a more informal basis and make a more gradual and natural transition to the start of class. Students began coming in earlier, too, allowing for questions or casual conversation.

In addition, whenever possible, I stayed longer in the room after each class session. Some students started doing that as well instead of making the wild dash to the stairwell. This provided even more opportunities for answering questions and developing relationships and goodwill. The simple changes I made allowed me to be more conversational in my presentations and interactions with students and appear less rigid and less robotic in their eyes.

My dismay at what I heard in the recording and my determination to address the issues were a direct reflection of the Clemson culture that values teaching. In retrospect, it was a good thing that a lackluster class session could ruin my day and set the wheels turning to help me make better connections with students. It became clear that more and/or better technology does not necessarily result in better teaching. I was fortunate to observe great teaching all around me in the Department of Management, and it had nothing to do with how much technology was in the room.

The larger lesson here may be that every instructor periodically needs to examine their approach to teaching. Over a long career, there may be several occasions when it is appropriate to evaluate, rethink, or even reinvent oneself as a teacher. It may sometimes be difficult for a college professor to know or accept when that point has been reached. I'm just thankful that my time of reckoning came in a wake-up call—from myself.

WHAT PROFESSOR DAY TAUGHT ME

Christopher A. Benson
Department of English
1990–2020

When I was at Clemson University in the 1980s, preparing to be an English teacher, I landed in a desk in a literature class taught by Professor Frank Day, who was a marvelous lecturer.[5] His lectures on British literature were some of the most exciting times in a classroom I can recall. Although at the time the lectures seemed linear to me, I later realized that Professor Day's knowledge of literature and culture was so broad and deep that he could begin with one topic and make connections between it and an astonishing array of literary ideas. His mind was an organic hypertext on literature and philosophy. In one class, for example, he presented the idea of mathematical geometry as a form of ideal beauty equal to that of Aphrodite, the Greek goddess of beauty, as presented in Edna St. Vincent Millay's modern poem "Euclid Alone Has Looked on Beauty Bare":

> O blinding hour, O holy, terrible day,
> When first the shaft into his vision shone
> Of light anatomized! Euclid alone
> Has looked on Beauty bare. Fortunate they
> Who, though once only and then but far away,
> Have heard her [i.e., Aphrodite/Beauty] massive sandal set on stone.

For me, this idea alone was enough to suggest the sublime possibilities of the human imagination, but then Professor Day leapt back twenty-four centuries, connecting Millay's poem to Plato's "Allegory of the Cave" and explaining the beauty of Plato's "ideal forms" of the mind as opposed to the mere shadow of that beauty that is perceived through human experience. He then ended the class by turning to William Wordsworth's 1807 poem "Ode: Intimations on Immortality" that describes how the

---

[5] A version of this was published in "Voices" column in *Teacher Magazine*, 1998.

Soul that rises with us . . . Hath had elsewhere its setting,
. . . But trailing clouds of glory do we come
. . . Heaven lies about us in our infancy!
Shades of the prison-house begin to close
Upon the growing boy.

Professor Day explained that beauty was real, although our understanding
of it might be imperfect and fleeting at best, unless you were Euclid, of course.
Although a self-professed skeptic and a cynic, I was stunned by the hard truth of
this lesson, and I listened with rapt attention.

My classmates and I prepared for Professor Day's class out of fear that he
might call on one of us spontaneously, as he often did, and ask for an opinion
about something we were to have read and thought about. He challenged us
individually, and each student was expected to be equipped with substantive
ideas and opinions to share with him and our classmates; it never occurred to us
that we should or could challenge Professor Day himself. In his class, we learned
to ask thoughtful questions because Professor Day—great teacher that he was—
did not conceal his disappointment over a question that bespoke a student's lack
of preparation. Over the course of the semester, some students stopped asking
questions; others continued to ask, despite our fear of being found to be inad-
equately prepared. Once, when two students were quietly talking in the back
row, Professor Day growled, "Hey, you in the back, there are no private conversations in this class unless they include me!" We were in awe of Professor Day: We
revered his knowledge and the man himself. Although we also feared him, Professor Day consistently enjoyed high praise from students who took his courses.

A few years later, I was an aspiring lecturer in English literature at Clemson University myself, and I wished to be the kind of teacher that Professor Day was,
to command the same authority. As a new teacher, I even imitated his growl
to hush students who talked in my class. But something was wrong: My students weren't in awe of me as I had been of Professor Day. My students were
sometimes uninterested, even hostile at times, and I wondered why. Around
this time, I began collaborating with my colleagues in Clemson University's
Communication-Across-the-Curriculum (CAC) writing workshops for faculty,
which promoted interdisciplinary teaching, research, and writing. These workshops were sponsored by Professor Art Young, Campbell Chair in Technical

Communication and professor of English, and attended by a growing number of forward-thinking faculty members at Clemson who encouraged one another to work together across disciplinary boundaries. Through these workshops and the ensuing collaborations, I learned that most of my colleagues, like me, had been inspired by great teachers and lecturers, but only a few of us had yet achieved those inspirational levels for our own students. Yet by working together as "team teachers" on collaborative curricula and by engaging in common professional pursuits, and writing about them, we became much better teachers, and many of us, I am certain, inspired our students.

My collaborations with other teachers introduced me to new disciplines and new ways of thinking about knowledge. With help from a biology professor, I developed a series of writing assignments called "A Sense of Place" that required close Thoreauvian transcendental observation of the natural world as part of scientific inquiry. In collaboration with a math professor, I taught my students the "invisible geometry" embedded in expressionist sculpture and painting. And from an engineering professor, I learned how to structure teams of students who could achieve cooperative goals that lay beyond the reach of any single student. As an English teacher, I helped my colleagues find ways to include a variety of writing activities in their courses, from art to accounting.

A few of my colleagues at Clemson became great lecturers like Professor Day through these collaborations, but all of us, indeed, became better teachers through discovering reasons to cross curricular boundaries and experiment with different pedagogies. I, too, was successful: After a couple years of unsuccessfully trying to impersonate Professor Day, I found my own stride and discovered that I did my best teaching when I encouraged students, as I had learned in the CAC workshops, to cooperate with each other, to inspire one another, and to help each other achieve collaborative success, something Professor Day, one of my favorite teachers, had not taught me to do.

THE TIME OF MY LIFE

Art Young
Communication-Across-the-Curriculum Program
1987–2009

The telephone rang early in my home in Clemson on the morning of August 17, 2000. A neighbor asked whether she could drop by with some important information for me. I said, "Sure." A few minutes later, I opened the door to Robin Denny, Clemson's director of News Services, who began, "Do you have a place to sit down?"

"Egads!" I thought, "What have I done now?" When we were both seated, she gave me the news: *TIME Magazine* had just announced that Clemson University was selected Public College of the Year for 2001 on the strength of its Communication-Across-the-Curriculum (CAC) program, which I had founded and directed since 1989. Robin was clearly excited and wanted to know whether I could be ready in an hour for a news conference at the Madren Center. The local media would be there, as would President James Barker and many top administrators.

As President Barker explained the purpose and importance of this national award, I could see that many Clemson folks in the room were as astonished by the honor as I was. To be named the Best Public College of the Year by *TIME /The Princeton Review* in its 2001 edition of *The Best College for You* would be not only useful to students and their families but a boon to Clemson's already-strong reputation as a leader in undergraduate education. The editors wrote that Clemson was selected for being "on the cutting edge of the Communication-Across-the-Curriculum movement and for excelling in teaching writing and communication skills." I was then introduced to explain the CAC movement and how it was implemented at Clemson.

As I surveyed the room of reporters, photographers, and television crews, I nervously tried to gather my thoughts. As a laid-back and reflective person, I had never been a good public speaker, especially when I did not have time to prepare, and especially when talking to television cameras. I began haltingly with a hem and a haw until I found my voice. I began something like this: "The key to Clemson's program is the phrase 'across the curriculum.'" Many disciplines and many companies say that being an effective communicator is as important as being proficient in technical skills. Graduates need to be able to explain their technical knowledge to colleagues, clients, board members, granting agencies, and the public. At Clemson, we not only teach writing and communication skills in English and speech courses but seek to integrate student writing and communication into courses in every subject and throughout the four-year curriculum. In our writing-across-the-curriculum (WAC) initiative, teachers in every discipline create writing assignments to enable their students to better understand the subject of study, whether accounting or zoology, electrical engineering or psychology.

Then, Dr. Patricia Connor-Greene explained how this approach worked in her psychology classes. She earlier had told *TIME* editors that students in her abnormal psychology class learn about mental illness as they write, design, and publish pamphlets that define a variety of mental illnesses. Students then distribute the pamphlets to local mental-health clinics. Students gain knowledge of mental illnesses, and they share that useful knowledge with a real audience outside the classroom.

Immediately after the news conference ended, a yearlong promotional campaign began to celebrate Clemson's commitment to undergraduate education, particularly in the areas of writing and communication skills, as recognized by *TIME*. No one was more surprised by these developments than I. In 1987, when I was being recruited to Clemson, Professor Dixie Goswami of the Search Committee had said to me, "Come to Clemson, you will love it." How right Dixie was!

In the summer of 2000, a *TIME* reporter-photographer showed up unannounced and asked whether she could visit my class in romantic literature for an article about teachers using a WAC approach. I did not suspect anything until a couple of months later, when I saw my photo featured in the *TIME* article that announced Clemson's selection as the "2001 Public University of the Year."

I joined the Clemson faculty as the Robert S. Campbell Chair in Technical Communications. This endowed chair position was thanks to the generosity of Bob (Class of 1937) and Betsy Campbell, and I was hired to work across disciplines to improve the communication skills of engineering students. An Effective Technical Communication program was already in place in the College of Engineering. As Campbell Chair, I joined this effort.

In 1989, with financial assistance from the Campbell endowment, I cautiously decided to test the waters to find out whether faculty might be

Peach Tent by Sam Wang (With permission of photographer Samuel T.M. Wang)

interested in the WAC concept in every discipline, not just engineering. I published a brochure announcing a full-day workshop at Clemson's Outdoor Lab, lunch included. To my surprise, sixty faculty from across campus volunteered to participate! I conducted a workshop for thirty faculty and a couple of weeks later for another thirty. These workshops became the centerpiece of our WAC program and then later our Communication-Across-the-Curriculum (CAC) program.

When we received the *TIME* award in 2000, several hundred faculty had participated in one or more workshops. Outstanding teachers and researchers attended, many of whom had themselves won teaching awards or been named alumni professors. They were eager to learn more about teaching with writing. Innovative faculty in science, math, nursing, business, agriculture, and the arts are role models who inspire their students to acquire the best communication practices of their professions. Clemson workshops were designed to offer these faculty ways to engage students in learning and communicating more effectively and to share their broad knowledge about teaching with instructors from other departments. Many participants said that being able to meet and work with colleagues from other disciplines was a strength of the WAC program. Together, they learned alternative ways of writing and thinking with students; they designed assignments with an emphasis on discovery and critical thinking, not on memorization and rote learning. Faculty created assignments in which students collaborated to create knowledge that audiences valued beyond the classroom. The university's current Critical Inquiry program grew out of these creative approaches to teaching and learning developed by faculty from WAC workshops.

In 1991, President Max Lennon asked me to make a presentation to Roy Pearce (Class of 1941), proposing a Center for Professional Communication that would support the university's growing WAC program. Mr. Pearce and I discussed the importance of oral communication in the workplace, and the proposal was revised from WAC to CAC, an across-discipline initiative to improve students' oral as well as written communication skills. Soon after this meeting, at a dinner I attended hosted by President and Mrs. Lennon, Roy and Marnie Pearce surprised all the guests by announcing a major gift to endow the Pearce Center for Professional Communication. Dr. Carl Lovitt was appointed the first director of the Pearce Center, and he and I worked together for most of the next decade to strengthen and expand the center's impact on faculty and students on campus, leading to the receipt of the *TIME* award in 2000.

Each department's faculty, with support from the Pearce Center, created communication-intensive courses in their disciplines, leading to a capstone course in the senior year. Students received instruction specifically in writing and oral communication in first-year English, second-year speech communication, and third-year technical or business writing. Teachers across campus came to realize that for students to write and speak effectively as accountants or engineers, they must learn the technical subject matter *and* be able to effectively communicate that knowledge to a variety of audiences.

Were there any difficulties along the way? Of course. One dean would routinely tell junior faculty not to spend too much time on teaching because getting grants was much more important, suggesting that "taking time to attend a workshop about teaching and learning will actually count against you at tenure time." Some faculty thought that their teaching evaluations would go down if they included writing in their courses. One teacher said, "Students hate my class now; can you imagine what would happen if I required writing?" For most faculty who participated in CAC workshops and programs, however, teaching evaluations went up because teachers and students were communicating and listening to each other more often in ways that created mentoring opportunities in a supportive atmosphere.

At Clemson, I have had opportunities to teach bright and talented undergraduate and graduate students and to collaborate on professional publications and presentations with dozens of teacher-researchers in almost every department. I had an amazing opportunity to see Clemson's history and culture through the eyes of alumni with a lifelong love of the university, including Robert Campbell, Class of 1937, and Roy Pearce, Class of 1941. In 2004, I received my most cherished award, the Class of 1939 Award for Excellence, and was inducted as an honorary member of the great Class of 1939, where I was awed by two great Clemson men from that class: Taze (Tee) Senn and James (Jim) Sweeny. My life at Clemson has been and continues to be full and rewarding.

WRITING ACROSS THE CURRICULUM

Victoria Ridgeway Gillis
Eugene T. Moore School of Education
1991–2010

Based on my own experience as an undergraduate, my view of college teaching was decidedly negative. I had spent years sitting through what I considered to be boring lectures, with professors who barely took a breath and rarely asked for questions. I frantically took notes in these classes and struggled to decipher my own handwriting as I studied for final exams, often the only evaluation of learning in a course in the middle of the twentieth century.

After teaching middle and high school science for twenty years, I returned to graduate school and completed a doctorate in reading education. I began my career at Clemson in the fall of 1991. I had been involved in a movement in literacy termed *content area reading* (today known as *disciplinary literacy*) and had conducted professional development for teachers. Although I had taught teachers in Florida and South Carolina, I was not sure how my active learning approach would fit with teaching in the *academy*, and so I participated in the Writing-Across-the-Curriculum (WAC) workshops offered at Clemson. When I signed up for my first WAC workshop, I assumed that participants would be other education faculty. Oh, how wrong I was!

It never occurred to me that faculty from other disciplines might be interested in teaching, much less in teaching well. My initial workshop included participants from modern language, chemistry, physics, English, engineering, and history. Clearly, my assumptions about higher-education faculty had been wrong. I was the lone education faculty member in that first WAC workshop.

The practices discussed were imaginative, insightful, and engaging for students. Exercises included having students write questions during the initial fifteen minutes of lecture and then turn to a partner to discuss them. This cycle was repeated throughout class, resulting in an interactive lecture that involved students in actively processing information. Other ideas mirrored the things I had done in my own high school physical science classes, including having students write questions at the end of class as an "exit slip" and beginning the next class with a discussion of those questions. I found kindred spirits in that WAC workshop and signed up for as many of them as time would allow. I adjusted my opinion about higher-education faculty. These faculty members, drawn from across the university, were focused on student learning and on helping students become independent learners. WAC promoted cross-curricular collaboration and assignments with students at the heart of generative activities that were congruent with students' learning. Assignments had an audience beyond the classroom and often involved problem solving. In a modern language class, students were directed to translate pamphlets found in doctors' offices into Spanish, French, or Russian.

Years later, as a consultant for a Maryland school district, I used this idea of an external audience with ninth-grade teachers who were struggling to create a collaborative culminating assignment. These teachers generated an assignment that produced a pamphlet for the Chamber of Commerce, available at Maryland welcome stations along interstate highways. Social studies students researched and wrote about the history of the area and identified sites and museums to visit; math students calculated the cost of travel, visits to museums and historical sites, and miles involved in trips; science students researched and wrote about the fauna, flora, and environmental issues of the areas; and English students revised and edited the pamphlets.

Based on my participation in WAC, I began to collaborate with professors in the subject matter methods courses in which my secondary disciplinary literacy pre-service teachers were co-enrolled. We created joint assignments with supervising teachers as an audience. Our preservice teachers assessed students in their internship, under the supervision of their cooperating teacher; evaluated students' disciplinary literacy; organized the results; prepared a summary of the data for their cooperating teacher; and created instructional plans for their internship based on assessment results. Before this interactive assignment, students in my classes had created notebooks of instructional ideas, an assignment that could be, and often was, completed in a mindless way, like generating a scrapbook. The new assignment enabled me to evaluate preservice teachers' ability to assess students, analyze and organize data, and plan instruction based on assessment results. It engaged preservice teachers in the process of minds-on teaching and provided them with a way to contribute valuable information to their supervising teachers.

My initial encounter with WAC was the continuation of a rich professional learning experience. In the late 1990s, I had been chosen to be a volunteer consultant in Reading and Writing for Critical Thinking (RWCT), a project that focused on helping newly independent Eastern European nations, which had broken away from the USSR, shift their educational system from the Soviet model to one that instilled democratic thinking in students. Twenty-nine countries in Eastern Europe participated in RWCT, and most of the projects continue twenty years after the initial RWCT workshops. I spent four years working twice a semester with teachers, professors, and ministry officials in Latvia. RWCT was based on principles involving active learning, collaborative work, and problem solving, as were the WAC principles and ideas. We encouraged lessons that involved multiple points of view; student involvement in actively constructing their own knowledge; and use of discussion and writing, as opposed to primarily listening, in classrooms. Volunteers conducted workshops with educational professionals (teachers, professors, and ministry officials), assisted as they planned for implementation, and observed these professionals as they incorporated the ideas in their own classrooms and later as they led their own professional development workshops. The original group of university professors was initially skeptical about the ideas discussed in RWCT. One philosophy professor had been imprisoned in a Soviet gulag for twenty years, and his opinions carried extraordinary weight with the other professors in our workshops. My involvement in WAC enabled me to provide explicit examples of RWCT principles in action in higher education for the professors in our workshops. These examples, from a variety of disciplines, convinced the philosophy professor to try our ideas. He became one of our most ardent supporters.

Looking back over a forty-nine-year career in education, I see how neatly my initial involvement in content area reading/disciplinary literacy as a K–12 teacher, WAC during my initial years in higher education, and RWCT fit together. These professional development programs shared essentially similar theoretical foundations involving active learning, collaborative work, and problem solving. What began with involvement in content area reading evolved to become a foundational theme throughout my career.

LITONLINE: Ahead of Its Time

Donna R. Reiss
Department of English
2004–2008

More than a decade before the pandemic forced unprepared, perhaps even unwilling, faculty to teach their classes online, Clemson's Department of English foresaw the potential for classes over the Internet. The year 2005 was the right time to offer students a way to take summer classes from their homes away from campus and at the same time remain connected with faculty in Clemson's Department of English. Thus began Litonline.

When I was invited by the Department of English in 2005 to design and lead a faculty development program to prepare literature faculty to teach summer classes online, I was honored to be able to bring my decades of experience with computer-mediated instruction to my new academic home. By the fall of 2005, the project we called Litonline began, with a group of enthusiastic lecturers who met monthly to share the results of our research into online education and to demonstrate the ways we were incorporating online activities into our face-to-face classes in preparation for fully online classes in the summer of 2006.

Despite early resistance to distance learning among some faculty and administrators, Clemson's Litonline was considered successful because it brought summer money to the department. Eventually, however, more faculty became curious about the advantages of teaching their summer classes from anyplace they might travel for research, writing, or vacation, as long as they had an Internet connection. Having taught my own online classes from Hawaii, Sweden, Australia, and New Zealand, I could speak to the flexibility of this approach for faculty and students. And as the Internet became increasingly important for their own research and publication, more faculty developed an interest in teaching hybrid classes, with some sessions face-to-face and some sessions asynchronous online.

Even before Litonline began in 2005, I had offered a number of workshops for Clemson faculty beginning in 2001. Here, a bit of history shows how I became a part of the Clemson family.

In 2000, I had a sabbatical from Tidewater Community College in Virginia, where I had developed for our four campuses a program on distributed learning at the request of the college president. For my sabbatical project, I chose to research other college and university programs on distance learning, in particular, at Clemson, for academic and personal reasons. For years, I had been collaborating with Professor Art Young of Clemson University and Professor Magnus Gustafsson of Chalmers University in Gothenburg, Sweden. Our students at these three institutions and three levels of learning (community college, master's, and doctorate, respectively) had been discussing poetry totally online in small groups composed of members from each class. Art, Magnus, and I spoke at conferences, conducted workshops, and gave keynote addresses in the United States and abroad about the benefits of these online communities for students to learn about literature. That's the professional part. As some of you know, my long professional connection with Art, including several publications together beginning in 1995, had by 2000 evolved to my moving to Clemson to marry him. That's the personal part.

I continued teaching online at Tidewater while living in Clemson, returning to Virginia Beach periodically to meet with colleagues and students until I was able to retire from Tidewater Community College in 2004 as associate professor of English emerita. Shortly after, I become a lecturer at Clemson, teaching what were then called laptop classes and becoming one of the first two English teachers to offer fully online classes. Even earlier, however, in 2001, I had been invited by Clemson's Office of Teaching Effectiveness and Innovation to offer workshops for faculty because of my extensive background in conducting workshops on computer-mediated instruction for any discipline.

Litonline grew to become English Online, and by the time I decided in 2008 that it was time to retire again, the program was offering all English Department faculty an opportunity to share ideas and experiences about teaching online. Even when Clemson established a university-wide certification program for online teaching, the English Department was able to continue its own successful training based on the Litonline model. This program emphasized a communication-intensive, highly interactive approach to online classes wherein students connected with each other through written discussion groups and multimedia presentations. Students in these online classes liked the connections, remarking that their teachers and classmates were actively involved in their learning. Whenever the college closed for weather or sports interference, English faculty were prepared to move online even if their classes usually met in person. And when the pandemic forced all classes online, most English Department faculty already had some experience teaching in that manner.

I am proud to have been an early adopter of technology for teaching and grateful that Clemson gave me an opportunity to share the experience from my decades of teaching hybrid and online classes with my new colleagues. The Litonline project has taken new directions since 2005, as technology changes and as more faculty and students come to appreciate the ways a learning community can develop among people who never meet in person.

For sharing their memories of Clemson's Department of English's development of online classes, I give my thanks to Sean Williams, Susanna Ashton, Lee Morrissey, Michele Martin, Elisa Sparks, and Barbara Weaver.

THE SKY IS FALLING!

VICTORIA RIDGEWAY GILLIS
Eugene T. Moore School of Education
1991–2010

In the fall of 2003, the Reading Area of the Eugene T. Moore School of Education was asked to deliver our master's in reading program to teachers in Horry County. I had a technology background and was generally comfortable with it, a trait not shared by all my colleagues, and so I was assigned to teach the first class in the program, which was READ 861, Foundations of Reading.

The delivery method was what we would call *hybrid* today; I had three students in front of me, in the face-to-face section of the class, and seventy-two teachers at a distant location in Horry County. I taught through the educational TV set up at the University Center in Greenville. I had no direct knowledge of how the teachers were being accommodated in the Horry County section but assumed that they were in a large classroom around tables, had a generous amount of space to work in, and viewed a large screen so they could clearly see and hear me. Oh, how wrong I was!

As in many classes in the beginning of the twenty-first century, the first class agenda included the syllabus; the course management system (a term that came into use much later), MyCLE, which was an excellent program, much better than any that came after; and my expectation that they use MyCLE to submit their work and use their Clemson email for all correspondence. The problem was that most, if not all, the teachers at the distant location didn't remember their Clemson email, many had not even set it up, and if they had set up the CU email, they did not remember their password. In those days, there was no app to remember passwords. Heck, there were no apps.

The first few classes were activity-based, with short fifteen-minute mini-lectures interspersed among student activities. I sent the texts that were the basis of these activities to the district administrator who coordinated the class; she duplicated them and then handed them out when directed. As I taught in front of the camera, we moved from one activity to another, developing the theories that formed the basis for the remaining weeks of class. After those initial weeks, the lecture portion of the class increased, and I used small-group discussions of common readings interspersed among those lectures. About four weeks into the class, I happened to ask a question and didn't get any response from the distant group, so I asked again. Thus, I discovered that all seventy-two teachers were sitting in an auditorium, watching a thirty-inch-screen television; most students could not see or hear me. I was furious and called the IT Department at Clemson. Eventually I got a large screen installed in the auditorium and had the audio broadcast through speakers. Great! Problem solved. Although I had acquired a negative reputation in the IT Department, I was relieved—but that relief was short-lived.

I had blithely used the traditional assignments for the course, which included five lesson plans constructed based on the theories and strategies students were learning and taught to their classes, accompanied by a reflection explaining instructional decisions made along with a rationale for them, an analysis of the success of the lesson supported by evidence from student work, and a reflexive look at what they would do next, based on what had transpired in the classroom. Five lesson plans from seventy-five students resulted in 375 individual papers that had to be graded. When their first assignments began coming in, via email rather than through MyCLE, I began to get an uneasy feeling in the pit of my stomach. Email became unmanageable, my inbox ballooned, and I got nasty little notes about its size from IT. I had directed students to upload their assignments through MyCLE because it identified who had submitted the work. It also made grading easier, as the original MyCLE had the capability of putting folders on your desktop into which you could drag and drop students' reviewed work. Unfortunately, these teachers were technophobic. They used their personal email addresses and sporadically put their names on their papers. How could I figure out who *beachteach@aol.com* was? Multiply this by seventy-two, and you can quickly see the nightmare. And this was just the beginning of the troubles.

About mid-term, the satellite used to beam the signals of the South Carolina Educational TV programs, the delivery vehicle we were depending on, fell out of the sky. This is not a joke—the satellite plummeted to Earth, and for a week or more, every SCETV program was scrambling. We were in the middle of the course, and I had no video link to the students. Ever inventive, I decided to send PowerPoint decks to the coordinator, and I taught by phone. I would call the distance location, and the coordinator would put me on speaker (remember, there were seventy-two students in a huge auditorium), and I'd move through the slides and activities by directing the coordinator to advance to the next slide.

Frequently, we lost the phone connection, or one or the other of us could not hear. Every time the connection failed, it took five to ten minutes to reestablish. Meanwhile, I had three students physically present in front of me. Class continued in this disjointed way through the end of the semester. Meanwhile, I had a serious grading glut on my hands. I cannot remember how I got everything graded and returned, or indeed whether I ever did; I only know that I got very little sleep that semester, although I did learn a lot.

From that time until the day I retired, I instituted a file-naming convention in my syllabus so that any assignment submitted for evaluation had information about the person submitting the file, the semester, the course, and the specific assignment. Another lesson was to minimize grading and at the same time maximize students' opportunity for active learning. Everything students produced did not have to be graded. In hindsight, I could have had students do the five lessons but choose only two or three to submit, having first had peers review their work, which would have engaged students in meaningful discussions about the ideas in class. This experience came a decade after I began my career in higher education, but I wish I had learned those lessons earlier. It might have saved my sanity in the fall of 2003.

RISE:
It's Critical Thinking Time

Laura J. Shick
Department of Mathematical Sciences
2005–2016

Anatole France once said, "An education is not how much you have committed to memory, or even how much you know. It's being able to differentiate between what you know and what you don't." It stands to reason that when students are engaged in curricula that promote critical thinking, student achievement increases, and they become better decision-makers. However, many college-bound students embark on their college careers with a lack of critical-thinking skills. Their educational experience prior to entering the university often consists of responding to standardized, multiple-choice tests. Simply put, for many, students' performance is based on their ability to regurgitate what they have heard via lecture or read in textbooks.

The need is clear: Students must engage in experiences that increase their attention and focus, motivate them to practice higher-level critical thinking, and promote active learning. Clemson's Critical Thinking Initiative (CT²) and the Faculty Institute were pathways to meeting that challenge. For four days, invited faculty members experienced intense training in the principles of critical thinking and strategies for intentionally integrating critical-thinking components into their courses, regardless of discipline.

The challenge was clear: Rework existing course syllabi to include critical-thinking measurables or design a new course. The task was motivating and challenging. Work was rigorously evaluated by institute peers and faculty, but it was also stimulating to be with like-minded professionals who were willing to put in the time to help students learn to think outside the box while making informed decisions, all while realizing the ramifications of those decisions.

As a participant in the CT² training, I began the work of designing a new course patterned after the book *How to Lie with Statistics*. I titled my course

"Looking Behind the Headlines: How Research Can Be Used and Misused to Influence Public Policy." My course design was reviewed and evaluated by my peers, and they were excited. The challenge was to find a "home" department for the course, and after much jockeying and debating, it was offered in the fall of 2014 as a "special problems course," CES 1990, for freshman students in the Residents in Science and Engineering (RISE) program. Offered at 8:00 a.m., this was usually the very first college-level course for many, and it was probably not quite what they were expecting.

Students enrolled in the new course were asked to consider news topics that were being hotly debated and had varying political or policy implications. One such topic was "transporting goods and services: rail, air, trucking, ship, and drone." Students were asked to address the topic at hand, keeping in mind the principles of critical thinking. They were divided into five teams consisting of four students each. Two students in each group would take the position in support of a particular stance; in the transportation example, what was the most efficient, cost-effective, environmentally friendly means of moving goods and services, and did that differ, depending on the product being transported? The other two would take the opposing viewpoint and support their positions. Students had to understand the difference between simple observation or news articles lacking a data source, peer-reviewed articles, or otherwise-vetted research and submit a position paper along with their oral presentation. These presentations were creative, including a series of "debates" that definitely would not have qualified them for the University Debate Team!

This classroom format took learning to a whole new level! There were no multiple-choice tests or "show-your-work" calculations. Students were able to see how their work was relevant beyond the classroom. A prompt for students to frame their presentations was "If I were a lobbyist, how would I reframe the question [restate the issue], and what evidence have I collected to convince lawmakers and decision-makers to support my side of the issue?" Students had to apply critical-thinking principles to separate factual information from inferences, cull relevant from irrelevant information, identify alternative positions/interpretations of the data, and evaluate evidence to support reasonable conclusions or refute inappropriate conclusions.

The class spent a good deal of time discussing the classic "vaccines and autism" challenge. Again, they took two sides and even went back to the original research. That study was never able to be replicated or validated, but that didn't stop the press and the alarmists. By the time the research was refuted, the damage had been done; to this day, many people are convinced that vaccines cause autism and avoid protecting their children or others around them by refusing the shots. How many millions of children have died from preventable diseases, all because someone grabbed onto false data?

Some of the other topics addressed by the class included a look at beef sustainability; income gap meets longevity gap (which led to a discussion of euthanasia); robotics and quantum computing; the materials genome project; energy: water, coal, solar, wind, nuclear, fracking, wave; 3D printing; and solar roadways. Relating statistics to real-world problems created a level of interest and engagement I had not previously witnessed. Students began to understand the value of research as they realized the detrimental effects of fake news and the impact it has on the attitudes of others.

Designing rubrics for the evaluation of student work in my class presented my biggest obstacle. I found it challenging, to say the least, to evaluate student engagement. All the work presented was well researched, and presentations were clear and concise. Additionally, writing was professional but still creative. Students worked cooperatively with other team members when engaged in debates. Defining an A in the course as opposed to a B was impossible for me. Because each and every student in the course was positively engaged in research and project delivery, there were no failing grades. Each student demonstrated growth in the use of critical thinking as they addressed the problems presented to them. The class met the goals for intentional integration of critical thinking into curriculum design. Students also met their goals of using critical thinking to address and evaluate the news and present findings. Scores on the standardized, required pre- and post-test of Critical Thinking Skills increased for all but one student; it clearly was test error, as her work demonstrated that she certainly had not regressed in her thinking skills!

Although the course I had designed taught statistics in a way that was challenging and meaningful to my students, it didn't fall neatly within my home Math Department, nor did Engineering (RISE) have the budget to "borrow" me from Math. The class was doomed and short-lived, lasting just one academic year. But in that academic year, I met some of the finest young men and women I've encountered throughout my academic career, and not just as students but as human beings. These future engineers showed such curiosity, creativity, and excitement that they will certainly make significant contributions to society. What a privilege it was to spend time with these young people.

TANKS FOR THE MEMORIES

DONALD L. COLLINS
College of Architecture
1972–2005

Jim Barker, dean of what was then the College of Architecture, was on a late-summer visit to Clemson University President Max Lennon's office on the second floor in the northeast corner of Sikes Hall when Lennon ventured off the agenda for their meeting. He began to speak about the view from his office window up the hill to the two "industrial-style" water towers located behind the Clemson House. He wondered aloud whether something could be done to the tanks to make them more attractive to anyone who might see them while in his office.

Barker, being in South Carolina longer than Lennon, made immediate reference to the infamous "Peachoid" water tank that sits alongside Interstate 85 near Gaffney. Barker instantly knew that the offending tanks behind the Clemson House presented a grand opportunity to raise the status and value of the College of Architecture in the new president's mind. He also knew whom he was going to call on to direct a design studio project concerning the appearance of the offending tanks—me.

On returning to Lee Hall, Barker sent a message for me to come see him about a possible project. It was a déjà vu moment: Could this be yet another fire-station design project? I thought. I had been summoned to two different deans' offices in late summer in the past to be presented with an opportunity to have my students explore fire-station designs. But this time, the "favor" I couldn't turn down proved to be different.

Barker was aware that I had a reputation for always beginning my fall semester design studio by issuing a short design challenge that was graphic in nature. He was also aware of and comfortable with my methodology of introducing "discovery" by having students understand and develop their own design process. He may not have been fully aware of my challenging students to think outside the box by giving zany titles to my project statements. For example, *Logo Loco* required each student to design a personal logo to be used throughout the semester on any final presentation drawings or models. *Stoolie Stools* required a graphic design to be painted on their worktable stool so they could identify their stool no matter where in Lee Hall the stool might migrate. *A Six Pack of Heroes* required the graphic design of a bottle carton and six bottle labels depicting their design heroes. *UPIGS*, which stood for *University Police Identification Graphic System*, required the development of a graphic scheme for university police cars, while *COPS*, standing for *Clemson's Official Police Symbol*, required the development of a logo to be used on the City of Clemson police vehicles. (A "winning" design was chosen by each department and graced the sides of each force's patrol units. Unfortunately, that is no longer the case. The "winning" students' graphics were far superior to what is in use today.) Perhaps my best title ever was *Pair of Dots Paradox*, a project for which I sent each student, before school started, a postcard with a red sticker dot and a green sticker dot as the only "message." In the studio, the dots were transformed in a series of design process steps into a graphic design. The graphic design's pieces were then extruded, morphing into an urban design complete with water elements and space-defining trees.

The project for the water tanks located behind the Clemson House was no different to me than any other project, and so it became *Tanks for the Memories*, with the challenge to propose a graphic design for the tanks that would live forever in one's memory of Clemson. The tanks would, however, be my first three-dimensional, 360-degree (3-D/360) graphic challenge. The 3-D/360 aspect was not an issue; it just became another "given" to grapple with in exploring the project.

When John Acorn, the head of the Art Department, got wind of the project and the reference that had been made to the Peachoid in bringing the Clemson tanks project to light, he let Dean Barker and me know that Peter Freudenberg, the installation artist for the "peach" design painted on the water tank at Gaffney, had an undergraduate degree in design from Clemson. Barker immediately asked whether there was any way to get him to come to Clemson. Within days, arrangements had been made to bring Freudenberg to campus as a short-term (two weeks) adjunct faculty member to work with me and the students in my studio on *Tanks for the Memories*.

Some clever proposals came out of the exercise, but the one that stood out was the face of a Tiger done in shades of white, orange, purple, and black, with the face spread across the two tanks. One eye was on each tank. You had to be on the axis to see the tiger's face emerge. Otherwise, you just saw the colors and pelt patterns. The tiger's nose was missing, but you knew it was there by implication.

The tiger's eyes were not a caricature; rather, they were piercing, the eyes of a fierce but elegant beast on the prowl. Imagine how much fun it would have been to take campus visitors to see the tiger's face and feel the steely eyes come into focus.

But the tiger on the tanks was never realized. Before they could be painted, the old tanks would need some repair, the surface would have to be sandblasted and reprimed, safety rigging would have to be installed, and paint would have to be purchased. Someone would have to do the painting. The Peachoid in Gaffney was painted when the tank was new; it took fifty gallons of paint in twenty colors and several months to accomplish. But what really killed the Clemson project was finding out that one of the tanks had already been decommissioned and that the other was scheduled to be taken offline as well. The tanks are gone now, as is the Clemson House, which was imploded several years ago.

The new water tank on Kite Hill replaced the offending tanks located behind the Clemson House that were viewable from President Lennon's office. The new tank is the culmination of the Clemson University Water Pressure Upgrade project, albeit many years later than planned. But think of this: Now we have a new tank, a single tank, one that would make a great place for an "Eyes of the Tiger" graphic statement. And one giant graphic on a single tank would be even easier to accomplish. Clemson University could have something special and iconic, something as impressive and easy to remember as the Tiger Paw. Heck, Clemson could have two ionic "Eyes of the Tiger" tanks for that matter—one on Kite Hill, and one on an identical university-owned tank located on the other side of Lake Hartwell! An opportunity exists to have a *Tanks for the Memories* experience added to Clemson lore.

THE CLEMSON EXPERIENCE IN PHOTOGRAPHS

SAMUEL T. M. WANG
Department of Visual Arts
1966–2006

Title: Peach Tent, ca. 1980
Description of the image:

It was always a pleasure to come across visually interesting objects or situations on campus, as in this case, the old experimental peach-growing area by the current golf course. It was probably part of an agricultural experiment, but to me the visual expressiveness was immeasurable. The round shape was the total

Silos and Plastic (With permission of photographer Samuel T.M. Wang)

output from a wide-angle lens on a five-by-seven film camera that I made to avoid cropping or eliminating any part of the available image area.

Title: Silos and Plastic, ca. 1980
Description of the image:

Another scene on campus, an advantage of a large university, where I could come upon unintended visual expressions. I believe that this was a prototype of bale-wrapping plastic near the cow pastures. The round picture was the total output from a wide-angle lens on a five-by-seven film camera that I made to avoid cropping or eliminating any part of the available image area.

Title: Sand Piles, 1978
Description of the image:

After I first constructed a five-by-seven film camera to capture the entire output from a wide-angle lens that was intended for a two-and-one-fourth-inch camera, I looked for subject matter on campus, partly to use as a teaching tool for my beginning photography class, to demonstrate that one could find interesting subject matter almost anywhere. These piles of sand placed near one of the dikes then became some of my teaching aids.

Sand (With permission of photographer Samuel T.M. Wang)

Time Magazine Sticker photograph by Art Young

CHAPTER 7

Airplane sculpture on Clemson's campus, photograph from files (With permission from the University Archives)

LET'S GO FLY . . . A PAPER AIRPLANE
(Or, How I Turned *Introduction to Statistics* into a Toy Shop)

Laura J. Shick

Department of Mathematical Sciences

2005–2016

Statistics: the course most students are required to take, most do not want to take, and most live in fear of taking. At the very least, many have heard that statistics is boring and useless. My challenge was to set the tone and expectations for the course on the first day of class. My mantra was that failing was not an option for students who were willing to put in some time and effort. Besides, failing created the illusion that I was a "lousy" teacher. I wanted students to have fun and conquer their fear. Cue eyes rolling.

A review of the syllabus provided students with an overview of the course. All went as expected until the students saw the last page: *SEMESTER PROJECT. You have been asked by a toy company to design a paper airplane that will be complex enough to challenge a young person but not so simple that an adult would be bored. You will produce a prototype and write a short description to put in the Christmas catalogue and produce a thirty-second TV commercial. You will work in teams of three students, and you will all get the same grade. This project will count as 10 percent of your final grade.* I saw looks of surprise, disbelief, "you're kidding," and a bit of excitement. "This is statistics?"

Students in Introduction to Statistics (I do not recall the course number—it kept changing) embarked on a semester of creativity, innovation, trial and error, application of statistical processes, teamwork, and, yes, fun. Their engagement in the class provided me with affirmation of my decision to teach. I saw students get excited about learning.

The semester was divided into four units, and the project steps fell neatly into those units.

Unit One: Experimental Design. Students had to figure out what kinds of planes they wanted to produce. They were required to use at least two types of paper or other flexible material, twelve-by-twelve inches square, and at least two different designs (models). This meant that they would have at least four different planes, using a two-by-two design. They could use staples, paper clips, or glue, and they could cut the sheet into smaller pieces but never use more than the original twelve-by-twelve-inch sheet. Attempts at flying the planes often required multiple redesigns—thus the term *experiment*.

Unit 2: Descriptive Statistics. Students were required to gather data. They recorded distance and noted trajectory, flight height, and success of flight. After ten attempts, students noted the condition of their planes and the likelihood that the planes would withstand being thrown by children. I recall getting a call from library staff, saying that students were flying paper airplanes in there. When asked about their actions, the students replied that they were flying planes for their class. I exclaimed, "Oh, that's fantastic. It's a great controlled environment." There was a stunned silence on the other end of the line, but in future semesters, I never got calls! Students calculated means and standard deviations and created graphs of their data. I realized that understanding of significant figures was lacking; you can't report an average to seven decimals when the tape measure was only in quarter inches!

Unit 3: Hypotheses and Inference. Students were required to conduct hypothesis tests based on those ten throws. How confident could they be that when the actual plane kit was sold, it would perform as advertised? Only *two* models would move on to the next step.

Unit 4: Two-Sample Testing. With only two planes left in the competition, students had to make their final decision. Did both semifinalists use the same paper with different models or the same model with different papers? Which statistical test was appropriate: Matched Pairs or Test of Two Independent Samples? Results of this final analysis would reveal the winning airplane.

I required a written report covering each unit, all data and analysis, a narrative of the decision process, anecdotal stories, all calculations and exhibits, and a formal conclusion. The last page of the report, the denouement, was a sketch of the plane and directions for its assembly and, finally, the print copy for the catalogue ad.

I've found that the week between Thanksgiving and finals, and again at the end of April, is the time for wrapping up the semester, in whatever form that might take. For this project, that meant producing and showing the commercials. And what a week that was! I was amazed and entertained by the creativity of the students. Early renditions of the project commercials were rather simple and plain, without a lot of color or action. However, subsequent classes tried to outdo the previous semesters' commercials. One trio of students even pulled some strings and got into Death Valley. *Tiger One* flew down the Hill with "Tiger Rag" playing in the background!

The hands-on engagement provided by the Paper Airplanes Project provided the format for my Introduction to Statistics class at Clemson for more than three years. Additionally, I created excitement and helped students understand relevancy by introducing current events. Election years were perfect for learning about sampling, probability, how to phrase a question, and how to (or how not to) present the data. Still, nothing compared to the Paper Airplane Project for excitement and the perfect alignment with each unit of the course. When doing her course evaluation, one student wrote, "I feel like I learned, and absorbed, more about statistics by doing this fun project than I ever would have in a traditional lecture class." It was affirmations like that that warmed my heart and kept me going.

Change is inevitable, and as more and more change came to Clemson, my airplanes were grounded. The student population at Clemson exploded. It seemed that introductory-level classes in many disciplines were changed to large lecture format. Coordinated courses with a common syllabus and schedule and common exams became the norm. The opportunity for students to participate in semester-long projects like the airplanes required flexibility in presenting the sequence of topics, and that flexibility didn't fit in the common course format. As a professional educator, I no longer felt alive in the classroom. The academic freedom I felt I needed to motivate students began to fall by the wayside. The question I found myself asking, repeatedly, was "How could I ignite that spark to get them excited about *t*-tests (for example)?" I'm too much of a traditionalist. I felt lost. And I knew that because I felt lost, it was time to move on. Retirement beckoned, and two years later I did just that.

Occasionally, as I'm cleaning out files at home, I'll come across the big stack of select projects that I saved. I wonder where those students are and whether they remember that crazy teacher who had them flying airplanes in the library. I know for certain that they conquered their fears and learned a little something about statistics in the process

A MOST UNUSUAL
THREE-LEGGED STOOL

Donald L. Collins
College of Architecture
1972–2005

In the late fall of 1976, a few years after arriving at Clemson, I was summoned to Dean Harlan McClure's office. I had no idea that the requested visit would change my career so profoundly. McClure instructed me to have a seat. Sitting down, he said, "Don, I seem to remember in your professional work or design teaching results you showed me when you were seeking a position at Clemson a fire-station project." His words created a near déjà vu moment.

McClure's memory was correct: I had indeed run a fire-station project at Ball State University's (BSU's) College of Architecture and Planning (CAP) for all third-year architecture studios. The project was indirectly the result of being summoned to CAP Dean Sappenfield's office because he had a memory of my hailing from a large fire-service family. Sappenfield wanted me to seek funding for a "fire-station locations" study being requested by the Muncie fire department.

McClure continued, asking whether I would be willing to run a fire-station project in my spring semester design studio to provide some insight to a nearby volunteer fire department. The fire department involved, Corinth-Shiloh VFD (C-S VFD), also known as Oconee County Station Three, had approached Clemson University about the possibility of building a new fire station on a small triangular parcel of Clemson University land on the west side of Lake Hartwell. The university's administration was favorably considering the request but concerned about the quality and appearance of the station to be erected. The administration turned to McClure for help. McClure, in turn, recalled my previous fire-station design experience.

The C-S VFD Station in use today, on Old Seneca Road, is a direct result of my studio effort, albeit with an addition that has changed its appearance a tad. C-S VFD acquired the right to use a favorite solution by making a small contribution to the College of Architecture Foundation and accepting the stipulations that the station would be built as designed and that a professional would be engaged to produce the required construction documents. The concept and schematic design phases for the project were completed by student Scott Collins (no relation), while the design development (DD) phase of the project was completed by student Joab Moore. Scott has an architectural office in Florence, South Carolina. Joab has an office in Greenwich, Connecticut. I still have a photo of Joab's final DD model.

To add "fire-service" expertise to the final faculty review or "jury" of the twenty-four student projects, I invited the CS-VFD fire chief and Charlie Owens, chief of the Clemson University Fire Department (CUFD), to participate. Afterward, Chief Owens asked how I knew the jargon of the fire service. I explained to him my connections to eleven professional firefighters, including my father, saying that firefighting was the "family business." Hearing my reply, Owens invited me to "join" the CUFD, to which I replied, "I thought CUFD was a career department." He stated it was, for the most part, but a few firefighters had other positions on campus and in town. He named Marvin Carmichael, then-director of Financial Aid; Steve Lightsey, a researcher in poultry science; and Jimmy Cook, future mayor of Clemson. I told Chief Owens that I would have to speak to Dean McClure about his proposition.

In meeting with McClure, I was completely surprised when he said, "You should do this. And let's redefine your land-grant college 'Three-Legged Stool' mandate of Teaching, Research and Public Service to capitalize on this opportunity. You continue your teaching as before, but let's now define your public service as working for the good of CUFD. As for your research, let it be related in some way to the fire service, but you define what that will be after giving it some thought." When I asked what would happen if I left class to fight a fire, he replied, "I know you, you already come back to the studios sometimes at night. I know you will make up any lost hours owed the students."

With McClure's approval, I contacted Chief Owens and was issued protective gear on a Monday in mid-May 1977. I responded to my first "working fire" on Thursday. Lacking any training, the professionals kept me at a safe distance. That midnight fire was on Jersey Lane on campus in one of the "pre-fab" married-student housing units that were once located where the Brooks Center and Strom Thurman Institute now stand.

As for the "Research" charge from Dean McClure, it did not take me long to settle on fire stations as a unique building typology to study and become "professorial" about. Since that time, I have visited for "Post-Occupancy Design Evaluation" more than three hundred fire stations throughout the United States and abroad. I have amassed a slide collection about fire-station functional design issues and details—good, bad, and ugly—that exceeds fifteen thousand images. At every station visited, I have presented myself as a Clemson University professor and a CUFD firefighter. As such, I have never been denied entrance to a fire station. I have come to understand and appreciate the universal camaraderie that exists among the "brothers and sisters" who take on the "red devil."

Shortly after Jack Abraham became CUFD's chief, he called me to ask whether I wrote construction specifications. My reply was "Not if I can help it, but why do you ask?" Abraham wanted to know whether I would take on the task of writing apparatus-construction specifications and bid documents to begin the modernization of the CUFD fire apparatus fleet. I did and have been involved in eight apparatus purchases since then under Chiefs Abraham, Riley, and Daniel. Although I handed the leadership over to a younger generation for the last three builds, I remained very involved in the process. Clemson University, with the city of Clemson as a contributing financial partner, now maintains a modern, updated fleet with outstanding operational capability.

One feature I called for in my very first specification document required nine "ground illumination lights" to be mounted beneath the apparatus. I did this after learning of an accident wherein a firefighter had a nasty leg break after stepping out of the cab at night. His foot and part of his leg went into a water meter box with a missing lid. By lighting up the ground at night, I hoped to avoid an accident caused by an unseen hole. My "ground lights" feature was subsequently presented to the National Fire Protection Association's (NFPA's) Technical Committee for Apparatus Minimum Standards. It is now required on all fire apparatus, becoming part of the *NFPA 1901 Standards for Motorized Fire Apparatus* in 1993.

At the time I received the initial specifications charge from Chief Abraham, the university's newest fire apparatus was fifteen years old, and all was red in color. I convinced the department to have all new apparatus henceforth painted white so it would be more visible at night and for easier cab cooling during the day. I wanted to add orange and purple reflective stripes but had to initially settle for red with a touch of blue. By the fourth purchase, they were delivered striped in the university's orange and purple colors that you see in use today. Auburn, University of North Carolina, and East Carolina, while served by municipal departments, have benefited from Clemson's lead, and are now also covered by "first-due" apparatus painted in their university's colors.

When our last aerial was constructed, I was there for the final inspection when the aerial platform was driven by the manufacturer a short distance over to

The Ohio State University. On the way over to campus, CUFD final inspection team members downloaded "Tiger Rag" to a cellphone, plugged the phone in to the apparatus's PA system, and blasted the OSU campus—payback, I suppose, for the time OSU's football coach slugged a Clemson player on the sideline at the 1977 Gator Bowl. While on the OSU campus, Sutphen, the manufacturer, had the rig photographed in front of the Buckeyes' football stadium. Sutphen used the photo in their next calendar of apparatus deliveries, marking the second time a CUFD apparatus was so featured. But when the apparatus arrived on campus, Sutphen employees had clandestinely placed small OSU stickers on the apparatus in a number of discreet locations. Out of respect for their audacity, one sticker remains on the truck to this day!

The fire apparatus specifications responsibility soon got me involved with the Fire Industry Equipment Research Organization (F.I.E.R.O.), an organization of individuals who often headed projects to improve an aspect of their respective fire departments. After Robert Tutterow, the safety officer for the Charlotte Fire Department, became F.I.E.R.O. president, he learned of my fire station design–focused slide collection and asked whether I would do a presentation for F.I.E.R.O. That discussion led to the development of a F.I.E.R.O.-produced National Symposium on Fire Station Design in 2000. The symposium proved so popular that it is now an annual event. In 2022, the event was held in Greenville, South Carolina. In 2004, again working through F.I.E.R.O., I conceived an international design awards program for fire stations and to this day remain the organizer and head judge. F.I.E.R.O. underwent a small name change and is now known as the Fire Industry Education Resource Organization, an IRS-recognized 501(c)3 nonprofit. In all publications pertaining to the symposiums and design awards programs, I am always listed as a professor and firefighter from Clemson University.

Although I had a few fire-station consulting roles before the F.I.E.R.O. symposiums began, I have had many more as a direct result of presentations I have made over the years at the symposiums. I have been consulted on fire-station projects in Manitoba, California, Iowa, Ohio, Virginia, West Virginia Tennessee, North Carolina, South Carolina, and Oklahoma. In Oklahoma, I was chided unmercifully about Clemson stealing one of "their" football coaches!

In the lobby of Human Resources is a picture of me standing in front of a CUFD apparatus. If you dig deep enough, you will find an old feature story on one of the university's websites. My teaching/research/public service career spanned forty-one years. In agreeing to come to Clemson, I never imagined that my Three-Legged Stool would morph into one so connected to the family business, but it was without a doubt a uniquely grand experience sitting on it!

OF DINOSAUR FOSSILS
AND A SABBATICAL

Michael F. Kohl
University Libraries
1982–2012

On Palm Sunday morning in April 1995, I was in a hotel room in Washington, D.C., working with John (Jack) McIntosh, emeritus physics professor at Wesleyan University, on a project that I hoped would see publication and permit me to receive a sabbatical. The project involved editing journals written in the 1870s by Arthur Lakes, an Englishman who helped discover dinosaur fossils in Colorado and Wyoming. The circumstances related to having the Smithsonian Institution Press publish the journals were improbable and fortitudinous.

My interest in paleontology spanned back to my childhood but had been rekindled through volunteering on paleontological digs in Montana during 1991 and Wyoming in 1993. The 1993 dig was sponsored by the Smithsonian Institution's Department of Vertebrate Paleontology. I found the digs to be an incredible adventure, although from a scientific assessment, they were helpful collecting projects but not groundbreaking. The Montana dig tried unsuccessfully to disprove the now widely accepted thesis advanced by Luis and Walter Alvarez, neither of them paleontologists, that an asteroid collision with Earth caused a mass extinction, including that of the dinosaurs. The Smithsonian dig in Wyoming found already well-known fossils from a site that had been disturbed by illegal fossil hunters.

Returning to my job at Clemson University Libraries Special Collections, I thought about how my dig experiences could be translated into the type of research that an archivist could undertake. During the digs, I became aware of the need to document the dig site's precise geographic location and stratigraphy. This need was essential in archaeology, with anthropology requiring accurate field notes as well. At the 1993 fall conference of the Society of American Archivists (SAA), I contacted some individuals who worked in museums and/or had participated in digs and were interested in presenting a paper during a session at next year's conference related to the creation and preservation of field notes. A session proposal was accepted by the SAA, which meant that a paper had to be written. During the summer of 1994, I spent a week or so in Washington, D.C., part of the time working to transfer papers from Senator Thurmond's office to Clemson's Special Collections and part of the time doing research at the Library of Congress and the Smithsonian Institution Archives related to field notes of paleontologists.

Among the collections I consulted at the Smithsonian were the journals of Arthur Lakes from 1877–1880, describing his discoveries of fossils, including some of the iconic dinosaurs from the Jurassic Period, such as the Stegosaurus and the Apatosaurus/Brontosaurs. Lakes was working as a collector for a paleobiologist, Leo Lesquereux, who published several volumes for the U.S. Geological Survey. During March 1877, Lakes and a friend were near Morrison, Colorado, when they found what they first thought were large pieces of petrified wood but quickly realized were huge, fossilized bones from creatures then unknown to mankind. The journals were not written by a scientist with dull precision and exacting mathematical detail; rather, they were written by a man who had attended Oxford University and had a flair for writing as well as being a sketch artist. At the time, my first thought was that these journals certainly had been published and that using a printed version with footnotes would be great. I knew paleontologists at the Smithsonian and contacted them. They indicated that Professor Jack McIntosh would certainly know whether they had been published because he had co-authored a large volume precisely about these fossils. I dutifully wrote a letter to Dr. McIntosh in August but heard nothing.

The SAA session and presentation in September 1994 were successful. After the conference, much to my surprise, Jack McIntosh called me out of the blue and exclaimed that those journals had been lost for decades. There is a long story related to their provenance; they were part of a huge collection, seven boxcar loads of Yale University's Professor Marsh's material that were determined after his death to belong to the United States and were transferred to the Smithsonian, even though the journals were created before Marsh began working for the Geological Survey. Jack suggested that the journals should be published. In a moment of boldness when the brass ring presented itself, I explained that I knew very little about paleontology compared to people like McIntosh and asked whether he would help edit them. He quickly agreed, and the following April, we examined photocopies of the journals.

Two things became clear from the initial reading of the journals and talking with Jack. He was an expert paleontologist related to the dig sites that Lakes describes in his journals. The second thing that soon became obvious was that Lakes sprinkles his journal entries with references to local geography; current events, local, national, and international; and matters that had occurred a decade or more earlier. A considerable amount of work would be required to untangle these references, and it would be up to me as the person with more familiarity with historical collections in research libraries to track them down. This would be a major commitment of my time and would no doubt involve trips to repositories in Colorado and Wyoming as well as other major collections of pertinent reference material.

By the mid-1990s, Clemson librarians had faculty status, which included peer review and the possibility for tenure. This had only been established during the previous decade, with faculty ranks only being established in the mid-1980s after I had been working for a year or two. Joseph Boykin Jr., dean of Libraries, supported faculty status, but with one exception, no Library faculty had ever received a sabbatical. That exception was the then–associate dean, who received a sabbatical in 1989. The library faculty was stretched thin, with few members in any part of the library. Including myself, Special Collections had only three faculty members.

This type of research could not be undertaken during one's spare time or all by distance. Most primary source collections had not been microfilmed, and digitization was in its early stages. Many nineteenth-century newspapers existed only in a few repositories and in some cases were not microfilmed. One would need to visit repositories in the West as well as national repositories, such as the Library of Congress. During the fall of 1994, I prepared a proposal for a sabbatical as well as working with Jack McIntosh on a publication proposal to the Smithsonian Institution Press. My sabbatical was approved in December, and the Smithsonian Institution Press approved the publication in January 1995.

Planning for my absence during my sabbatical evolved during the spring semester of 1995. The two remaining faculty in the unit shared the unit's responsibilities. I planned projects that I believed that staff could successfully undertake. My sabbatical began on August 11 and was to encompass the fall semester of 1995, lasting until January 8, 1996.

The semester was a whirlwind of travel to repositories for research; attendance at conferences, including presentations; and hectic searches to identify obscure references made in the journals. In August, I spent most of my time in Washington, D.C., at the Smithsonian Archives, tracking down information about Lakes and the Yale professor he worked for, O. C. Marsh. There, I discovered the existence of another journal, an oversized sketch book that was separated from Lakes's other journals. Despite the efforts of Smithsonian paleontologists, archivists, librarians, and other staff, this sketchbook—which no doubt illustrates what is described in the journals—has never been found.

After attending the SAA meeting, I spent September traveling to repositories in the West and Midwest as well as meeting paleontologists, archivists, and historians who were of great help. I camped in my pavilion tent and stayed with friends and in B&Bs while going to small repositories, such as the Arthur Lakes Library at the Colorado School of Mines, as well as major repositories, such as the Denver Public Library and the State Historical Society of Wisconsin. In early November, I gave a poster session at the Society of Vertebrate Paleontology's annual meeting, which was well received. Later that month, with the manuscript deadline approaching in January, Jack flew down to South Carolina, and we worked on last-minute edits. These included revising some of the sidebars and footnotes, which often resulted in my spending time in the Cooper Library,

On January 8, I returned to my full-time duties in Special Collections. The manuscript draft was mailed to the Smithsonian Institution Press before the end of the month. Through the winter and into the spring, further revisions were made, including obtaining permissions from repositories and working on the maps. Later that year, the book was published and received good reviews. In January 1997, I gave a presentation at the Strom Thurmond Institute auditorium to a packed house. By then, I had begun working to edit the journals describing another paleontological dig in Wyoming in 1895. For the next decade, I would be involved with the history of paleontology, which was truly interesting and enjoyable.

SIMPLE EVENTS CAN
LEAD TO BIG OUTCOMES

William C. Stringer
Department of Agronomy and Soils
1984–2011

The first class I taught at Clemson was Agronomy 423, a senior-level course in Forage Crops Management. I loved it because my master's and doctoral work involved forage crops, and ironically, I had previously taught the same course, under the same course number, at Penn State University. The course integrated physiological and morphological aspects of pasture and hay crop plant species with characteristics and needs of forage-consuming livestock species (cattle, sheep, goats, and horses). Students from plant science and animal science as well as agricultural engineering and agricultural economics disciplines enrolled in the course, so we had some very interesting discussions in class.

In 1990, after teaching the course for five years, I felt the urge to try something new on opening day. I settled on posing this question: "If you were here in 1491, what would your livestock be eating?" The significance of 1491 is that all the plants on the landscape were native, by definition. So, to make sure that I had some answers to my own question, I spent a week rambling around South Carolina, exploring old roadsides, powerline and railroad rights-of-way, and old cemeteries—areas that had not been cultivated and that contained surviving remnant native grass and native wildflower populations.

Well, in the words of the old TV show, that was the week that was! I noticed for the first time many native grass, wildflower, and shrub species that I had learned about in a course that I had taken in the 1970s and promptly forgotten. A particularly exciting roadside event was spotting a small clump of Indiangrass (*Sorghastrum nutans*), a very common grass in midwestern tall-grass prairies. I leaped out of the car with pin flags and ribbons and created a colorful fortress around the clump. As soon as I returned to the office, I called the South Carolina Department of Transportation in that county and asked them to please not mow that plant, as it was very rare, and I wanted to collect seeds from it.

The very next week, I hustled back down the road to check on my new plant best friend. I left Clemson and had no sooner gone rural when I started noticing clump after clump of Indiangrass on the roadsides, all the way to my discovery site. I had an epiphany from that experience: You do not start noticing something until you notice it. Several things evolved from this experience:

- I started watching roadsides closely. This made long trips around the state more fun.
- I diverted part of my research effort to native plants, particularly native grasses.
- I started reading the diaries of early (mid-16th-century) European explorers of our region. They reported "leagues and leagues" of grasslands in country that is now forest and subdivisions.
- When a new grassland group in the state proposed to petition the legislature to establish a state grass, I lobbied for Indiangrass. The grassland group agreed, and the idea of bermudagrass, an imported grass, was left in the dust. Result? South Carolina's official state grass is Indiangrass, *Sorghastrum nutans*.
- In 1995, I received a letter from a fellow I had never met, asking whether I would be interested in collaborating to establish a native plant society. I replied, "Count me in." That fellow was Rick Huffman, and Rick, along with me and a dozen more folks, established a 501(c)3 nonprofit organization called the South Carolina Native Plant Society in 1996. We now have a statewide presence and are a key part of environmental protection and preservation in South Carolina.
- In 2008, the SC Native Plant Society and Clemson University, with collaboration from other organizations and agencies, hosted a national event, the Sixth Eastern Native Grass Symposium, to Columbia.

Lesson: Life is a participation sport. Be open to new ideas and opportunities that life sends your way. Participating energetically can take you in unanticipated directions and yield good outcomes.

IT'S A LONG WAY TO RIO

JAMES H. PALMER
Department of Agronomy and Soils
1970–2000

When I first became a faculty member in the Department of Agronomy and Soils at Clemson, little did I know that in March 1989, I would be sitting in the middle seat on a direct eleven-hour flight from Miami to Rio de Janeiro. The trip was a study mission to assess the potential expansion of the soybean crop in Brazil and Argentina. Soybean growers in the United States also wanted to know how future competitiveness of South American soybeans would affect the world price and potential profitability of their crop. Sponsors of the mission were the American Soybean Association and ICI Americas Agrichemicals (now Syngenta). Along with agronomists were agricultural economists and engineers, plant pathologists, weed scientists, and entomologists from land-grant universities and the United States Department of Agriculture (USDA). Also, various U.S. agricultural media personnel were present. Altogether, about thirty individuals were involved.

Flying into Rio, I noticed Sugar Loaf Mountain and the Statue of Christ, major tourist sites that we would visit later in our trip. I thought, with a tinge of homesickness, "We aren't in good ol' South Carolina anymore." Before we could stop to catch our breath, we got on another plane for the three-hour flight to Buenos Aires, Argentina, our first stop on the mission. Our objective there was to attend the World Soybean Research Conference, held at a convention center adjacent to our hotel. At the conference were soybean research personnel from around the world, presenting the latest technology in production, marketing, and utilization information. The three-day program was interesting but also included many breaks that I and others in the group used to slip away and walk to downtown Buenos Aires to explore shopping, eating, and entertainment venues. At that time, the president of Argentina was Carlos Menem, a member of the Peronist political party, established during the administration of Juan Perón. After a military coup in 1976 deposed Perón's wife, Eva, the ruling government pulled thousands of dissidents, intellectuals, and anyone suspected of left-wing ideology off the streets and into government-owned Ford Falcon automobiles, never to be seen again. These people were known as *the disappeared*. By the time we got there, most locals had ceased to fear Ford Falcons. In fact, Ford had a factory in Argentina that built *only* the Falcon. In our rides around the city, every cab we saw was a Falcon. During our time in Buenos Aires, tourists like us could wander around the city with little concern about meeting anyone intent on doing us harm. Merchants in the markets were nice and tried hard to persuade us to purchase their wares, especially when they learned that we had American currency. When searching for places to eat, we had to keep in mind that restaurants there didn't even open until 8:30 p.m., and most people didn't start eating until 9:30 p.m.; they sat around and talked over drinks until then.

After three days at the conference, we boarded a bus and began touring various soybean production areas in Argentina, including the large farm of Hector Diaz. His farm was in the Pampas Region, covering almost five hundred thousand square miles of low-lying terrain with some of the most fertile soils in the world. It is also home to gauchos, the famous Argentine cowboys, and pampas grass, an ornamental grass that almost everyone in the U.S. regrets planting. Interesting animal sightings from the bus included rheas, an ostrich- or emu-like bird that stands almost six feet tall, and pink flamingos on their migration to areas in Chile and northwestern Argentina. Farmers in Argentina are mostly of Italian origin, and at one stop we were hosted by several farmers who had prepared a fantastic barbecue meal for us. It was interesting how the kids there hung around us, asking for American coins, which we gladly shared. After touring many Argentine farms, we headed to Rosario City, the third-largest city in Argentina and the birthplace of Che Guevara and global soccer star Lionel Messi. The highlight of the evening was a meal in a great restaurant, a short bus ride from our hotel. Interestingly, my agronomist friend from Ohio State and I decided that we would walk back to the hotel and got terribly lost. Almost in a state of panic, we stopped to ask directions to our hotel from a group of folks walking toward us. Fortunately, they were extremely nice and gave us clear directions back.

Our next stop was on the border between Argentina, Paraguay, and Brazil—the Itaipu Dam on the Parana River and Iguazu Falls on the Iguazu River in Argentina. The Itaipu Dam is one of the Seven Wonders of the World and the second-largest producer of hydroelectric power in the world. Iguazu Falls are the largest system of falls in the world and the site for multiple movies, such as *The Mission* and *Raiders of the Lost Ark*.

After the tourist stops, we bused to the southern Brazilian town of Curitiba in the state of Parana, where the soybean crop was first introduced. The soils there were redder in color (like southern Piedmont soils in South Carolina) and more susceptible to erosion than those we saw in Argentina. The farmers we met were of European origin, mostly German and Dutch, and very technologically adept. To our surprise, they were practicing no-till planting in crop residue to lower costs, decrease erosion, and increase yields. They also practiced the latest fertilization and pest-control methods for top yields. Although farms there were very large, the farmers efficiently used all daylight hours for planting, spraying, and harvesting operations (i.e., same equipment, but different operators). This meant lower costs for equipment, but higher labor costs. However, labor costs there were very low (e.g., only about $400 per month). We were told that some farmers used hand labor, paying US$1 per day for cleaning their fields of weeds.

In Londrina, also in southern Brazil, we met several soybean scientists at Embrapa, equivalent to the USDA's Agricultural Research Service. Most of the soybean research for Brazil is based in this large facility. At Embrapa, the scientists discussed their backgrounds (many had received their graduate degrees from American land-grant universities) and what they were doing to help sustain and increase the profitability of Brazilian soybeans. Nearby, we toured a coffee plantation and met the farmer (not Juan Valdez); there were five hundred acres of coffee on the rolling hills and no burros!

In southern Brazil, the climate and growing season for soybeans approximates that of the southern U.S., except Brazilian farmers plant in October and November and harvest in March and April. Therefore, the soybean varieties, pests, and other considerations are like what we southern soybean scientists deal with here. The entomologists found similar insects, and weed scientists found the same weed species that we have in the U.S. Our main finding on the trip was that farmers there, and those who advise them, were using basically the same technologies as we do in the states. The same was true in Argentina.

The major disadvantage for farmers in South America, especially Brazil, is infrastructure. Ports on the coast of Brazil are more than one thousand miles from the major soybean production states, and transport of the crop is by caravans of trucks, often on bad roads. However, progress is being made, though, especially now that more than 70 percent of Brazilian soybeans are exported to China, and the Chinese have aided in building railroads and a new port on the coast.

In Brazil, soybean production has increased nine-fold since 1990 and has now surpassed the U.S. in production. This fact is a fulfillment of our prediction that the potential for expansion of soybeans as a crop in South American was almost unlimited. We concluded that, like all science, technology cannot be put in a lockbox or kept from any one entity or country. Once South America established a large acreage, interest in securing the most up-to-date technology was clear. World agrichemical, seed, equipment, fertilizer, and marketing companies established a presence there, and farmers there now have at their fingertips on smartphones or computers the same information to guide their production and marketing goals as do U.S. farmers.

Of course, there is wide concern that the growth of soybeans as a crop, especially for export, will require clearing much of the critical rainforest area in the northern states of Brazil. However, a 2021 report from Embrapa claims that the government has protected the rainforest areas and that further expansion of soybeans will not threaten this important ecosystem and national resource.

Our last stop on the fifteen-day trip was in Rio, where we stayed in a hotel on the Copacabana Beach, rode the cable car to the top of Sugar Loaf, and bused to the Statue of Christ, which looks over the city. The desk clerk at the hotel was quite adamant that we not go out alone on the streets of Rio. Crime there is rampant due to, we were told, "poverty of the people that live on the hills around the city."

Our plane left Rio the next afternoon and flew four hours into a thunderstorm as we arrived in Manaus, a city in the middle of the Brazilian rainforest. After a short delay, our plane left Manaus for the long flight to Miami.

Kate and the children had put up a wall-size map of South America in the kitchen when I left and stuck colored pins in it to record every stop I made. It looked colorful when I returned, and I was glad to be home.

MEMORIES AS DEPARTMENT OF CHEMISTRY CHAIR

Adolph L. Beyerlein
Department of Chemistry
1967–2001

From the day I was hired as an assistant professor of chemistry, I have always felt privileged to be a Clemson University faculty member. I have fond memories from all those years, but the memories I cherish the most are from my last six-and-a-half years as the Chemistry Department chair. Perhaps one reason these years are so memorable is that I did not expect to serve the department as chair, particularly in my last years as an active faculty member. I applied for the position at the last minute with the encouragement of one of our newly hired faculty and was indeed surprised when Dean Thomas Keinath called me into his office to offer me the position. I immediately accepted because I believed that it would provide opportunities and challenges I would never experience as a regular faculty member. I was not disappointed; the chair position did just that. During my tenure as the Chemistry Department chair, the department experienced unprecedented growth in research funding and scholarship, and I experienced challenges I would never have had as a regular faculty member. Meeting these challenges was a learning experience that spanned my entire tenure as chair.

The departmental growth I experienced as chair began on my very first day in the role. I realized immediately that the department was poised for growth based on the work of our prior chairs, R. A. Abramovitch, Darryl DesMarteau, and John Petersen. It was up to me to keep the growth going that my predecessors had started. This began with Alex Kitaygorodskiy, director of our nuclear magnetic resonance (NMR) facilities, obtaining National Science Foundation (NSF) funding for a new 500 MHz Japan Electron Optics Laboratory (JEOL) NMR instrument. With this acquisition, organic chemists could obtain carbon-13 NMR spectra within five minutes that would have taken more than an hour on our older instruments. This equipment made research proposals from our organic faculty much more attractive to funding agencies. The result was an immediate research-funding increase in organic chemistry and other related areas.

In the year immediately following the acquisition of the JEOL NMR instrument, William Pennington obtained NSF funding for an X-ray diffractometer with an area detector, and Shiou Jyh Hwu obtained NSF funding for a Super Conducting Quantum Interference Device (SQUID) magnetometer. The X-ray instrumentation equipped with an area detector made it possible to obtain a crystal structure in less than a day, whereas older instruments required several days to one week. The SQUID magnetometer provided a means of studying extremely subtle magnetic fields in a variety of compounds. The acquisition of these three instruments over a period of two years initiated the unprecedented growth in research funding that we experienced over the next six years. The new funding included support for undergraduate and graduate research and produced substantial growth in our undergraduate (BS graduates increased from twenty to thirty per year) as well as our graduate programs.

I realized very early that funding of proposals for external grants and major departmental instruments written by faculty is the primary driver of department growth. Therefore, the department chair's highest priority is to provide faculty with what they need to achieve success. One type of faculty need is departmental support to compete for peer recognition, awards, and professional activities, such as serving as an officer in a learned society or journal editorships. However, the greatest challenges for me were providing funds for matching money for major instrument grants, faculty start-up funds, and costs associated with space and the building facilities. The department has a discretionary budget to cover some costs that arise with faculty needs, such as travel, but normally will not be able to cover costs of matching an instrument grant or new faculty start-up costs, which often are more than $100,000. For example, the matching funds required for the purchase of the JEOL 500 MHz NMR instrument were about $200,000. We had $60,000 from departmental funds, $40,000 from the college, and another $40,000 from the University Research Office. The problem was "to find the remaining funding." Fortunately, we were able to obtain the remaining funds from the Greenville Hospital/Clemson University Research Cooperative by offering to provide the Research Cooperative high field NMR services on the new 500MHz JEOL instrument. Requesting matching funding was not always this complicated, but each case provided a memorable learning experience.

Perhaps the most challenging need I faced as the department chair was getting the ventilation on the fourth floor of the Chemistry Building (Hunter Hall) up to Occupational Safety and Health Administration (OSHA) standards. This required changing the main ventilation duct in our organic research labs and adding an exhaust fan. The cost for doing this was more than $1,000,000, and we were advised that it would require at least a year to get approval for this kind of expenditure. In the meantime, the organic research labs would need to be shut down, which would have resulted in a major loss in research funding and a loss in confidence in our ability to fulfill research goals set forth in our research proposals. I had almost given up on finding the funding support when the university administration found a way to begin work on the renovation immediately. This was like a surprise gift. I learned that if one is vigilant, help will come.

As time passed, the annual externally funded research expenditures increased to above $2,000,000, causing the department to experience space problems. At that time, $2,000,000 in research expenditures supported the stipends of sixty researchers, who normally include graduate students and postdoctorates. These researchers needed space in addition to the space already allocated for forty student researchers supported on teaching assistantships, bringing the total space needs up to one hundred researchers; our building (Hunter Hall) only has space for about ninety researchers. Darryl DesMarteau came to the rescue by agreeing to move his research group to the Clemson Engineering Technologies Laboratory (CETL) at the Clemson Research Park, freeing up 1,200 square feet of space in Hunter Hall.

During my final year as department chair, our research expenditures exceeded $2.5 million, which was double the research expenditures at the beginning of my tenure as department chair. In this position, I had the opportunity to hire five outstanding faculty, Dvora Perahia, Steven Stuart, George Chumanov, Dev Arya, and Dennis Smith. All were highly successful and rose through the ranks to full professor. I announced my retirement to the faculty in August 2001, effective on December 31, 2001. I was given a surprise retirement party at the Café Rendezvous in Seneca, South Carolina, on January 26, 2002. More than eighty persons attended the event, including my wife, Anne; my daughter Irene; and her husband, Jesus Ilundain. The department gave me a Heritage Family Tree Chair with an engraving of a Clemson University Seal and my name engraved on the backboard. Dr. Dvora Perahia, my first faculty hire as department chair, presented me with a framed poster creatively listing my scientific publications and pictures highlighting my career at Clemson University. Perhaps of all the memories as department chair, the retirement party with the gifts was the most vivid.

AN ALTERNATIVE IN HIGHER EDUCATION IN THE MATHEMATICAL SCIENCES

CHRISTOPHER L. COX
School of Mathematical and Statistical Sciences
1984–2018

The title of this essay is also the title of a National Science Foundation (NSF) grant that funded innovative changes in the Clemson University mathematical sciences graduate program during the latter half of the 1970s. The vision implemented during that period profoundly affected numerous students and faculty members, including me. This write-up is an expression of my gratitude for opportunities, related in no small part to the impact of that vision, that I was given while working at Clemson.

A history of the Mathematical Sciences Department (originally the Mathematics Department and, since 2020, the School of Mathematical and Statistical Sciences) that covers the period of 1893–2002, written by Professor Gil Proctor, is on the web at https://www.clemson.edu/science/departments/math-stat/about/history/toc.html.

As I heard many times, and as confirmed by Gil's firsthand account, the prime mover in the redevelopment of the math sciences graduate program was Dr. Clayton Aucoin. In the early to mid-1970s, there was a declining demand for doctoral mathematicians in academia, particularly those with training solely in the pure math fields. Clayton and colleagues, including Professor Ted Wallenius, proposed broadening the master's and doctoral programs so that students would gain knowledge in the applied fields of computational mathematics, operations research, and statistics and probability in addition to the traditional areas of algebra and analysis. Today, master's students take at least one course in each of the five areas, and doctoral students are required to take two. A variety of measures attest to the effectiveness of this program. For example, when I retired, there were 128 graduate students in the department. Even more telling are the many successful careers, in academia as well as business, industry, and government, that graduates pursue. I recall return visits of alums from, for example, National Security Agency, Lockheed-Martin, National Institution for Standards and Technology, DisneyWorld, and Sandia National Labs, seeking more of our graduates to hire. One of the keys to the program's success was that graduates who became faculty members would regularly refer their undergraduate students to our graduate program. Professor Rich Ringeisen established a tradition of periodic recruiting visits to a set of "pipeline" schools (e.g., St. Olaf, Manchester, SUNY Fredonia, Baldwin Wallace, and Indiana University of Pennsylvania).

It was my good fortune in 1984, as a new doctorate in computational mathematics, to apply for and be hired into a department whose faculty and degree programs reflected the breadth of mathematical sciences. A friend from graduate school recommended that I apply to Clemson, believing that the position would likely be a good fit. He was right. I'll share some examples of how the department provided an environment for intradisciplinary and interdisciplinary collaboration.

At an early point in my Clemson career, Professor Virgil Quisenberry, a soil physicist in what is now the Plant and Environmental Sciences Department, was looking for someone to collaborate on problems in groundwater modeling. That effort led to journal articles and shared advisement of graduate students, plus some fun conference trips. Colleague Bill Moss and I coauthored (at Bill's initiation) a couple of papers in the area of numerical linear algebra, which provided a boost in my research output. The major Office of Naval Research (ONR) grant that Charlie Johnson, Dan Warner, and others secured in 1986 led me to broaden my horizons into parallel computing.

A mid-career turning point for me occurred in 1998, when Clemson was awarded an NSF Engineering Research Center grant. The driving force behind the Center for Advanced Engineering Fibers and Films (CAEFF) was chemical engineering professor and CAEFF founding director Dan Edie. Dan's invitation to co-lead the CAEFF Modeling Thrust launched a wide set of fulfilling experiences in research, administration, and professional travel. The positive effects of educational opportunities for students and research alliances between CAEFF personnel at multiple universities (including Clemson, MIT, Lehigh, McGill [Montreal], Bradford [UK], and Minho [Portugal]) and industry partners (Dupont, Procter and Gamble, Dow, Celanese Acetate, plus several more) are still being realized.

A major change in the format used for instruction, which began in 2004 at Clemson, deserves mention. Around that time, the upper administration was urging science, technology, engineering, and mathematics (STEM) departments, including Clemson's Math Sciences and Mechanical Engineering Departments, to find a remedy for the high grades of D, Failing, or Withdrawn (DFW) rates in introductory courses. Gaining attention during that period was a model for instructional change with the acronym SCALE-UP (Student-Centered Activities for Large Enrollment Undergraduate Physics), introduced at North Carolina State University to engage students through active learning. SCALE-UP was designed to enable a large classroom to incorporate small-group activities and provide a student-centered cooperative learning environment for classes of one hundred or more students. With the instructional leadership of Bill Moss and administrative support from Department Chair Bob Taylor and Associate Chair Rick Jarvis, the Clemson version of SCALE-UP (Student-Centered Activities for Large-Enrollment Undergraduate Programs) was implemented in the fall of 2006 in all twenty-seven sections of first-year calculus. Several of the larger classrooms in Martin-M were redesigned to incorporate multiple projectors from computers on smart podiums, along with round tables that each accommodated nine students, who formed three teams to work on in-class assignments. The change in instructional format was accompanied by more intentional course coordination, common exams, and a math placement exam that Rick, with help from others, including faculty member Judy Cottingham, designed and implemented on the web. DFW rates that were in the 40 to 50 percent range in Calculus I and II in 2001 were less than 20 percent in the spring of 2009. Bill was an integral part of an interdisciplinary team of faculty members who introduced SCALE-UP in multiple departments, including Engineering, Chemistry, Physics, and Secondary Education.

In the fall of 2011, the Mathematical Sciences Department gained nine applied statistics faculty members when the university deactivated the Department of Applied Economics and Statistics. This brought to Math Sciences another productive and collegial set of faculty members, expanding the impact of the program with respect to instruction and research. This merger also allowed the School of Mathematical and Statistical Sciences (SMSS) to later become a partner, with Management, in the creation of a new master's degree program, whose curriculum consists mainly of courses in applied statistics and business management. The online MS in data science and analytics program, co-directed by Ellen Breazel in SMSS and Russ Purvis in Management, officially started in 2020 and has received national recognition, as noted in the Clemson News article at https://news.clemson.edu/clemson-data-science-and-analytics-masters-program-ranked-among-top-in-the-nation/.

I see in these reflections a department (now a school) that has been suffi-ciently flexible and resilient to enable change and growth to best meet the needs of its students, faculty, and those they serve outside the university. It was an envi-ronment that allowed me to grow and thrive.

I'm grateful for the opportunity to put these memories of Clemson in writ-ten form. The Twentieth Anniversary Project is one of many ways that the Clem-son Emeritus College is a significant resource not only for retired faculty but also for the university, and a role model for other universities to follow.

CHAPTER 8

R.M. Cooper Library and Reflecting Pond from files (With permission from the University Archives)

A CLEMSON MEMORY FROM 1989

RICHARD H. KLEIN
Department of Finance
1981–2005

One of my most wonderful memories from Clemson University occurred in the fall of 1989. From 1981 until 1997, I was the faculty advisor of the Hillel Student Organization, the organization for Jewish students at Clemson University. I was also the only non-clergy member of the Clemson Campus Ministers Association. We were asked to put together the history of our denomination at Clemson University in commemoration of the 100th anniversary of the university in 1989. We had about eight organizations that were represented, and each religious denomination told a story of their activities during the hundred years of Clemson. The presentation was held, I think, in Tillman Hall. It was wonderful experience, showing the fellowship and respect that each religious organization had for the others.

In doing research for this endeavor, I visited the Clemson University Library Archives where a wealth of information is available. Personally, I researched the activities of Jewish students at Clemson University and found out that the first Jewish students attended Clemson in the early 1900s. In 1940, the editor of *The Tiger* was Jewish. From about 1940 until 1948, the Jewish students met at the Fort Hill Presbyterian Church. The minister of the church—I think it was Reverend Sidney Crouch—was the faculty advisor for the Jewish students. Both Presbyterian and Jewish students had their meetings on the same evening of the week at the church, and I read that the Presbyterian students were told to go to one room and the Jewish students went to another room on the same floor. In 1944, a Jewish organization visited Clemson University and thought that the minister was doing a terrific job.

Around 1950, the Jewish student group was officially founded, and it was called the Hillel-Brandeis Student Organization. My wife, Joyce, and I changed the name of the organization in 1981 or 1982 to the Hillel Student Organization to formally affiliate the group with the B'nai B'rith Hillel Organization that had offices in Washington, D.C. No money was involved, but one year Joyce and I did attend a conference of faculty advisors of small Hillel groups in Washington, D.C. Over the years, many wonderful students belonged to the group. I am still in touch with a few of them.

My wife and I held a meeting for the Hillel Student Organization about once a month. She prepared a wonderful Sunday brunch at our house at the beginning of each semester. Typically, we had about twenty-five to thirty students attend the event at the beginning of the semester. By the end of each semester, we had only about ten students attending the monthly meeting because of the "crush" of exams and term papers. My guess is that there were no more than one hundred Jewish students at any one time during my tenure at Clemson. Essentially, our house became the Hillel House at Clemson. We had one activity per month, including a pizza night; trips to Atlanta to attend meetings of Jewish organizations, such as American Israel Public Affairs Committee (AIPAC); and interfaith meetings with other religious organizations. It was at those interfaith meetings that the Jewish students felt most at home on campus.

My wife hosted several Seders, a Jewish ceremonial dinner at Passover time, for Clemson students. She hosted interfaith Seders on different years at St. Andrew's Catholic Church, the Clemson United Methodist Church, and the Clemson Lutheran Church, and it was a wonderful experience for everyone involved. Joyce had attended a Jewish day school in Albany, New York, through the eighth grade, and she was very knowledgeable and qualified to conduct services. I remembered this once we began using the facilities of the Methodist Church for Joyce to conduct a regular Friday night service.

We were blessed to have the very active cooperation and support of the leaders of the various religious groups on campus, and I am in touch with a few of them to this day. They included Father Joe Ciccone and Lynn Pallazo from St. Andrew's Catholic Church, Reverend Tim Willis from the First Baptist Church of Clemson, Reverend Ron Singleton from the Clemson United Methodist Church, Reverends Ron Luckey and Chris Heavner from the University Lutheran Church, and Reverends Jim Richardson and Laura Conrad from the Fort Hill Presbyterian Church. Our friend from the Holy Trinity Episcopalian Church, Reverend Tom Davis, has passed away. Dr. Peter Cohen took over from me as faculty advisor in 1997. He has the records, while I am just trying to remember. My wife, Joyce, passed away in 2021.

In any case, the celebration of the religious organizations at the 100th anniversary of Clemson University in 1989 remains ingrained in my memory. It was an extremely inspiring, inclusive, and warm ceremony.

"TRUST" OPENS DOORS OF OPPORTUNITY

Yuji Kishimoto
Department of Architecture
1980–2011

It was thirty-five years ago, when I was still active as special assistant to the president at Clemson University. This episode begins with President Constantine Deno Curris. Everyone called him "Deno," including me. One day, at Deno's request, I was playing my ten-string classical guitar for the dinner meeting of the Board of Trustees. After I had played one hour of background music, one of the trustee members asked a waiter to bring me a full-course dinner and invited me to eat at their table. I was very appreciative of his kindness. When I was about to finish my delicious dinner, suddenly Mrs. Curris stood up at the distant table and, walking toward me with her arms opened, said, "Maestro Yuji Kishimoto, we enjoyed your music so much. Now, we have a request for you. Today's keynote speaker from Atlanta suddenly could not come to this meeting. We would be extremely appreciative if it would be at all possible for you to play your guitar for us on the front stage." I had five seconds to think about it and then said, "Yes, I am honored to play for you." I decided to play a piece of traditional Japanese music, "Sakura (Cherry Blossom)," arranged for classical guitar. I knew that I had to play very well for the Board of Trustees. I requested a chair without armrests for me to sit on while I played.

Mrs. Curris then formally introduced me as a professor of architecture, with a degree from Harvard Graduate School of Design. That seemed to have surprised the audience because they might have thought I was just a hired musician. I sat on the chair and placed my left foot on a footstool while thinking how to explain the Japanese piece I had decided to play. This particular arrangement was composed in five parts, starting with an introduction, the main theme, the first variation, the second variation with pizzicato, and finally tremolo variation. By the time I was playing the final tremolo variation, I knew that my audience was moving with me emotionally. When I finished playing my music, I received a

Reception in the Emeritus College. Note the figure to the right and his Japanese guitar. (With permission of the artist Lynn Craig)

more enthusiastic response than I expected. I stood up and bowed several times. This happened to be a very important moment for my future activities, especially international, academic, cultural, and economic, because I gained their confidence and trust.

I began pursuing a variety of international activities, particularly between the United States and Japan. Many members of the Board of Trustees were leaders in a variety of national and international organizations, but they did not know then that they would be collaborating with me in a variety of functions and situations.

I initiated the creation of several organizations, including the Japan America Association of SC (JAASC), the U.S. Japan Alliance with Clemson (UJAC), the U.S. Japan Sport Exchange, and the Fuji Film–Clemson–Ohnishi Endowment (FFCOE). I also represented the state of South Carolina and Clemson University at the Southeast U.S. Japan (SEUS Japan) meeting. Members of the Board of Trustees in the audience that night were very supportive of my international activities. In fact, President James Barker has been to Japan, once as president of the Association of Collegiate Schools of Architecture (ACSA), once as dean of the College of Architecture at Clemson, and twice as president of Clemson University—all four times accompanied by me.

Another story relates to how FFCOE was established. The support from U.S. and Japanese industries was essential to start such community organizations as JAASC and UJAC. The largest Japanese industry in the Upstate of South Carolina at the time was Fuji Film, Inc. I was acquainted with Chairman Ohnishi of Fuji Film because we had met so many times at annual SEUS Japan meetings in the United States and in Japan. Because of his variety of contributions to South Carolina, I recommended that Chairman Ohnishi receive an honorary degree from Clemson University, the first foreign recipient. A year later, I phoned Chairman Ohnishi to ask whether he would support the idea of creating a Fuji Film–Clemson endowment. He immediately asked, "How much do you need?" I was not prepared to say the amount then, but I sensed that I had to come up with the right amount in a few seconds, which would be slightly more than what he might have expected. After a few seconds, I said, "One half million dollars." After a moment of silence, he said that I would receive the check in the mail in a week.

I soon reported the news to Clemson's president, who then suggested creating a committee to make the endowment a reality. I told him that the committee was not necessary, but he decided to create one anyway. I went to the first committee meeting the next day. While I was trying to explain the background story of how it had happened, the chair of the committee said that they did not need to know. I was astonished and left the meeting. I soon received a check for $500,000 from Chairman Ohnishi, and that was how FFCOE was established. This episode reminds one of how important mutual trust can be and how one good result opens more doors in a chain reaction as long as you continue to achieve good results. The essence of this story is mutual trust. Chairman Ohnishi trusted me, and I trusted his word.

Several years later, the Japanese government became aware of what I had been accomplishing culturally, economically, and educationally between Japan and the United States, which would generally be accomplished by a successful, official Japanese ambassador to such major nations as the United States, England, or France. The Japanese government, through the Japanese emperor, awarded me a National Medal, which provided me with even more doors of opportunity, although I began slowing down because of my retirement.

Mutual trust played a major role in my activities, particularly international ones. "Creative ideas" had to be understood by all the collaborators; therefore, an idea creator must spend extra effort in communication, so that all collaborators can share the same ideas that I call "Commonsense (commonly sharable sense)." In other words, "Creativity," "Commonsense," and "Collaboration" are what I call the "3C" triplet. It also is important that all three aspects be considered simultaneously. **3C** was been the main concept in my architectural teaching for more than forty years. I would state that the Emeritus College at Clemson University provides me with a variety of intercultural environments in using the **3C** concept because of its membership and rich experiences.

POSSUMS

Cecil O. Huey Jr.
Department of Mechanical Engineering
1969–2006

I was parked outside a dark house in a somewhat sketchy neighborhood along with Becky Bowman, our director of athletic compliance, and an all-business NCAA (National Collegiate Athletic Association) enforcement rep. It was an unfamiliar vehicle to me, and although the enforcement rep phoned around to learn why no one was there for a planned meeting on a delicate and confidential matter, I resolved not to carelessly leave the keys inside should we eventually get out. I removed them, intending to put them in my pocket, thereby triggering the interior lights and some exterior courtesy lights to boot. No matter what I frantically tried, they wouldn't turn off. The lights alerted the neighborhood dogs, which converged on us in full voice, and there we sat, for all the world looking like a poorly cast surveillance team from a B-movie stakeout in a brightly illuminated soccer-mom van. Treed possums came to mind.

Somehow, our minds curate memories according to their own whims, and often the most sharply recalled particulars are but minor fragments of larger, complex matters. They seem to just pop into our consciousness without summoning and are usually imperfect reconstructions. A measure of significance is neither necessary nor sufficient to bring them to the fore. Such is the case when I reflect on my thirteen years as Clemson's faculty athletics representative, and the episode described above is just one example. I suppose that most memoirists are prompted by motive—otherwise, why bother? My motivation here remains vague, even to me, but perhaps a suggestion of it is embedded in another sharp, fleeting experience that still evokes a sigh.

Shortly after my successor had been named, I bumped into a colleague who in years past had been involved in faculty governance and had served as president of the faculty senate. His greeting included something to the effect of "I guess you will miss all the fun and tickets and travel and perks." I sigh again with the realization that many likely shared his sentiment—that giving up such things would be my primary regret. I have yet to miss them. In fact, I came to detest resort hotels, the insincere flattery and greetings that often accompanied having some sort of athletic credential, and the general excess of it all. Nor do I miss the rather onerous task of personally reviewing the application folder of every single student-athlete in all sports to confirm their athletic eligibility (well over a thousand files in the thirteen years of my tenure), or responding to letters from unhappy fans and calls from aggressive reporters, or feeling the exasperation occasioned by one internal skirmish or another, or, especially, reading the *ad hominem* online criticisms, usually related to academic eligibility matters fomented by athletic talk radio. For example, here's an "insult" posted online and addressed to the Board of Trustees: "Cecil Huey, Becky Bowman[,] and several others want Clemson to be Duke Monday through Friday[,] but that will never happen because of perception. However, if you don't fix it, Clemson will become Duke on Saturdays in the fall." Followed by this: ". . . Huey has been an extremely influential member of the academic movement at Clemson[,] . . . represent[ing] how far removed from the real world Huey and his academia cronies have become." Maybe this person was right about the real world; many agreed with him and said so, often in less polite language, and they have long memories. One rant that I received— *three years after my retirement*—ran on for some five hundred words, starting with "They must not know what a fraud you are" and ending with "You['re] too chicken to respond[,] but remember[,] what goes around comes around."

Once, we received a routine notice from the NCAA regarding an allegation that one of our most recognizable football athletes had been provided an automobile by a "representative of the institution's athletic interests" and requesting that we investigate the matter. As it turned out, there were no untoward circumstances, and the whole issue was settled quickly and easily. However, one particular moment haunts me.

I prefaced my conversations with those involved by explaining, apologetically, that we were following up an inquiry from the NCAA and that it was our responsibility to do so. The young man's father, sensing my discomfort at the circumstances, responded in the most courteous and polite manner that they understood, and he told me not to worry but to just continue with our "due diligence." He then added, "But we all know that none of this would be happening, and we wouldn't be here, if we weren't a Black family." He was right, and I agreed with him, and the truth of it still pains me.

There were, however, bright, gratifying moments, some affording enduring satisfaction. My relatively long tenure in the position led to opportunities of the sort that come with some years of experience, such as serving on the Search and Selection Committee for the Atlantic Coast Conference (ACC) commissioner and as Clemson's voice within a very confidential group that oversaw matters related to the expansion of the conference from nine to twelve members. I spent six years, one as chair, on the NCAA Student Athlete Reinstatement Committee, the body that dealt with infractions having potential eligibility consequences for individual athletes. A year or two before my retirement, I was invited to join an NCAA group, termed the Academic Consultants, who developed the basic structure of the national academic standards for athletic eligibility that are still in place. I also served two stints as president of the Atlantic Coast Conference. Fast friends from those days remain scattered about the campus and the larger college athletic community, and I am grateful for having found them along the way.

An especially pleasant instance from Dr. Curris's tenure as our president comes to mind. I had been heartened already by his kind and thoughtful efforts to involve former president Bob Edwards in campus events, in my view, a courtesy that had been neglected in the recent years. On this occasion, he had invited Dr. Edwards to travel to College Park with the team for a football game against the University of Maryland. On such occasions, polite protocol included brief visits between opposing teams' box seats and sometimes a little "business," *sub rosa*. I'm sure I had an agenda myself, but it is now forgotten.

We traveled to the stadium by bus and got out at field level, right by the statue of Testudo, the turtle mascot, to start a long trek up the stadium steps to the press-box level—a lot of steps. Others in our party scurried off to attend to whatever business they had, but I was one of the last off the bus and realized immediately the challenge before President Edwards as we confronted those stairs. Dr. Edwards wouldn't permit me to find an alternative to climbing to the top, so we started off on our upward trudge. Every few steps, I invented a reason to pause—to study recent stadium improvements, to recall past games there, and the like. Eventually, we huffed and puffed our way to the top, and I immediately went to the Maryland box and arranged for a golf cart to help us out following the game. All in all, it was a pleasant and unexpected interlude, and it was my last extended interaction with Dr. Edwards. I treasure the memory.

My thirteen years spanned an especially fraught period in Clemson athletics and all or part of the tenure of three provosts and four university presidents. I lack a concise answer to a still frequently asked question: "Why did you do it?" Simply put, it seemed bad form to reject a call to an important duty, even if that duty is neither sought nor desired and might be onerous at times.

WHO CHOOSES SELF-STUDIES AND ACCREDITATION AS A CAREER PATH?

Debra Broadwell Jackson
College of Nursing and Department of Public Health Sciences
1991–2017

Who would choose a career in doing self-studies and accreditation for a university? No one. So, how in the world did I end up chairing not one but two self-studies for Clemson University in its quest for regional accreditation through the Southern Association of Colleges and Schools Commission on Colleges (SACSCOC)? It is not a pretty story.

In the summer of 1998, as I finished an academic year as the interim dean of the Graduate School, I was sitting in a meeting with Provost Stef Rogers and the other academic deans. The topic of the upcoming SACS self-study was on the agenda. "The university needs to identify a leader for the project," Rogers said. Everyone, including me, knew that an external candidate would be selected for the graduate dean. What they don't know was that I had an in-hand offer to be the graduate school dean at another southeastern university. My husband and I had discussed the next steps. Should we move, or should we stay? I was incredibly quiet during this meeting. Unexpectedly, Dean William (Bill) Wehrenberg announced that I should be appointed to lead this project. He thought that I would be perfect. It seemed that he had actually looked at my vitae and read it, learning my dark secrets. I had been involved in nursing accreditation and site visits in my past, actually writing standards for accreditation of nondegree programs. It's not a life's profession; however, it was a job needed for an international nursing specialty association. I even was versed in hospital accreditation processes. But I had never been involved with regional accreditation.

Within two weeks, Provost Rogers offered a salary that exceeded the graduate dean offer, and I agreed to stay. Little did I know that I'd be moved to the basement of Hardin Hall, with its rolling floors, drafty windows, and creatures living in the file cabinets. But there I was, and what I learned was not good: The university had followed *none* of the SACS processes and procedures for the last ten years. Yes, the university had an assessment program (more or less), but it had made no efforts toward notification of substantive changes. Being out of compliance seemed like a minor deal; a letter should clear things up with SACS—or not. I learned that Georgia Tech, the university we were striving to emulate, had been placed on public warning by SACS. Public warning by SACS only occurs if an institution fails to correct cited deficiencies after private warning and reviews over a period of time.

What you might find the most interesting is what I discovered moving forward. In the ten-year time period since the last self-study in 1988–1990, the university had:

- Four presidents (Lennon, Prince, Curris, Barker)
- Four provosts (Maxwell, Jennett, Rogers, Helms)
- Six strategic plans and related activities
- Total Quality Management (TQM) (1992)
- Kellogg Initiative Redesigning Land-Grant Universities (1992–1993)
- Reorganization of the University (1994–1995)
- ACT 359 Performance Funding Criteria and Measures (1995)
- Commission on the Future of Clemson (1997–1998)
- Barker's Top Twenty Goals (1999)

I spent the first year in my role meeting with faculty and academic leaders across the campus. We expanded assessment activities and pushed all departments to have workable and usable assessment activities. In the midst of this, I presented a report to the Board of Trustees. Two things happened: First, Thornton Kirby included me in administrative meetings, and second, Trustee Les McCraw was appointed to the SACS Steering Committee. If you knew Trustee McCraw, you know that he loved Clemson, was a tough administrator and leader, and was the former chair and CEO of Fluor Corporation. He was also involved in the hiring of President Barker. Trustee McCraw was on the subcommittee on Vision, Mission, and Strategic Planning. Other members included Neil Cameron, vice president for Advancement; Bart Palmer, Professor of English; and me. Les said that we could talk all we wanted, but the only thing that mattered was that Jim Barker had laid out his ten-year plan for the university, the board had accepted it in hiring him, and it would be the basis for the SACS section of the report. Our job was to take President Barker's points and turn them into SACS language.

I was able to assemble a wonderful group of faculty, staff, and administrators to serve on the steering committee and on each of the subcommittees needed to pull together the report. At this time, President Barker, Thornton Kirby, and Doris Helms were in leadership positions, and their support was invaluable. The Steering Committee met every Friday for more than a year. We received full accreditation, two commendations for our report, and ten years with no follow-ups.

I was appointed as an assistant to the president and worked closely with President Barker on his quarterly Board of Trustee report cards. It was a joy to pull together quarterly reports showing progress toward his ten-year goals. With the support of President Barker and Provost Helms, we put processes in place that would keep Clemson moving forward, managing all current and future SACS guidelines and procedures. I spent time doing special projects as needed. Provost Helms wanted to focus our research priorities, and Teresa Henry and I planned workshops for faculty by emphasis areas, with hundreds of faculty participating in one or more of these discussions.

Special projects were often assigned to me. I helped Provost Helms organize meetings between Clemson and Tri-County faculty to explore what would become the Bridge to Clemson program. What would be required to make the program successful? Where would students live? I worked with Student Affairs and Student Housing in discussing options. At one point, three of us involved in these discussions were accused in the news reports of taking "kickbacks" from a local developer for selecting his housing project. I had to seek legal advice and prove no involvement. It was not fun or true, but we all still laugh about the charge that we each got a free condominium out of the deal.

On another key project, I worked closely with a group of faculty (Jens Holley, Thomas Kuehn, Bill Hare, Alan Grubb, and Steven Marks) who were establishing the charter for the Phi Beta Kappa chapter for Clemson. Our office, Teresa Henry, Melissa Welborn, David Knox, and I planned and helped host an on-campus site visit and ultimately planned the first celebration of a new Phi Beta Kappa chapter at Clemson. Teresa and I were made honorary members of PBK that first year, and another of President Barker's goals was completed. We continued to provide staff support for PBK annual events until our retirement.

Sometime in the mix of all the activities, I was assigned to activities with the SC Commission on Higher Education for the approval of new degree programs. I am not sure why, but I guess someone needed to oversee the process and make sure that the pieces were in place that ultimately went to SACS. In the process, I worked with faculty across the campus. It was an interesting and rewarding experience.

It was a quick ten years and time for the SACS reaffirmation process to start. This time would be different. SACS had revised the rules and requirements. We no longer needed the level of involvement by faculty and staff. It was about students and student achievement. We needed a Quality Enhancement Plan and a Compliance Report. I assembled a group of academic and nonacademic leaders for the compliance report. Kathy Headley, who was the associate dean for research for the College of Health, Education and Human Development (HEHD), served on the committee. Randy Collins (Engineering and Sciences), Constancio Nakuma (Arts, Architecture, and Humanities), and Ted Whitwell (Agriculture, Forestry and Life Sciences) were also part of the group. Frankie Felder provided all the strategic materials needed from the Graduate School. It was a university-wide effort to document compliance with all the SACS criteria.

The key to the 2013 visit was the Quality Enhancement Plan (QEP), which required widespread campus involvement. Dr. Bill Surver was my co-chair. Trustee Alan Wood served on the committee as a representative of the Clemson Board. The committee worked in circles for months until we finally reached a consensus to develop the QEP around the area of Critical Thinking. Clemson Thinks[2] was an ambitious experiment in critical thinking designed to transform learning and teaching through developing a cohort of faculty scholars, faculty development, rigorous assessment, and scholarly research. The program was implemented in 2013 and is still active, hosting its ninth Faculty Institute in 2022 under Dr. David Knox's leadership.

People often ask me what I did in my job. Well, now you know a bit of it!

BUILDING OPPORTUNITY

M. Elaine Richardson
Department of Animal and Veterinary Sciences and Academic Success Center
1972–2014

When I graduated from a small South Carolina high school in the mid-1960s, I had no idea what I wanted to do next, except I knew that I did *not* want to teach. Imagine my surprise when life's events (including several moves and a broken leg) over the next few years led me directly to that path! I realized later that those earlier years were actually building blocks for the next steps in my career.

Fast forward to 2002. I had reached my ultimate goal of earning a doctorate and becoming a full professor at Clemson. Now what? I knew that I needed to grow and expand but did not know what direction to take. When I saw the university ad for a position as the director of the newly formed Academic Success Center (ASC), I was intrigued but unsure whether that was the direction for me. I knew that I loved teaching and helping students discover themselves and their direction. So, I decided, what the heck! I would apply and see where it went. As I headed for the interview that spring day, enjoying our beautiful campus, I was excited yet apprehensive. Did I really want to leave my "comfortable as an old pair of jeans" office in the Poole Agriculture Center (P&A building)? But was I not in somewhat of a rut, with no future aspirations? I loved working with the students in ag majors, but this new position would give me so many more opportunities to work with more students in supporting their hopes and dreams. I would be able to build a program from the ground up, but little did I know at that time that the opportunity to actually help build a *building* would be a part of this new direction.

That summer, after I had accepted the position and moved to my new office in the "temporary" (we would remain there for ten years) location in Cooper Library, enter the Class of 1956, with dreams of how to give back to the university in honor of their Golden Anniversary. I sat in awe at my first meeting with the Golden Anniversary Committee as they planned their ambitious goal of building a center to support students in their quest for a Clemson degree, a

"Vickery Hall for all"! These alumni had a goal: "We want to do something to help current students succeed." Providing a permanent home with all the dedicated space required for programming fit the bill for them. It was indeed an ambitious goal, but this class had the spirit and the drive to make it happen. I was so honored to collaborate with them and to support their goals. We attended many meetings with their classmates around the state. I was able to share student success data from Clemson students using the center with them that encouraged more support for the project.

The class never waivered in their determination, even when the "great slump" of 2008 came, and the first groundbreaking ceremony was canceled. The university administration began exploring other options, such as remodeling space in several existing buildings. Through it all, the class was adamant that they were going to build a building—nothing else would do! They shared memories of academic struggles and failures and seeing many classmates drop out; these memories were a driving force in keeping them on task. And raise money they did! This small but mighty class raised more than $3.5 million, far exceeding the amount required to name the building. It would be more than ten years before their dream was fully realized, but in the summer of 2012, the dedication ceremony was held on the lawn outside this beautiful building, and the doors opened for service. The chair of the Golden Anniversary Committee said, "It was Elaine's guidance during the planning for the ASC, and serving as the first director, that has contributed to its status as a world-class support center for the students." A building opportunity for sure!

The biggest reward during my time as the ASC director was the opportunity to work with this amazing class and support their fundraising. Although I have received multiple local and national awards, the recognition most precious to me was being named an honorary member of the Class of 1956. I am so grateful for that recognition and honor.

Now, on to building opportunity for students. Students found their way to the ASC for many reasons: failing a class or not earning an A, maintaining their scholarships, having difficulty understanding class material, setting goals for attending veterinarian or medical school, and dealing with sundry other reasons. Asking for help is a complex process—most students were highly successful high school students, and college was presenting unique challenges they had never faced before. One of my most memorable students was a young lady from Pickens who transferred to Clemson after attending Tri-County Tech and Southern Wesleyan University. She was a very successful high school student and an A student at both of these institutions. But when she transferred to Clemson, she quickly realized that she could not use old study habits in this more rigorous and demanding environment. She ended up on academic probation after her first semester. She heard about the ASC and the role of CU 101 (now CU 1010) in supporting students on probation. So, she enrolled in the course, and I was fortunate to have her in my section that semester—our first semester to hold classes in our new building. She learned new study habits and how to use the resources available to her and had a very successful second semester at Clemson. Shortly after that, we hired her as a peer academic coach, and she began helping other students on probation. She always talked about finding her best career path—she knew that her chosen major was no longer the way she wanted to go. Well, one day she burst into my office and said, "I have finally figured out what I want to do. I want your job!!" Wow—the ultimate compliment!

Many success stories like that come out of the ASC every day. Because of the dedication and determination of the Class of 1956, a dream initiated by then-Provost Helms, and support from the university administration, the ASC now has an impressive and functional world-renowned home with programs and services that are making a difference in the lives of Clemson students, from getting off probation to keeping scholarships and graduating! Thanks to the Class of 1956 for this invaluable gift to Clemson University students, and thanks for the "building opportunities" given to me.

SKETCHING WORKSHOPS:
Memories from Online to In-Person

LYNN G. CRAIG
School of Architecture
1981–2015

I have always enjoyed teaching freehand sketching no matter where I am, professionally as an architect and as a design studio faculty member at Clemson University. When Nicci Hanewald and Debbie Jackson approached me about teaching sketching workshops in the Emeritus College, I jumped for joy, and we were able to begin scheduling them in 2019. Well, we all remember the spring of 2020, when COVID-19 virtually shut down our academic teaching lives as well as every other aspect of how we carried on our normal daily routines.

But COVID was not going to stop the aggressive service nature of the Emeritus College. Nicci, Debbie, and I set about scheduling the initial sketching workshops as two-hour sessions on Zoom. I sat at home with my dual monitors, web camera, sketchbooks, and sketching tools—oil pastels, watercolors, black Sharpies, and a variety of pens and pencils—while Emeritus sketchers followed my sketching techniques on their laptops as we sketched the view together in our sketchbooks. Our first workshop focused on the variety of landscape features of Clemson University, such as Bowman Field and the Scroll of Honor Memorial Park.

University COVID restrictions began to loosen up a bit later in 2020, and sketching workshops were moved to the Pendleton Town Square. These were followed by large attendance at Vince Jackson's "Birding Sessions" at the Clemson Bottoms and the Botanical Gardens. I thoroughly enjoyed these in-person gatherings, and I must say that as I sketched, I mostly enjoyed watching the bird watchers in their colorful outfits, using marvelous telescoping cameras and super big binoculars.

Our last freehand sketch workshops of 2022 were at Clemson University's new Caden Chapel and the roof terrace of the Watts Innovation Center. We started on the inside of the beautiful newly opened Caden Chapel.

Birding at the Bottoms Sketch (With permission of the artist Lynn Craig)

Sketch of Caden Chapel (With permission of the artist Lynn Craig)

Using the Watts Innovation Center roof terrace., our sketching that day focused on seeing the campus from above—"a bird's-eye view" of the landscape and buildings. It was a great surprise to everyone to discover the roof terrace and to be able to take advantage of its elevated views. We always share our sketches during an informal wrap-up. Members from the Blue Ridge Arts Center in Seneca joined the emeritus faculty for a great sketching workshop.

I wish to thank Nicci Hanewald, as she was instrumental in presenting the idea to establish freehand sketching workshops for the Emeritus College and always reminding me that "It is time again to schedule one of your exciting sketching workshops." I always enjoy sketching during all social gatherings, and in-person sketching is a fulfilling experience, such as Nicci's promotion to a new position in the President's Office.

In summary, the Emeritus College sketching workshops started with a collaborative idea as a virtual online educational program and transformed to in-person, interactive, creative sketching workshops of the Clemson University campus.

Throw Down--Important part of any sketching workshop (With permission of photographer, Debra Broadwell Jackson

FAILING RETIREMENT

M. Elaine Richardson
Department of Animal and Veterinary Sciences and Academic Success Center
1972–2014

I'll be the first to admit that I retired for the wrong reason, but financially, it did not make sense to *not* retire. I had more than thirty-five years of service to Clemson University when I learned that the TERI (Teacher and Employee Retention Incentive) program was going to be phased out, so I was eligible at any time. The purpose of the program was designed to allow eligible employees in the SC Retirement System to retire and to continue working for five years. The person's retirement (pension) payment was placed into an escrow account and held until they completed their years of service. In essence, it allowed SC employees a chance to save five years of retirement funds. I waited until the last minute to sign up, wanting to make sure that I maximized my opportunity. I signed up so I would be the last group to get the full five-year plan. My TERI time was up in June 2014, so at that time, I officially left the university—sort of! That fall, I was nominated by Joe Dickey to be a member of the Emeritus College Advisory Board. Joe was my mentor, former supervisor, and long-time friend who spoke so highly of the Emeritus College (EC) and all it has to offer faculty. I accepted, and that was the first step in my failed retirement.

Retirement is described as when someone leaves the workforce for good—or maybe not! I was not really ready to retire—I loved my position as the director of the Academic Success Center and how I was able to interact with undergraduate students, supporting them and seeing them successfully complete their degree program at Clemson. So, how could I move forward? Immediately becoming involved with the EC was a good step for me. Before my Board term was over, I was elected to serve as the vice chair and then chair of the Executive Committee for the board and the college. To continue interacting with students, I volunteered to serve as a mentor for the Conversations with International Students (CIS) program. Over the next few years, I worked with two international graduate students, an amazing experience. These two young men, both from

China, were so eager to learn and to improve their English-speaking skills, and they taught me so much in the process. This led to working with others in the EC to submit a nomination for the Association of Retirement Organizations in Higher Education (AROHE) Innovation Award for the CESP/CIS programs, and we were selected. How exciting to see the Clemson program receive this recognition!

During this initial "retirement" time, two friends from the National College Learning Center Association were determined that I would continue collaborating with them on the Learning Centers of Excellence (LCE) program we had developed together. So, I moved into a reviewer position for the LCE applicants. This is such an exciting program, showing how institutions of higher education are moving to use best practices to more effectively support students academically. I just saw it as an extension of what I had done in the Clemson Academic Success Center, and it provided a meaningful way for me to still be involved in the learning center arena.

Back on the home front, I have lived in the downtown area of Clemson since 1976, and I have observed how the explosive growth of Clemson University has affected quiet neighborhood life; our sleepy little town isn't so sleepy anymore. I felt called to action and applied to join the city Planning Commission. This led to involvement with ClemsonNext, a project of the city of Clemson to develop a strategic plan that addresses growth and its effects, particularly as they relate to high-density multifamily development. In Clemson, that means "luxury" student housing, and that has been a challenging process! I co-chaired the committee on housing and learned so much about housing opportunities, or lack thereof, for so many. Growing demand was driving prices up and pushing many of the minority residents in small neighborhoods out of their homes. That process continues today and has influenced the work of the Planning Commission. We are continually addressing requests for new projects, but they are not for affordable housing, and that is a major concern not just in Clemson but nationally. Now, I am serving as chair of the Planning Commission, and we are gearing up to write a new and much-needed comprehensive plan.

As I learned more about the minority neighborhoods, the housing problems in Clemson, and how "studentification" was affecting these neighborhoods, I got involved with several other folks who were also concerned about these problems. As a result, we created a new nonprofit to help address housing concerns in minority neighborhoods. The George and Rozsena Shaw Center for Housing and Economic Growth was formed, and I was elected as vice chair for the board and serve as the Governance Committee chair. The Shaw Center has now repaired five homes to ensure that their elderly owners can age in place. We have several more homes in line for repairs, and we are also planning programming to ensure that these residents have wills, accurate titles to their property, and correct property lines. We have received many donations, and local churches are partnering with us on individual homes. To supplement our fundraising efforts, in the first year, I have written three grants that received additional funding—but all of this effort has not been without growing pains.

Now, flipping back to the EC—as I transitioned off the advisory board, I was asked to chair the Undergraduate Support Committee. This has resulted in hosting several sessions with emeritus faculty serving on panels for new freshmen and for incoming transfer students. I partnered with the transfer student academic programs coordinator to present several of the sessions with transfer students. We actually presented together on our panel discussions at the AROHE virtual conference. Our next steps were to present at the National College Learning Center Association (NCLCA) conference in 2021, but the program director left the university, and we have not yet connected with her replacement. But that is part of future plans for the Undergraduate Support Committee.

Tired yet? Me neither. My next venture has some very personal connections. My son, adopted at age six, was diagnosed with several mental illnesses. Long story short, he pled guilty but mentally ill to several charges and ended up in prison at age twenty-four. He had taken several courses at Tri-County Tech after high school but had successfully completed only a few of them. After he was incarcerated, he and I discussed options for him to be able to continue his education. Because the facility in which he is housed does not have access to any higher-education opportunities, we explored other ways. The best option was to enroll him in special programs for incarcerated individuals, which used paper-based correspondence. It didn't take me long to see what a challenging process that was. From my experience in student learning theory, it was apparent to me that this isolated way of taking college-level courses was challenging, to say the least. I started thinking on a broader scale about how I could help change or better support incarcerated people like my son. What were possible ways for the EC faculty to support prison education in South Carolina facilities? This led to my appointment to the Palmetto Unified School District Board, the state board that oversees education programs in South Carolina prisons. The majority of its emphasis is on the GED and vocational training. However, in recent years, more attention has been given to higher-education opportunities, and several South Carolina colleges are working on ways to offer courses in several of the state's prisons. This interest led to the formation of the EC Prison Education

Task Force, a committee that has led the way in planning and presenting a symposium at Clemson, resulting in an outstanding program with nearly fifty participants, including representatives from the state's Department of Corrections (DOC) along with representatives from several two- and four-year colleges in South Carolina and others with interest in prison education. As a result of the symposium, the DOC deputy director will be presenting a training opportunity for anyone interested in working with the DOC facilities and programs. It will be exciting to see where this venture will lead in the future.

"Retirement is a blank sheet of paper. It is a chance to redesign your life into something new and different," said Patrick Foley. I have taken that blank sheet of retirement paper and begun to fill it with new, different, and exciting areas. I can't wait to see what comes next!

CHAPTER 9

Clemson Across Lake Hartwell (8/7/01) (With permission of artist Clemson President Emeritus James F. Barker)

HELPING BUILD A DREAM

John V. "Dick" Hamby
Department of Education
1973–1991

Have you ever been dragged kicking and screaming into a situation you would never have chosen on your own, only to find it to be a most enjoyable one that ends up changing your career and your life forever?

In the late spring of 1986, Dr. Gordon Gray, department head of Elementary and Secondary Education in the College of Education, called me into his office and asked, "How would you like to be the director of the new National Dropout Prevention Center at Clemson University?"

When I finally managed to raise myself off the floor and collapse into a chair, I replied, "What? Gordon, I don't know anything about dropout prevention. I have a research project I want to pursue, so I can get promoted before I retire in 1991."

"Well," Gordon responded, "this is bigger than that. Ms. Esther Ferguson from New York—a native South Carolinian—has promised to raise $20 million to fund a center at Clemson. Her husband Jim is CEO of General Foods. Lots of money.

"She's organized a group of influential people called the National Dropout Prevention Fund to help with dropout prevention in New York City. They couldn't find the information they needed, so they want to establish a clearinghouse for dropout data and research here at Clemson. Ms. Ferguson initially wanted to house it in the Strom Thurmond Institute because she and Jim are personal friends with Horace Fleming, the director. Horace said he felt that the Department of Elementary and Secondary Education would be a better fit.

"Ms. Ferguson has a big dream, and now that they've dropped this in our lap, she expects us to make it come true. I know you are a details person. You handle the paperwork, and I'll deal with the folks from New York."

Thus began my five-year adventure as acting director—and later assistant director—of the National Dropout Prevention Center at Clemson University (NDPC).

After lots of ups and downs and communication mishaps during that summer, October 28, 1986, was set for the big public announcement. In attendance at the Alumni Center were Ms. and Mr. Ferguson and some members of the NY Fund. President Max Lennon, Provost David Maxwell, College of Education Dean Jim Matthews, Gordan Gray, and a host of Clemson administrators represented the university. The guest list included South Carolina Governor Dick Riley, State Superintendent of Education Charlie Williams, several state legislators, and a number of local and state educators. And, of course, several media staff from area newspapers and television stations were in attendance.

After speeches by all appropriate dignitaries, I was asked to tell everyone what the center was all about. As I stood before that august body, my mouth was cotton-dry, sweat soaked my underarms, and my hand that held my notes was shaking so badly, I could hardly read them. Why was I so nervous? Well, at that moment, I felt that this was all a big joke, and I was a big fraud.

You see, at that time, the NDPC was my office in Tillman Hall. Our resources were a stack of note cards with names and phone numbers of educators and agencies around the country and a file folder with about twenty articles and pamphlets I had collected. Our lone piece of literature was a leaflet produced by the New York Fund describing what *it* said the NDPC would do. When members of the media started asking questions, I had to think fast and talk about what we *hoped* to do and what we *planned* to have in place in the near future. To put this in perspective, this was the time before widely available Internet connections, smartphones, and personal computers.

On that momentous day, none of us there really knew what lay ahead. However, with lots of hard work and late nights during the next couple of years, we went from a staff of me, a part-time secretary, and a part-time graduate assistant to a cadre of nine permanent staff and several graduate assistants.

Under the leadership of our new executive director, Jay Smink, and with a competent staff of Linda Shirley, Marty Duckenfield, Mary Polen, and many others who came along from time to time, we were able to develop many of the items I had talked about on the day of our announcement: a public telephone hotline, a database of dropout prevention programs, many research-based publications, a national conference, an outreach program of staff development and school improvement, and a variety of other products and processes.

One of my favorite accomplishments was bringing the NDPC together with the National Dropout Prevention Network, a group struggling to organize at the same time we were at Clemson. When the network had funding problems, we proposed a merger, and in October 1987, the National Dropout Prevention Center/Network was born.

The NDPC/N operated for thirty years before Clemson decided to cut the cord. It survived for a while in Anderson County under the direction of Dr. Sandy Addis and is now located in Roxford, New York.

Although I was with the NDPC/N for only five years, I continued to serve as a consultant for more than a decade after my retirement. I am proud and honored that I had a small role in making Ms. Ferguson's dream come true and helping establish an organization that is still operating today. Not only did my position at the NDPC/N give me a whole new perspective on public education and teacher training; it allowed me to form life-long friendships with some of the most dedicated, hardworking people I have ever known.

NATIONAL DROPOUT PREVENTION CENTER:
Getting Started

JAY SMINK
National Dropout Prevention Center
1988–2011

Students were leaving our public schools long before the National Dropout Prevention Center (NDPC) was conceived at Clemson University. Although the university was recognized as a leading land-grant institution for higher learning, it mostly addressed the state's population and their issues found in South Carolina. Thus, it was very evident in 1883 that Thomas Green Clemson executed his will to improve the economic environment of South Carolina. With Clemson's will in place, the stage was set to expand the university's reach not only in the state but beyond the borders to other states with similar needs to guide students to earn a high school diploma.

One other significant event that gave direction to addressing the needs of high-risk students was the 1983 special report *A Nation at Risk*. This highly promoted and studied report provided evidence that America's schools were failing and creating large numbers of high school dropouts. The report warned school and political leaders to focus on improving our schools and graduation rates. Thanks to the data in this report and other critical evidence, the conditions were in place to focus on fixing America's schools.

Welcome to several initiatives that collectively were forming and setting the stage for the NDPC to become a reality at Clemson University. In 1985, the National Dropout Prevention Network was being developed to serve local school districts and state education agencies by focusing on model dropout prevention programs designed to increase graduation rates across the nation.

During the same time frame, the National Dropout Prevention Fund (NDPF) was formed in New York City by Esther and Jim Ferguson to serve the desperate needs of several high schools in New York City. The fund was guided by fifty representatives with experience in project management, legal issues, logistics, and communications. The fund's board of advisors offered recommendations to Fund Chair Esther Ferguson regarding business protocols, communications, and fund-raising. Jim Ferguson, a former CEO of the General Foods Corporation, was helpful in securing financial assistance to help start the NDPF and later the NDPC. An example of revenue development was the Gala Dinner Dance, hosted by Bill Cosby in the NYC Waldorf Astoria, which raised $450,000. One other notable recommendation by the board of advisors was to align the NYC-based fund to a prominent institution. Dr. Max Lennon, the president of Clemson University, and Dr. Horace Fleming, the director of the Strom Thurmond Institution at Clemson, were two of the board members advocating for moving the NDPF to Clemson University.

During this same period, a dropout prevention center was being designed by Professor Dick Hamby and Dr. Gordon Gray, Dean of the College of Education. It is worth mentioning that assisting the Clemson design team was Nancy Peck from the University of Miami, Ray Eberhart from the California state education agency, and myself from The Ohio State University. My responsibilities at the National Research Center for Vocational Education at OSU included developing a database of highly successful vocational technical programs to serve students in need. As the programs and services continued to be developed at OSU, it was obvious that a similar database would be appropriate at the developing NDPC. Several other programs and services developed at OSU were easily transferable to the new NDPC at Clemson.

With all the preliminary design work completed, the NDPC was launched with great fanfare on October 28, 1986. Many dignitaries, including State Superintendent of Education Charlie Williams, several state legislators, and South Carolina Governor Dick Riley, were present for the ceremony. Although much of the NDPC design work was completed, the biggest effort was now focused on finding a full-time executive director.

At this point, I found myself a candidate for the executive director position and was scheduled for the traditional set of university-based interviews, with the final interview scheduled with the president of Clemson University, Dr. Max Lennon. The final interview with Dr. Lennon turned out to be focused on one of his key areas of interest. He was very much aware of all the roles and responsibilities of a land-grant university and expected the NDPC services to be rendered to school and political leaders in South Carolina. However, his most important request to me was based on his keen interest in responding to the similar state needs in the remainder of the nation. In other words, he wanted to have the

NDPC provide all the services and programs available to every state. Quite honestly, his goal was to have Clemson University recognized as a national leader in the arena of serving high-risk students. His request to show Clemson University as a national leader clearly meshed with the NDPC's goals and objectives. Furthermore, many of the programs and services used at OSU clearly coincided with the NDPC's direction and mission. It seemed like a natural fit, and in 1988, I was chosen to help steer the continued development of the center. President Lennon asked me to report regularly and directly to the university provost, David Maxwell.

The NDPC at Clemson University had become the organizational anchor for the various institutions designed to address the high school dropout crisis. Therefore, one of the major services the NDPC had to address was the collection of highly successful dropout prevention programs; these programs would likely offer several common strategies to serve high-risk students. A collection of more than four hundred successful programs was given a thorough review, allowing the NDPC to identify the fifteen most effective strategies to help high-risk students graduate from high school. These strategies turned out to be some of the most prestigious and useful assets available from the NDPC. The strategies, well documented in the publication *Helping Students Graduate, A Strategic Approach to Dropout Prevention*, served as the basis for skill-development workshops, conference topics, grant-writing themes, local school-improvement efforts, state program requirements, and state and federal legislation. In addition to this basic publication, more than one hundred other publications, newsletters, professional journals, and other supportive documents were developed and became part of the NDPC revenue streams. All these efforts supported President Lennon's goal for the NDPC to meet state and national needs.

Since the beginning, the NDPC was fortunate to have a board of advisors to help guide the direction of the services provided to its clients. Those experienced leaders from various corners of America, representing businesses, legislators, community leaders, and educators, were also instrumental in fund-raising and helpful in finding new partners and new program efforts. Stuart Udell, the CEO of Catapult Learning, served as board chair for several years and was one of the more active board members, raising funds from his company and other businesses. Approximately seventy-five advisory board members were active over the life of the NDPC. I worked closely with these advisors, and these relationships were among the reasons I accepted the NDPC leadership position.

In closing, I must acknowledge that examples of the dropout prevention programs and services offered by the NDPC are endless. The programs are an integral part of every success story found in South Carolina and all other states. The mandates given to me by President Lennon are now readily visible in hundreds of dropout prevention programs in school districts across America.

Postscript: In 1986, a business owner offered the university a rent-free building in which to house the NDPC in downtown Clemson. After two years, the NDPC's growth required additional space—hence, the university moved the center on campus to a house at 209 Martin Street. The house, built in the early 1950s, was originally occupied by several university academic officials. Dr. David Maxwell was the last provost to reside there, and the Strom Thurmond Institute occupied the house temporarily while its new building was under construction on campus. The NDPC occupied the house from 1989 to 2019, when it moved off campus.

ALL ROADS GO THROUGH IOWA

Marty Duckenfield
National Dropout Prevention Center
1988–2018

I was standing in front of our director's desk in his wood-paneled office at the National Dropout Prevention Center on Martin Street, the impressive white house where the provosts once lived. I'd innocently come downstairs at his request, only to receive this unexpected news: "I need you to represent the center at a conference in Iowa and present a session on effective strategies. I know you can do it. You helped us by doing the research and helping us do the write-up." This was a shock. My heart skipped a few beats, and no wonder—after all, I'd been hired less than two years before as a data management and research analyst.

Nevertheless, six weeks later, I was on my first solo assignment. This time, I found myself standing anxiously at the gate at Greenville/Spartanburg Airport. On that fateful day in October 1990, I was about to board the first leg of a long day of travel, a flight to Washington, D.C. This was my first solo assignment, and going on my own was a bit unnerving, but as I looked out the window of the boarding area, what really had my nerves jangling was the large prop plane awaiting me on the tarmac.

The secretary at the Iowa Department of Education had booked my flight to Des Moines. When we had talked on the phone about schedules, I explained that I did not fly on "commuter" flights. I'd had a few prior bad experiences with commuters and had vowed, "Never again!" She seemed sympathetic, and I had few doubts that my request was understood.

A week later, I received the tickets in the mail. Looking at the itinerary, I noticed with chagrin that it would take three flights for me to get to Des Moines. I must have had at least one doubt, so I did some quick research: I called my friend Mark Malmgren, at Small World Travel, and asked him to verify that none of these were commuters. He promptly went into action, but the news was not good: The first airplane was a large prop plane—to me, a commuter flight. I turned pale and went into panic mode.

I immediately called the secretary back and requested that she change the flight. Although she apologized, she referred me to her boss, the director of Alternative Education and the conference host. She apparently told him about my request to change the flight, mentioning the cost of the ticket, before she connected us.

In our conversation, I told him about my deep-felt concerns. He listened attentively, but he pointed out that from his perspective, if they canceled my ticket, it would cost that much or more to rebook a flight, and he was not going to do it.

"Marty," he advised, "just take a Dramamine and get on the damn plane!"

Nice though he was, he was firm. I was cornered. It looked like my heartfelt appeals to his compassion had utterly failed. I would have to get prepared for the challenge. I bought the Dramamine.

Now at the gate, I took the drug. With all the courage I could muster, I boarded the steps to the door of the plane. Within minutes of my taking my seat and buckling in, the Dramamine kicked in, and I fell asleep before take-off. The next thing I knew, I was jolted awake as the plane made its noisy and bumpy landing. To my complete astonishment, we had arrived, safe and sound, in D.C. I can't even begin to tell you what a tremendous relief it was to have that first flight behind me.

The next leg of the trip was to Chicago's O'Hare Airport. The remainder of the long journey was full of delays and even a required overnight, but after the initial fears of the prop plane had been conquered, I found the strength to deal with the rest. The next morning, I finally got an early flight to Des Moines, arrived safely, took the shuttle, and checked into the hotel. The dreaded travel to Iowa had ended, and I had conquered my fears and successfully arrived. Nevertheless, the following day, it was time to enter the next even more frightening phase of this novel adventure.

Barely two years had gone by since I had been teaching at-risk fifth graders at an elementary school in Walhalla. Yet on that fateful Monday morning, I walked into one of the largest conference rooms in the old Hotel Fort Des Moines, a room filled with a noisy crowd of seventy-five Iowa alternative-school teachers, counselors, and administrators. They were waiting for me to present our specific dropout prevention solutions, as recently revealed in our new research publication, *The 12 Effective Strategies in Dropout Prevention*. Also awaiting me was an overhead projector and screen. I opened my briefcase, took out my handouts and transparencies, and signaled to the moderator that I was ready.

Over the years, I'd become comfortable speaking in front of groups, but this felt different. Suddenly, the stakes seemed so high. What had become a familiar conference scene when I was a member of the audience now was reversed as I became the speaker. I began to realize that because I was representing the NDPC *and* Clemson University, I had a temporary protective shield of credibility and respect. In addition, being a researcher for the past two years and a coauthor of the *12 Effective Strategies* gave me the credentials and the confidence in the results of that work. Although inside I still felt like an imposter, it soon became obvious that my audience accepted me as the real deal. I was dealt a strong hand, and it was time to play it.

In the remaining moments before I was introduced, one of the superintendents came up to talk with me, handing me his business card. He apologized that he'd have to leave early but requested that I please send him the information and transparency masters for the whole presentation. This was heady stuff, but it was just the beginning. As I was introduced and began my presentation, the talking suddenly ended, transformed into a courteous, respectful silence. It had to be magic! I'd never discovered such powers with my fifth graders. These educators seemed to hang on to my every word, as if each syllable possessed great pearls of wisdom. They were taking notes from every transparency, believing each unveiled the mysteries of how to keep kids, and especially alternative-school kids, in school. This apparent acceptance and appreciation of our research stunned me. I had found an audience who found this work valuable and important. Afterward, many of them came up to me to express their appreciation. Their words seemed sincere and heartfelt; for me, this unique experience was so rewarding. Maybe we could make a difference!

Once my official duties had ended, I was able to attend a session of my choice—to do as I had at other conferences, learn about education programs that might qualify as dropout prevention. The main thing I had already learned about conferences was that they were a place to find new ideas. I sat in on a session on service learning, my last stop before the long trip home. The trainers had come from Minnesota to conduct an introductory session on service learning. I was mesmerized. Service learning impressed me more than anything I had learned about in the past few years. Its experiential approach to authentic student engagement in their learning met so many of their needs. A seed was planted, and with so much to contemplate, I collected their materials, said my farewells, and headed to the airport.

I had much to ponder and three flights on which to mull it over. I thought about these two years of research and data collection, developing the effective strategies. Through this new center, Clemson had entered a field with a scarcity of research and even less material for actual practitioners. Due to the NDPC leadership of Dr. Jay Smink and Dr. Dick Hamby, our director and assistant director, practical answers had been revealed that became the *Effective Strategies*, the foundation of our center's work. I had just witnessed the value of these efforts for real educators.

At my session, I had observed with my own eyes how important these research-based solutions were to the educators. I became aware of how Clemson's role in supporting our center's efforts lent us the aura of credibility. I was beginning to understand the benefits of what a land-grant university does at its best—taking research, translating it into practical solutions, and making it easily accessible to those who thirst for it.

In addition to this powerful takeaway, there was so much more. In retrospect, the Iowa trip's series of experiences not only reflected a significant role the center would come to play in the K–12 education world but also defined and prepared me for my future activities beyond the research desk. All my subsequent roads emerged from that trip to Iowa: providing useable knowledge-based outreach through multiple avenues of professional development and creating my own area of expertise with a new effective strategy, service learning.

From that point on, I came to believe that the university's role in outreach was a great and good mission. I was privileged to be a part of it.

NATIONAL DROPOUT PREVENTION CENTER: Operate the Mission

Jay Smink
National Dropout Prevention Center
1988–2011

In 1990, I was approached in my Clemson University office by Dewey Blackledge, a Mississippi school district leader. Dewey had traveled to Clemson to have lengthy face-to-face discussions about how the National Dropout Prevention Center (NDPC) could help the Southeastern Mississippi Regional Alternative Education Cooperative (SMRAEC), a newly formed consortium consisting of eight separate school districts. The critical need for school improvement and reduction of the school dropout rates was, and is, perhaps more evident in Mississippi than in any other state.

By that time, the NDPC was only just beginning to develop its package of professional services for such clients as Dewey Blackledge. Typically, schools and school districts, state education departments, businesses, legislators, and interested local communities and organizations would call or write with a vast variety of inquiries. These inquiries revealed three ways we could respond.

First, these early clients initially sought information in many arenas, such as dropout statistics, successful programs, availability of funds, classroom teaching strategies, or best practices for working with students with disabilities. Second, if the NDPC didn't have the answers to the client's initial set of questions, we would make referrals to the relevant organizations with the specific expertise needed. Such an example is the Intercultural Development Research Association, where successful programs are available directly to Hispanic families with high-risk students. Third, the NDPC could offer help in the way of guided processes, whereby local school needs could be identified and diagnosed by participating in the NDPC-developed Program Assessment and Review (PAR) process.

The PAR process provided an on-site assessment and guidance service that worked with an assigned local school action team assisted collaboratively with skilled NDPC staff. The result of this process provided program options for the client to assess and implement. Once again, specific referrals were offered to the clients as needed. This assistance became characterized in several other dimensions, such as revenue development, grant-writing skills, links to successful community-based programs, classroom teaching strategies, assistance in partnership development, and skill-based instructional workshops available in local districts or at statewide or national conferences.

When the NDPC started to provide its services to numerous clients in Mississippi, the dropout rate was among the highest in the United States. After looking at the set of dropout statistics, it was an easy decision to offer our collective services to numerous clients in Mississippi. More than three decades later, it is exciting to see positive reports from varied groups, including a recent statement from the state agency leader: "The trend lines show that we are making improvement in our graduation and dropout rates."

I am pleasantly encouraged by the continuous efforts by each state education agency and the leadership they provide to their local school districts. Much work remains to be done, and the need for funds is greater than ever. However, the fifteen most effective strategies to increase graduation rates remain as a basic set of positive initiatives offered to each school and community to follow as their plans and actions are initiated and successfully completed. The fifteen effective strategies remain a treasured gift and guide to use while working with high-risk students not only in Mississippi but in every other state.

SPRING FEVER

Janice "Jan" G. Comfort
R. M. Cooper Library
1992–2019

It was spring break in 1994, and the Clemson campus was empty and covered with a powdery layer of yellow-green pollen. It was unnaturally quiet without the students, but that was about to change. Cooper Library was open and fully staffed. On this day, we were hosting a group of grade school students, which was unusual. Normally our tours were intended to educate, not entertain, but this was back in the day when we indulged local public school teachers and their young students who had spring fever. The kids were very excited to be on campus, even if it was just the library, and their excited chatter filled the lobby. To channel their energy, we sorted them into groups—two groups of girls and one group of boys. You know the drill. Librarians were strategically stationed throughout the space to give brief talks.

The interior looked quite different than it does today. The main floor was dominated by ugly orange carpet and large wooden tables with orange chairs, surrounded by many ranges of tall bookshelves with orange endcaps. The large card catalog had recently been replaced by an online catalog, so there were computers. And, of course, the circulation desk was featured prominently near the entrance of the building, with a reference desk and a security desk near the exit doors. I don't think that the students really believed that all six floors were full of books, but they were enthralled with the building. It was the first time many of them had ridden in an elevator. I pondered that thought as my group of girls marched in a crooked single-file line to the next stop on the tour.

We met the other group of girls in the Byrnes Room—named for a notable historical figure, not for a character in *The Simpsons*. This was to be the last educational stop on the tour. Next up was the Poole Agricultural Center (P&A Building), so we were all that was standing between the kids and their ice cream. The girls were getting restless, and they milled about sullenly as we waited. The tour leaders were trying desperately to keep their attention. We chatted informally about Mr. Byrnes to try to fill the time productively until the others arrived.

Finally, the boys strutted into the room. There was a noticeable change in the atmosphere. The girls were now full of smiles, posing and vying for attention. One particular boy was the object of their desire. I could see at once that he was the class leader. He had an air of confidence about him, even at the tender age of nine. When he realized that he had not learned why Mr. Byrnes had his own room, he gestured to one of the girls, as if to ask, "What'd I miss?" She summed up succinctly, "He dead." I looked over at my colleague Peg to make sure that she had heard this adorable exchange, and we shared a quiet laugh. This was to be a topic of conversation for many years to come.

One of the teachers finally goaded the students into silence. We stood together on the sidelines by the portrait of an unsmiling Mr. Byrnes as Peg took center stage. The students crowded around her, trying hard to avoid the glass display cases housing memorabilia and furniture that was not meant to be touched. The young class leader brushed past me until he was facing Peg, close enough to put his arms around her. He looked at her with rapt attention. Clearly, she'd

School children on a tour of the R.M. Cooper Library These photos (available from https://digitalcollections.clemson.edu) were taken in the Byrnes Room in 1966, so they do not fully reflect the reality of 1994. But they capture the flavor of a most memorable Library Tour. (With permission from the University Archives)

made an impression. She launched into her spiel. We never experienced listening at this level from our own students, and she warmed to her task. When she was done, the student looked up at her with an awed expression. He wanted to say something—he was nearly bursting with it. I could hardly wait to hear what it was. I braced myself, but nothing could have prepared me for his words: "You sure got a lot of fillings."

This time our laughter was *not* subdued. Peg and I howled. Once the teachers realized that there were no hard feelings, they joined in. Soon, the students were laughing, too, and the small room was filled with joyful noise. Who says that a library should be a quiet place? Even now I can hear the laughter, and the memory of the experience still brings a smile to my face.

I often wonder what happened to the kids in that group. The young class leader would be nearly forty years old now. Did he attend Clemson? Is he happy? I sincerely hope so. And I hope that he remembers his tour of R. M. Cooper Library at Clemson University in the spring of 1994.

The James Byrnes Room (available from https://digitalcollections.clemson.edu) (With permission from the University Archives)

THE LAND OF OPPORTUNITY AND AN HONEST WOMAN

Donna S. London
Strom Thurmond Institute
1987–2015

After serving as a local government planner in Charleston and Greenville, my initial employment with Clemson University began in 1987, under contract with the Strom Thurmond Institute (STI). Among the projects I worked on was a Consolidation of Services Study, which looked at issues facing university communities across the country where larger universities overwhelmed surrounding communities. This study led to the long-standing Joint City of Clemson and Clemson University Committee. My last project under this contract followed 1989's Hurricane Hugo, when I served on a Department of Energy–funded project to develop Energy Emergency Plans for the U.S. Virgin Islands and Hawaii. After a 1994 Australian sabbatical year with my husband and primary-school-age children, I took the position as director of Planning and Codes Administration for the city of Clemson. In 2000, I was hired back at the STI by Director Bob Becker to contribute to the research efforts of the institute and the Jim Self Center on the Future (JSCF) that was housed therein and to coordinate the activities of the Sustainable Universities Initiative (SUI), a consortium effort of the University of South Carolina, the Medical University of South Carolina, and Clemson University. Alan Elzerman was Clemson's SUI principal investigator. Later, I was named director of the JSCF, funded by the Self Family Foundation. In all, the research was challenging, interesting, varied, and, in my mind, a land of opportunity.

In addition to numerous other projects, we conducted a study and prepared guidelines for Tree Cities U.S.A. and the U.S. Forest Service on tree canopy preservation and expansion and how programs are administered and funded. The Southern Growth Policies Board commissioned a Visioning Handbook for local communities across the south. Other projects included assistance on a state plan for South Carolina Commerce Department's Recycling Market Development Council and Industries and a network scaling plan for Greenville-based Liberty Foundation's Fellows Program. One of the long-standing mainstays of our work was a biannual survey conducted in partnership with the University of South Carolina's Survey Research Lab that tracked citizens' perspectives relating to government, the economy, health, education, climate change, and other current or anticipated issues. The survey results guided the Self Center's research agenda and the Citizens' Guides that were posted online and distributed to state and local officials, libraries, and other affiliated organizations. Speakers and issue forums were hosted in conjunction with the Self Foundation and the Pew Charitable Trust. Particularly interesting was annual training for first-time political candidates, to help them prepare for campaigns and to promote respectable campaign behavior even when faced with heated situations. Studies showed that below-the-belt campaign tactics were having a dampening effect on voter turnout.

About the radio: Just after I joined the STI staff, Becker and I had a meeting with Bob McAnally, the director and producer of Clemson Radio Productions. McAnally was embarking on a daily radio magazine program airing on South Carolina Educational Radio, an affiliate of National Public Radio. Weekly segments on bugs, food, science, gardening, music, and two policy segments were on the agenda. Becker and I were tapped to cover the policy segments. Given the multidisciplinary policy work of the STI and the Self Center on the Future, contacts with a breadth of government and industry leaders, and many on-campus experts, the radio made sense from a communication and outreach standpoint. Any concerns about not having enough interviewees or worthwhile material were quickly dispelled. People doing interesting and meaningful work wanted to share their information and findings.

There were serious interviews on climate change, education funding, housing, health care, social security, taxation, food insecurity, and land and wildlife protection. South Carolina legislation, politics, and human-interest stories were shared. Likewise, a listener might hear from filmmakers, scientists, preachers, political cartoonists, authors, a tall ship captain, or an around-the-world sailor. Interviews were held with current and former governors, university presidents, mayors, and other state and national leaders. The list continues, and, to me, the program was a gold mine.

Another addition to the programming began in 2003, when the Public Broadcast System (PBS) and Educational Television (ETV) launched the South Carolina Channel, the first digital channel, with a rollout of a few years of road trips to all parts of the state. I am not sure how many cities and towns were visited, but all forty-six counties were included; it was an all television and radio hands-on-deck production. The television folks came in with their bright lights, cameras, big trucks, and equipment, and the Clemson radio folks came in with the same, minus the big trucks. It was an exciting production to my eyes, with live television/radio productions midday and in the evening. Histories of the state's settlements, railroads, waterways, town characters, and dignitaries were highlighted. Every road trip was a new, different, and enlightening experience. People brought their horses, llamas, and cows to the courthouse and their best pies, pickles, and barbecue to the park. Musicians and dancers performed, dignitaries spoke, artists displayed their creativity, and a variety of community fixtures helped us better understand what made their communities sparkle and different from the next. When I mentioned that our traveling radio show was headed on a road show, I would get a thrill when people would say it was their favorite show on PBS. Come to find out, they were talking about the more broadly distributed *Antiques Roadshow*. At the time, only a few of us were antiques, so we did not even try to compete on that front.

How did Clemson University Radio Productions help me become an honest woman? I didn't think of myself as dishonest. However, by not quelling a household rumor, I guess I was guilty by omission. It had started years earlier, when I was living in Charleston and went to the Hampton County Watermelon Festival with my family. We took many grainy, Instamatic photos that day, including one of the watermelon queen on her parade float. A few years passed, and my daughter came across a photo of the watermelon queen and asked someone in our family whether it was me. I don't remember the answer, but somehow she came away with the impression that I had been the watermelon queen. Several years later, we were headed to Hampton County for the road show. I mentioned to McAnally and Bob Schuster, my coworkers, my earlier trip to the Watermelon Festival and the photo, while downplaying any transgression. Later that week, at the midday show, I finished my on-camera segments, and while standing on the sidelines, I was approached by the guys and maybe the mayor or festival chair with a crown in hand. I was crowned the watermelon queen for the day. There was applause, or maybe I just thought that I heard it, but it was a big day for me. I held my head high the rest of day, and yes, the crown made me feel taller. When the evening show started, the so-called *real* watermelon queen was interviewed by someone else. I was incensed with that imposter! Then, I got a grip and tried to be cordial. Although I had long since set the record straight with my daughter,

I learned some lessons that day. First, be grateful for friends who try to make an honest person out of you when you should have fessed up earlier to your daughter. Also, everyone needs a crown at some point in life.

Production of the South Carolina ETV and Clemson University's *Your Day* radio program sadly ended after fourteen years, on November 13, 2014. I was happy to have had the opportunity to be a part of the program for that time period. I am grateful to Bob McAnally for including me on the journey into radio and to Bob Becker for insisting that it was okay to upset a listener if our interviews represented a variety of perspectives and attempted to broaden the public's understanding of the issues.

TRANSFORMATIONAL MOMENTS IN HABITAT FOR HUMANITY LANDSCAPE DESIGN SERVICE-LEARNING PROJECTS

MARY TAYLOR HAQUE
Department of Horticulture
1978–2010

One of the great gifts of teaching at Clemson University is getting to work with a wide variety of students from varied backgrounds. After teaching landscape design in the Department of Horticulture from 1978 to 2010, it's enjoyable to recall students, classes, projects, and a few of the surprises that spring up when working with college students.

Specializing in landscape design meant that I taught about sixteen different courses, ranging in size from design studios, which were necessarily and delightfully limited to fifteen students, to lecture classes, where seventy students were compressed into one of the larger P&A Building classrooms with the fire marshal's permission. The "P&A," otherwise known as the Plant and Animal Science Building or Poole Hall, houses a wonderful collection of classrooms, laboratories, and offices, but it is not the most architecturally interesting building on campus. One semester, I was struggling with the difficulties of getting to know seventy students in a long and narrow classroom that could be entered from doors at the front and back. Students in the front half of the class were recognizable and could be called by name, but it was hard to identify those sitting in the back rows. The task was made even more difficult in the dark setting necessary when showing slides or PowerPoint presentations to illustrate lectures.

One beautiful spring morning during turkey season in April, several of my "back row students," dressed in camouflage and most likely arriving straight from an early morning turkey hunt, slipped in late through the back door. I was presenting a slide of my brother's yard, which was located in the middle of the family tree farm in Fairfield County. The lecture topic for the day was sustainability and low-maintenance landscapes, and the grass in my brother's yard consisted of a golden field of broomsedge (*Andropogon virginicus*), a native pioneer species grass used to help with erosion control, water-wise landscapes, and wildlife habitat. Wild turkey and quail like the cover it affords their nests, and the photograph captured a gobbler and two hens in the broomsedge field, beautifully illustrating plant/animal relationships. As the slide came up and the hunters sat down, they spontaneously let out true-to-life turkey calls that made me feel like those turkeys had walked straight out of the picture and into the classroom! The calls elicited an uproarious laugh from the class, and I finally got to associate a great memory with the previously anonymous back row students in a large class!

Over an academic career spanning thirty-two years, I particularly enjoyed promoting sustainable landscape architecture through interdisciplinary partnerships and integrating student experiences that promoted education beyond classroom walls, thereby creating effective practitioners of the professions of horticulture and landscape architecture. My teaching has been grounded in the conviction that producing students who can think critically, communicate effectively, and develop professionally requires engagement with the world beyond campus. In my classes, students grappled with real problems and provided solutions that withstood the scrutiny of their peers and their chosen profession. Students learned not only the methodology of the discipline but also the ability to synthesize, think creatively and systemically, and collaborate with their peers and clients. The following project illustrates how my classes and our interdisciplinary teams here at Clemson translated the philosophy "think globally, act locally" into action.

When volunteering on Habitat for Humanity teams, I observed that local affordable housing projects focused only on constructing homes and, in the process, were eliminating wildlife habitats, grading without thought to stormwater runoff or erosion, and bulldozing existing trees that could have been saved for climate control, wildlife food, shelter, and aesthetic purposes. With local partners and colleagues, my students and I began working to spearhead landscape architectural solutions to the many problems that were being created. Classes with long afternoon studios and labs are a natural fit for hands-on community projects. It's more difficult with lecture classes, but I was determined to let one of them also participate. When working on a Habitat for Humanity construction site only five minutes from campus, I concluded that it was feasible to arrange for a seventy-minute lecture class to participate in a landscape implementation exercise. Imagine my delight when two students who had not scored well on tests or papers and who never spoke up in class unless called upon jumped into action and demonstrated superb leadership skills by organizing their classmates, assessing the site, seeing what needed to be done in a glance, doing it, and leading their peers by example with enthusiasm, energy, and insight. They were kinesthetic learners, and the traditional classroom geared for visual and auditory learners did not begin to showcase their skills and talents.

After several years of designing successful local projects, which included teaching volunteers how to embody the concepts of sustainable site design and teaching new homeowners how to become environmental stewards, a nationwide demand for these services began to grow. In response to demand, we formed interdisciplinary partnerships with the National Wildlife Federation, Habitat for Humanity International, the Sustainable Universities Initiative, the USDA Forest Service, and the Pew Charitable Trust, which enabled my colleagues and I to research, write, and distribute a book titled *Tree Conservation and Home Site Development Guide*, featuring student work, that was published by the National Wildlife Federation and distributed to all Habitat for Humanity Affiliates nationwide. Our goal was to have a "toolbox" of sustainable landscape architecture and horticulture techniques and principles available to the more than two million Habitat volunteers per year. With this publication, volunteer teams from all socioeconomic backgrounds nationwide are empowered to work together to create better habitats for people and wildlife.

Clemson University students, faculty, and staff, together with our many community partners, were honored with six awards between 1998 and 2002 for our various "Habitat Partners" projects, including a 2002 American Society of Landscape Architects Tri-State Merit Award for the book mentioned above, a 2001 SC Public Housing Award, a 2000 Clemson University Student Affairs Collaboration Award for the "Blitz-01: Student Community Development Project," a 1998 South Carolina Wildlife Federation Conservation Award in the Organization category, and a 1998 Housing Achievement Award from the SC State Housing Finance and Development Authority for the "Red Hills" project.

A disciple of the Communication Across the Curriculum Program at Clemson, I often invited students who demonstrated exceptional interest and ability to hone their communication skills through independent study courses, which culminated in giving presentations at professional society meetings. It was a proud moment for me to watch one such student receive first place in the 2000 American Society of Horticultural Science Collegiate Branch Oral Competition in Orlando, Florida, for her paper titled "Educating the Public about the Design and Implementation of Sustainable Landscapes for Low-Income Communities."

This approach to teaching students to help solve problems that are global in scale through collaboration and service-learning work on local projects, combined with broad dissemination of knowledge through publications, teaching, and speaking engagements, has been the hallmark of my teaching career. It has provided me with many pleasurable opportunities to get to know and appreciate not only those scholarly students who excel at writing, public speaking, and test taking but also those anonymous "back row students" who metamorphose out of their silent classroom cocoons into active community leaders in an informal, outdoor, service-learning setting.

ORIGIN OF THE STUDENT ORGANIZATION CLEMSON ENGINEERS FOR DEVELOPING COUNTRIES

LANSFORD BELL

Glenn Department of Civil Engineering

1989–2011

About twelve years ago, I was sitting in my office grading papers. Three civil engineering graduate students knocked on my door and asked to speak with me: "Dr. Bell, we would like to apply what we are learning in the classroom outside the classroom. Perhaps work in an underdeveloped country." I responded, "Okay, just what country do you have in mind?" Blank stares. I continued, "And just what exactly would you like to *do* in this underdeveloped country?" More blank stares.

I suggested that the students attend meetings of a local chapter of Engineers Without Borders. They did so and reported back to me that they did not want to be dictated to with respect to what projects to undertake and where. Instead, they wanted to start their *own* student organization.

We then soon discovered that the local Episcopal Church had a long-term presence in Cange, Haiti. When we contacted church members, they shared the tremendous need to somehow bring clean water to the village of Cange. The women in Cange were spending entire days hauling water up a steep mountain with jugs on their heads.

An informal agreement was reached with the church: We would design and help construct a clean water system, and the church would purchase the pumps, pipes, and purification system components. The students would fund their own travel.

The students then decided that they needed to become a formal Clemson University student organization so they could apply for Creative Inquiry Program funding. I agreed to serve as faculty advisor. The students, who by this time had grown to twenty or more in number, decided to name their organization

Clemson Engineers for Developing Countries (CEDC). CEDC polo shirts were distributed to all, which helped advertise our presence on campus. A generous amount of Creative Inquiry Program funding was soon forthcoming.

Work began immediately to design and construct a system that would pump and chlorinate water from the lake, uphill to the village of Cange. We recruited engineers from Flour and other organizations to assist us with our designs. Many students worked in Cange during their fall or spring break, and others as summer interns. Approximately one year after the organization was formally established, CEDC was the recipient of the Clemson University Service-Learning Project of the Year Award. It has since received numerous other national and international awards. Approximately ninety students currently serve as members of CEDC, representing more than thirty academic disciplines on campus. After completing the clean water initiative and numerous other projects in Haiti, CEDC is now working in other countries and to some extent (as a result of limited travel due to COVID) on public service projects here in the United States.

In my opinion, one reason for the success of CEDC is the fact that the students themselves took ownership of the organization. They devised their own organizational chart and selected their own officers and project leaders. I told the students that it was my job is to sign the paperwork and battle the CU administration, but they had to do everything else—and they did. It should be stated that the organization would never have flourished without consistent Creative Inquiry Program funding and the partnership with the Episcopal Church. It is interesting that numerous other university administrators and students have contacted CEDC officers, asking how they could replicate the CEDC concept at their institutions.

I have so many fond memories of my time serving as the first CEDC faculty advisor. Needless to say, I received many telephone calls from parents: "Is it safe for my daughter to spend her spring break in Haiti?" The answer was yes, for the Episcopal Church had a facility in Cange to house and feed the students.

One particular memory is fresh in my mind to this day. An outstanding civil engineering student named Lucy asked to speak with me, stating that she had just recently joined CEDC. She had no interest in designing pipes, pumps, or filtration systems; instead, she wanted to serve as head of CEDC public relations, recruiting other students and giving presentations to various civic organizations. My response: "Lucy, there is no way you can promote the work we are doing in Cange unless you personally have experienced our work in Cange. Telephone your parents tonight. Ask their permission for you to spend your spring break in

Cange." She did. One of my favorite photos of all time is of Lucy hugging two young children there.

Over the years, many former CEDC students, upon graduation, joined the Peace Corps. All former CEDC students received multiple employment offers long before graduation. To this day, I still receive emails from former students saying, in effect, "My CEDC experience changed my life."

CHAPTER 10

Reflection at the Vietnam Monument (With permission of photographer Delbert L Kimbler)

OUR TENTH BIRTHDAY

Delbert "Del" L. Kimbler
Department of Industrial Engineering
1987–2008

A high point of my time in the Emeritus College (EC) was the publication of a book memorializing the first ten years for the EC's tenth birthday celebration. I was a part of the team that produced this book, which depended much more on my photography than on my career in industrial engineering. Part of that story involves how I moved from engineer to photographer, and this began a few years before I retired.

My lifelong interest in photography got a new boost with the development of digital cameras—no more wondering where to put the darkroom! So, my photography took this new direction in late 2000 with my purchase of a Canon G1 (all of three megapixels) and an inkjet printer. The Canon was roughly the size and shape of a half-frame thirty-five millimeter I had in 1968; it was light and easy to carry. My process turned to camera and printing, with that messy film processing a thing of the past.

That camera became a constant companion in 2001. Travel, my back yard, and still lifes made of whatever was at hand became my palette. My darkroom became a computer, which not only took up much less room but didn't smell bad. Some of my first works (not very artistic) were of my film cameras, to be sold on eBay. I began exhibiting in the Upstate, mostly in Greenville and Clemson. By 2008, I had been juried into a few shows in the Upstate, had a few winners (and sales), and had enough prints to show my plunge into the digital art world. My retirement at Clemson University was celebrated at the Clemson Arts Center and included a show of some of my photography.

My entry into the EC brought with it closer contact with Cecil Huey and Sam Wang. Cecil and Sam were promoting the idea of emeritus life as an opportunity to take new directions, and I took this to heart. Photography became not just making pictures and showing the good ones but a creative process involving finding inspiration, making art, and displaying it with others. Around this time, the Clemson Photo Club was founded, and my volunteer work at the Clemson Arts Center came to include this new opportunity. Created by Karin Emmons and Russ Warmath, photography enthusiasts in staff positions in the Department of Parks, Recreation, Tourism Management, this new club was a great opportunity to network, learn, and exhibit.

All of this led to an opportunity from Larry Abernathy to create a photography book about Clemson. This became *Seasons of Clemson*, a book of photographs by volunteers who went out and took photographs on four scheduled days, one in each season, published by the Clemson Arts Center. I had written articles and a couple of books as an engineering professor but had never published one, so this was a highly educational process. Produced entirely by volunteers, with a publishing team of Debbie (Pagano) Feiste, Cheryl Lecroy, Beth Kimbler, and me, we had significant help from Hub City Press in Spartanburg and book design by Matt Merkle, a friend in advertising in Charlotte. The result was that we learned how to create a book a little bit at a time, and then we did it, thanks to the sixty-two photographers, most of them amateurs.

And now this narrative comes back to its title. In preparing for the EC's tenth birthday, Diane Smathers had the idea of publishing a book about the first ten years. Fred Sias, Deborah Thomason, and I were tasked with creating this book. Diane had a collection of photographs taken at EC events, Jerry Reel wrote a history of the first ten years, and we had photos of the distinguished emeriti over this period. Deborah, Fred, and I put together these and other pieces to complete the book.

My contribution, other than getting it published and printed, was an interview with Jim Barker and a collection of photos of new buildings on our campuses over the same ten years. This combined my experience as a journalism major decades ago, my enthusiasm for photography, and my brief experience in photography in book form. We did our own book design, and my desktop photography program was where the book creation took place.

And now, back to Cecil and Sam. It was their thesis, years before, that emeritus years are ripe for cultivating new interests and skills. Their influence on me was that part of my years that began just making pictures progressed through exhibiting and publishing and ended as serving a member of the Art Gallery on Pendleton Square. Including the evenings and weekends before retirement, my career as a photographer lasted almost eighteen years.

And what's next? New kinds of hobbies that stimulate the mind with less demand on the body. Acoustic mountain music, to complement banjo playing I learned in 1964. Watch repair, to satisfy my mechanical urges with things that are easy to lift and don't take up much space. Social action, with a local nonprofit that needs some help that my wife, Andi, and I are capable of giving. Just another step in what I believe that Cecil described as growing old in interesting ways. My deep appreciation to the EC for being the place that can allow that to happen. May the next ten years prove to be interesting as well.

THE NEW KID ON THE BLOCK MEETS THE ODD COUPLE

JOHN R. WAGNER
Departments of Chemistry and Geology
1976– 2010

I was the newly hired geologist in the fall of 1976. At that time, the geology program was housed in the Department of Chemistry and Geology in the old Brackett Hall. There were only five geology faculty when I arrived, all full professors: Paul Birkhead, Villard Griffin, George Haselton, Bob Hatcher, and Dave Snipes. We had no graduate program (and therefore no teaching assistants) but were experiencing a rapidly increasing enrollment in our introductory service courses. So, I was brought in to teach some lecture classes and labs and manage the labs. Not only was I new to the department; I was new to the South, having lived my whole life in Pennsylvania. Of the five other geology faculty, only George Haselton had not grown up in the South, but he was on sabbatical that year, and his position was filled temporarily by another southerner, Hugh Mills. So, I was the outsider, based on age, rank, experience, and cultural background.

In the midst of navigating all the complexities of teaching and functioning in a new department during my first semester, I learned that Bob Hatcher had enlisted the geology faculty to assist with a professional field trip he was leading for the Georgia Geological Society along the Blue Ridge Front and the Chattooga River that October. Different faculty would oversee different logistical aspects of the trip, which involved several stops and short hikes to view unusual rock exposures in the area. A key component of the day's activities was providing lunch for about one hundred participants at the Whitewater Falls Picnic Area in North Carolina. Bob Hatcher, as trip leader, would be involved with most activities at the different field locations; Dave Snipes was assigned to prepare and set up the lunch at Whitewater Falls and drive the food truck. Because Hugh Mills and I were new to the area and didn't know much about Blue Ridge geology at that time, we were assigned to help Dave Snipes with the food.

Although Bob Hatcher and Dave Snipes were both accomplished and well known in their fields and generally worked well together and got along most of the time, they were as different as night and day. Bob was strait-laced and serious about everything—a hard worker who was meticulous about details. Dave was the stereotypical absent-minded professor, whose office disorder was legendary and who was known for misplacing items and occasionally even forgetting to come to class. They resembled TV's "odd couple," Tony Randall and Jack Klugman, in so many ways, including physical appearance, dress, and demeanor.

One unusual event from that field trip has never been told. Only three people knew the story. Dave has since passed on, and Hugh and I were sworn to secrecy, but I believe that the statute of limitations has expired by now. At our penultimate field stop—before the group proceeded to Whitewater Falls for a hike to the falls, to be followed by lunch—the participants, led by Bob Hatcher, were loaded up into several vans to head to the falls. Dave, Hugh, and I stayed behind to drive Bob's pickup truck (which carried all the food) to the picnic area. I don't remember which of us discovered that the truck was locked and that the keys were inside, still in the ignition. There were no cell phones in those days, so there was no chance of contacting anyone who might have a spare key. Panic set in. I had always heard that you could sometimes open a locked car by threading a coat hanger wire between the window glass and the rubber molding and pulling up on the locking knob, but I had never tried that trick before. I'm sure this procedure could never work on today's cars, but we could come up with no better plan. The immediate problem was that we did not have a coat hanger. The three of us scoured the entire parking area until Hugh found a piece of wire in the bed of the pickup truck. I tried several times to hook the lock knob without success until, finally, I was able to get the wire in the correct position, and the lock opened. I'm sure that achievement was my greatest contribution to departmental esprit de corps during my first semester at Clemson. The rest of the story was noneventful. We got to the picnic area on time and had lunch ready when the crowd arrived. And Bob Hatcher never once asked why we were so late getting there.

CECIL, KATE, JIM, AND STEVE'S NOT-SO-EXCELLENT ADVENTURE

Stephen H. Wainscott
Honors College
1976–2010

The Scene: 1989 Citrus Bowl, Orlando, Florida
Principal Dramatis Personae: Steve and Sue Wainscott, Jim and Kate Palmer, and Cecil and Louise Huey

The events surrounding the 1989 Citrus Bowl in Orlando, Florida, will live in infamy for several of us emeriti faculty. We were members of the Clemson Athletic Council that year. The day before the game, consultations among the men about where to go for dinner favored nontouristy, "local" hangouts. We settled on an establishment with the promising name of "Ev's Oyster Bar," about twenty minutes outside Orlando. Ev's could have been charitably described as a seafood dive: Upon arrival, our party of twelve was immediately charmed by the screen door and the jammed gravel parking lot. Ah, this must be a great place! (It is well known that the best barbecue places sport "C" ratings from the Health Department. And flies. Lots of flies.)

The menu at Ev's featured just about everything a seafood lover could want: flounder (broiled and fried), grouper, tuna, shrimp, scallops, gator tail, and more. But the main attraction was oysters—baked, steamed, fried, broiled . . . and especially on the half shell. Heaven! Seven of us started out with a dozen each. Cecil and Steve each had two dozen more. Kate, on the other hand, had just two raw oysters.

She recalled later that she should have stuck with steamed oysters, but instead she wandered down to the end of the table where she was offered two raw oysters on the half shell, which she happily accepted. (By now, you probably know where this story is going.)

When we boarded the bus the next day for the game, those who had eaten the raw oysters, whether it was two or thirty-six, looked a bit green in the gills. When we got to the stadium, Cecil had turned a nice, deep lime color and

Citrus Bowl: Ev's Oyster Bar (With permission, original art by Kate Palmer)

immediately made his way to the first-aid station, where he remained for the entire game on a cot next to a woman who was "fourteen months pregnant," he reported. The rest of us managed to find our seats. Steve's was next to a friend of his who was not part of the Clemson Athletic Council group. Shortly into the game, he got up to get beers. A bit later, and not having taken a sip of his beer, Steve heard his friend's girlfriend whisper to him, "I don't think your friend likes me. He hasn't spoken a word to me." The friend looked over and, seeing that Steve's beer was sitting by his feet untouched, he replied, "If he's not drinking his beer, he must be sick."

At the end of the game, we managed to retrieve Cecil (who by this time had turned pea green) from the first-aid station and boarded the bus for the return to our hotel. By this time, all the oyster eaters had experienced numerous visits to the restrooms and couldn't wait to get back to our hotel rooms to die in peace.

Kate didn't go to the game. Instead, she and Louise Huey took their four children to Epcot Center. The oysters began to turn on Kate about midday, but she thought that she was "just getting a migraine." It wasn't until the group was in the World of Motion that Kate realized that she urgently needed to get back to the hotel! The group miraculously arrived there without incident, even with a rapidly deteriorating Kate at the wheel. Bursting unceremoniously into her hotel room, Kate caught a glimpse of Cecil's legs laid out on the floor behind the far bed (more on this later). By then, the unafflicted had noticed that some of the party were violently ill, but nobody yet suspected the oysters. Louise took the four kids to stay with her in the Hueys' room across the hall, in case it turned out to be a contagious stomach virus. Louise was horrified when the children all ordered pizza for supper!

When folks who attended the game arrived at the hotel, the unafflicted, having realized that a minor epidemic might be at hand, decided it would be best to quarantine the soon-to-die oyster eaters in separate rooms. This was because those of our group who could still think rationally still didn't suspect the oysters and thought that it could be the aforementioned contagious stomach virus. So, quarantine seemed to be a good idea. Of course, this entailed a goodly amount of "spouse swapping"—for example, Cecil Huey and Kate Palmer were designated as roommates for the night. Kate recalled telling Cecil later that spending the night with him was "not all she had dreamed it would be."

Jim Palmer, being of sound mind and body and having access to a car, was designated to call Byron Harder, the Clemson team physician, to ask whether he could provide some anti-nausea/diarrhea medicine for the corpse impersonators. Byron called back and said to come down to the team hotel at SeaWorld, and he'd have some meds at the desk. So, Jim left Kate and Cecil in their sickroom, drove to SeaWorld to pick up the meds, and then headed back to Orlando, where he rationed them out to the sick ones.

Meanwhile, Steve was left in a hotel room to die alone. Sue and their eleven-year-old daughter, Stephanie, decided to ride out the night elsewhere. At one point, maybe about 2:00 A.M., Stephanie came to the room and asked her dad whether she could get him anything. In his misery, Steve said, "Yeah, bring me a gun." The next thing they knew, Stephanie was running down the hall, shouting, "My dad wants to shoot himself!"

Back in Cecil and Kate's room, Cecil lay on his back with his hands in the pockets of his khaki pants on one bed, and Kate suffered on the other. Cecil never moved a muscle all night. He never got off that bed, stoically keeping all his bodily fluids to himself—a feat that it was not within any other human's power to achieve. Jim lay on the floor in the room. Neither Cecil nor Kate could bear the flickering light from the silent TV Jim tried to watch.

Sue Wainscott came into the Palmers' room at one point, stood at the foot of the two sickbeds, and announced that she knew that they all felt bad, but the least they could do was to "try not to scare the children." It didn't make sense to Kate and Cecil until later, when they learned of Steve's earlier request for a firearm.

The next day, the oyster eaters had recovered enough to make the drive back to Clemson, but all were too weak and sleep-deprived to do the driving. After they checked out, Sue went back to the hotel desk to ask whether she could buy a pillow for Steve so he could sleep in the back seat. After being told that pillows could not be sold, she drove to a discount store and bought one.

With the Palmers' two children in the back seat of the car, Jim kindly released the front passenger seat to an almost reclining position. By then, the meds prescribed by Byron Harder had given Kate a more positive view on the prospect of continuing to live. She stayed in a semi-fetal position for the entire trip home.

Epilogue:

Ev's Oyster Bar no longer exists, but we are fairly sure that our experience there thirty-three years ago was responsible for today's restaurant warnings about consuming raw or undercooked shellfish.

And time has tempered our caution; in the manner of "getting back on the horse that throwed us," we do look forward to oyster roasts these days. And some of us have even been known to enjoy a raw oyster (or several) on a saltine with a little seafood cocktail sauce.

In 1989, as we sufferers lay there in our world of misery, none of us would ever have believed that our Citrus Bowl misfortunes would one day be the slightest bit amusing. But now, so many years later, whenever we get together, the Citrus Bowl story remains a staple of conversation. It has become the stuff of legend. From the constant retelling, each of the "characters" knows the others' experiences almost as well as our own. And we laugh. A lot.

FROM HERE TO EVERYWHERE

CHARLES W. DUNN
Department of Political Science
1972–1998

The year was 1972, and I was on the faculty of the University of Illinois in my home state, the Land of Lincoln, having no desire to leave. But the telephone rang from a totally unexpected place, Clemson University, best known for its football teams, with H. Morris Cox, Dean of the College of Liberal Arts [name] asking whether I would come for an interview to become the head of its soon-to-be-created Department of Political Science. Well, I thought, why not visit that faraway place? And so, I came.

My first impression was not what I expected. These people in the foothills of the mountains were friendly, respectful, and serious about Clemson's academic reputation, and I enjoyed everyone I met. But that did not seal the deal on my interest in Clemson. It was that second interview, which my wife, Carol, and I had with Clemson's Dean of Liberal Arts Morris Cox, a southern gentleman and scholar whose demeanor and desire, especially as a senior professor of English, spoke eloquently about his aspirations for Clemson. Oh, and he just incidentally housed us on the top floor of the Clemson House, with its commanding view of campus.

Yes, all's well that ends well. But would the final stop along the way of that second interview end well? For, you see, Dean Cox had to usher me into the President's Office for a meeting with President R. C. Edwards, a business executive and active Democrat. I was neither. But we both rose to the occasion. I left there a believer in Dean Cox's leadership ability and President Edwards's unexpectedly high regard for the academic community. And so, I returned home, ready to accept Clemson's offer.

EARLY YEARS

My background before coming to Clemson included two years at the University of Illinois, one year as a postdoctoral fellow for the governor of the state of

Washington, four years as an administrative assistant to members of the U.S. House and U.S. Senate, counsel to the Legislative Committee of the Illinois Constitutional Convention, and speech writer to the convention president. By virtue of these and other countless opportunities over the next twenty-five years, Clemson became the guiding light of my career.

Illustrative of these opportunities during my first two years was the privilege of delivering "My Last Lecture" at the annual liberal arts honors and awards convocation, where I tested my Christian faith against the university's intellectual antagonists and scholarly critics. And in the political realm, I well remember the morning before a major football game when President Edwards called to personally ask me to introduce the governor of South Carolina, live at halftime on television that afternoon on the fifty-yard line. Opportunities like these came early and often.

Unannounced, for example, Dr. A. M. Moseley, of Greenville, South Carolina, showed up in my office, carrying with him an offer to begin the Robert A. Taft Seminars in Government for high school teachers from throughout South Carolina. He said that he wanted Clemson and no one else to host these seminars, which would be funded by the Taft Institute in New York City. So it was that every summer, thirty high school teachers came to Clemson to personally meet with South Carolina's leading political authorities, including the governor. And afterward, we televised the seminars on ETV.

Now, why does Clemson have a Thurmond Institute and not a Byrnes Center?

Some years ago, Clemson's then–academic vice president, Victor Hurst, asked me on behalf of President Edwards to develop a proposal for a new institute that would strengthen Clemson's identity with government and public affairs for faculty and students. The completed proposal, which I delivered to Dr. Hurst, bore the name James F. Byrnes Center of Government. And why not? Byrnes had served in more prestigious positions than almost anyone anywhere, including governor of South Carolina, U.S. senator, U.S. congressman, assistant to the president of the United States, and U.S. Supreme Court justice. And he was also a member of Clemson's Board of Trustees.

But time passed, and nothing happened—until Harry Durham in Clemson's Communications Office hurriedly came to my office early one morning in need of help, ASAP. "Word on the street was out": Senator Strom Thurmond planned to donate his papers to the University of South Carolina, and to counter that, President Atchley planned to fly to Washington the next day to make a counteroffer. When Mr. Durham left my office that morning, I went to my files, pulled out the file for the James F. Byrnes Center of Government, and replaced it with the Strom Thurmond Institute of Government. President Atchley delivered that proposal, and Clemson once again upset South Carolina.

LATER YEARS

Four words highlight the later years of my North Star experience at Clemson: *Fulbright, travels, television*, and *books*. Who would have thought that someone sitting in a small office in Daniel Hall would receive a call from the White House, asking whether he would be interested in a presidential appointment to the U.S. J. William *Fulbright* Board, a twelve-member board that governs the Fulbright Program worldwide? After catching my breath, I said, "Yes," but then I was told that I must undergo all FBI and other intelligence checks for this position.

Time passed slowly, oh so slowly, so slowly that I began to wonder whether I had passed the intelligence checks. And then, finally, the call came: "The president will appoint you to the Fulbright Board tomorrow."

Now, what did I know about the Fulbright Board? Not much. I had grown up on the wrong side of town, a block from the railroad tracks. My father was a railroader, my mother was a maid, and neither had finished the eighth grade. But I soon learned that Clemson had well prepared me to debate the issues of international scholarly exchange with Fulbright Board members from America's most prestigious institutions: Harvard, Yale, University of Chicago, and others. I had the privilege of setting three records of service on the Board: serving eight years as a member, acting six years as chair, and serving under three presidents, Ronald Reagan, George H. W. Bush, and Bill Clinton.

Travels for the Fulbright program took me to many countries, including China, Russia, Austria, Indonesia, Italy, Mexico, Israel, Japan, and others. And, of course, quarterly board meetings to Washington were always on the travel schedule. Another venue, *television*, gradually began to offer other opportunities, first locally on WYFF-Channel 4 and then nationally on ABC, CBS, NBC, and FOX.

Finally, the fourth word, *books*, represents the publication of some twenty-two written and edited books published by Pearson Prentice Hall, The University Press of Kentucky, Scott Foresman, Rowman & Littlefield, Madison Books, Addison Wesley Longman, HarperCollins, and others. The book titles include *The Seven Laws of Presidential Leadership*, *The Future of the American Presidency*, *The Scarlet Thread of Scandal*, *American Democracy Debated*, and *American Culture in Peril*.

From Here to Everywhere

I write these words as an expression of gratitude to Clemson, the North Star or guiding light of my career, which two of Abraham Lincoln's best, but not-so-well-known, quotes put in proper perspective:

- "In the end it's not the years in your life that count. It's the life in your years."
- "I will study and be prepared should my time come."

MY JOURNEY WITH CLEMSON

B. Merle Shepard

Department of Entomology and Charleston Research and Education Center
1971–2017

I met my colleague Dr. Dan Janzen at a Tall Timbers meeting in Florida while I was a doctoral student at Texas A&M. Dan told me about a project on tropical ecology that he oversaw in Costa Rica under the auspices of the Organization for Tropical Studies, which has its headquarters at Duke University. Every year, students could apply for National Science Foundation (NSF) funding to attend the tropical ecology course. I applied for funding for the course and was lucky to be accepted.

I graduated from Texas A&M University in 1969 and took a job as assistant professor at the University of Florida's Research and Education Center in Sanford, Florida. I was there for about a year, and during this time I met Sydney Hays, who was head of the Entomology and Economic Zoology Department at Clemson. Syd and I were attending an entomology conference in Mobile, Alabama. After a brief conversation, Syd hired me on the spot, and we shook hands. In those days, the department head did the hiring and firing; there was no Selection Committee. I resigned my position in Sanford, Florida, and started working at Clemson in 1971. Shortly thereafter, I developed and taught two graduate courses: Insect Ecology and Insect Pest Management. I also conducted research on insect pest management (IPM), supported by a grant from the NSF. My research focused on developing pest management strategies and tactics that did not rely on insecticides. My close colleague at Clemson was Dr. Gerald R. "Gerry" Carner. Gerry was an insect pathologist and carried out research using microbial agents that specifically target pest insects without harming the naturally occurring beneficial species, such as predators, parasitoids, and pathogens.

After directing the graduate programs of more than twenty master's- and doctoral-level graduate students, I left Clemson in 1971 to join the International Rice Research Institute (IRRI) in Los Baños, Philippines. IRRI is one of about twenty international centers around the world that are funded through the Consultative Group on International Agricultural Research (CGIAR) via support from the NSF and multiple other donors. Examples of other CGIAG centers include the International Center for Tropical Agricultural Research (CIAT) in Calle, Colombia. During my time at IRRI, I published more than twenty refereed papers and four books and directed the graduate programs of about ten graduate students who were studying at the University of the Philippines at Los Baños (UPLB).

I rejoined Clemson as director of the Coastal Research and Education Center in Charleston, South Carolina, and remained in that position until I retired in 1998. Even after retirement, I still kept my office and lab at the U.S. Vegetable Laboratory. This lab was constructed with funds from a special grant from Congress, due largely to help from Senator Ernest Hollings, who actively lobbied Congress to support a proposal to build a new vegetable lab on Savannah Highway in Charleston. The lab is shared by Clemson and USDA scientists, and many collaborative projects take place there.

I continued to carry out international agricultural research during my time here in Charleston with several of my colleagues at Clemson. Mike Hammig, professor of agricultural economics at Clemson, was the principal investigator on the projects in Brazil and Indonesia. More recently, I visited Cuba with a group from Virginia Tech. We visited many farms where no pesticides were used. When Russia stopped subsidizing pesticides in Cuba, the farmers and agricultural researchers there had to find alternatives to chemical use. As a result, they became leaders in more ecologically stable and sustainable methods of pest control.

ADDRESSING ISSUES OF THE DAY

JAMES LONDON
Department of City & Regional Planning
1985–2013

As I look back on my academic career, there are a lot of memorable experiences. Particularly rewarding was the opportunity to contribute in small part to the long history of Clemson's research and consultation on important state policy issues. As a land-grant institution, the university from its earliest days provided significant research and extension support to the state's important farm sector. Significant contributions have also been made to the state in terms of economic development policy and natural resource management.

Clemson faculty led by George Aull were very much involved in articulating the state's rural industrialization effort, which proved successful over time in raising living standards in the state. Over the middle decades of the twentieth century (1930–1970), the state had the highest percentage gain in per-capita income of any state in the United States; granted, the starting base was low. The driving force was the shift of New England textile manufacturing to the Carolina Piedmont and with it the ancillary activity that included apparel, fabricated textile products, chemicals and synthetics, and textile machinery. Clemson's textiles and industrial management programs were important in supplying management talent as well as technical support.

I came to Clemson in 1975 as a doctoral student in applied economics. My master's thesis at the University of South Carolina, focusing on the role of the textile cluster in affecting economic development in the state, paralleled some of the work that Jim Hite and his students were doing at Clemson. My first research project as a doctoral student was to work with Jim Stepp on the impact of the proposed Richard Russell Dam and Lake on South Carolina. That project was my first, and Dr. Stepp's last, project before he retired. Because of the study, the project was reauthorized to include pumped storage, an oxygen injection system to minimize fish kills above and below the dam, and other concessions to offset the loss of option value on the land lost to the state. This project continued the involvement of Clemson faculty in natural resource issues going back to Dr.

"

Aull's consolidation of the Clemson Experimental Forest in the 1930s and the university's role in shaping state water policy during the drought years of the 1950s.

Following in the footsteps of Drs. Aull and Stepp, by the 1970s, Jim Hite was an important sounding board for state policy makers. The road was well traveled to what Hite referred to as "Baghdad on the Congaree." My dissertation project came at the request of the Governor's Office to Jim to look at future higher-education needs for the state, given industry and occupational projections over the next twenty years, including what academic areas were most likely to be in demand in the twenty-first century. Meanwhile, Jim was pulled over to a local government tax study with Horace Fleming and Holly Ulbrich that would lay the groundwork for the Strom Thurmond Institute (STI) to follow.

Although I had left Clemson to take a faculty appointment at the College of Charleston, I was asked by Jim to work on the state's coastal erosion plan through the relatively new State Coastal Council. The research team included faculty from the University of South Carolina's (USC's) Geology Program with Miles Hayes, one of the country's top coastal geologists; the Civil Engineering Program at Clemson with Billy Edge and John Fisher, both leaders in the field; and USC's Law School with John Montgomery, the associate dean. That level of collaboration across disciplines as well as institutions to address emerging issues was indicative of much of the policy initiatives undertaken over the years.

I came back to Clemson in 1985 with a joint appointment in city and regional planning and the STI. At the institute, I joined Jim Hite on a four-year water project for the state, looking at long-term needs and options. Project collaboration in this case included geography and economics programs at USC as well as water resource engineers, economists, demographers, political scientists, and planners at Clemson. Led by the USC geographers, the project set up for the first time a GIS database within one of the state agencies, layering watersheds, political boundaries, water flow data, and current and projected water demand.

That project was followed by an STI study on the impact of infrastructure on economic development, in collaboration once again with the same USC partners. The project mapped water and sewer lines as well as transportation infrastructure statewide along with industry locations and geo-referenced economic and demographic databases. It was the first such statewide database in the United States and was later replicated in other states. In South Carolina, the information base was incorporated into the state's target industry focus, which included access to infrastructure, workforce availability, and other socioeconomic indicators.

A three-year project for South Carolina Department of Transportation on funding options examined current state funding that at the time included the second-lowest gas tax in the country and simulated alternative funding mechanisms to determine how each individually or in combination closed the funding gap in meeting projected transportation needs. The project was instrumental in the enactment of a long-debated increase in the state's gas tax.

The earlier work relating to coastal shoreline management continued over the years, including a follow-up project through the STI looking at the state's Beachfront Management Plan twenty years after enactment. Later work focused on climate adaptation, including applications in Caribbean Island states that turned full circle from the early work on shoreline change in South Carolina.

Along the way, in the early 1990s, I had a chance to work with Bill Ward on a World Bank study to look at options for reducing greenhouse-gas emissions in China, the first country study for the United Nation Intergovernmental Panel on Climate Change following the Rio Conference. With Chinese partners and European industrial engineers, we conducted twenty-five industrial case studies to examine the cost and potential emissions reduction of introducing energy-efficient industrial technology. Twenty-four of the twenty-five cases were no-regrets projects with positive economic and environmental benefits. What the bank referred to as "the Clemson model" would serve as an assessment framework in other country studies.

As for the state policy initiatives, that work unfortunately began to lose momentum for a number of reasons. The core of the STI faculty pool, including Jim Hite, Horace Fleming, Bruce Yandle, and Holly Ulbrich, was disappearing. Meanwhile, the political winds were shifting, and state leaders seemed less interested in in-depth policy analysis. Tight agency budgets curtailed multiyear projects that had been the lifeblood of the institute. Although the Experiment Station had once provided support for some of the projects, that level of support had disappeared much earlier. The university, also feeling a pinch from reduced state funding, tightened its belt and began requiring institutes and centers to be self-supporting.

Still, looking back, not many universities, land grant or otherwise, were involved over the past century in addressing emerging state policy issues to the extent that Clemson was. I am indebted to those who laid the groundwork and am happy to have participated in some small way in that effort. I hope that the university can play a meaningful role assisting the state in addressing emerging issues going forward.

NOT EVERYONE NEEDS DUCKS . . .

Richard M. Kaminski

James C. Kennedy Waterfowl & Wetlands Conservation Center

2015–2021

Not everyone needs ducks, but everyone needs wetlands that produce clean air and water, plus plants, ducks, and other waterbirds and wildlife. So, what are wetlands? Wetlands are landscape depressions that have hydrology, hydrophytic plants, and hydric soil; the prefix *hydro-* means "water." Thus, wetlands are wet places on Earth, temporarily, seasonally, or permanently flooded, that support aquatic life.

Wetlands and their intrinsic plants help produce clean air and water, lessen impacts of hurricanes and floods, capture carbon to reduce greenhouse gases, and provide habitats for invertebrates, fish, waterfowl, and other wildlife. They also enable people to enjoy beaches, fishing, oystering, hunting, boating, and watching wildlife. Collectively, these diverse wetland ecosystem services contribute billions of dollars annually worldwide. Incredibly, South Carolina is vastly and diversely rich in wetlands, from the Piedmont to the Lowcountry.

I'm a waterfowl and wetlands ecologist and conservationist. I've practiced this profession since the early 1970s, working as a research biologist for Ducks Unlimited-Canada and as a waterfowl and wetlands professor at Mississippi State University (MSU) and Clemson University (CU). I served MSU from 1983–2015 and CU from 2015 until my retirement in October 2021.

In the 1990s, I began observing a significant decline in the number of university-based waterfowl and wetlands programs across the United States and Canada, despite the importance and values of these natural resources; about 40 percent of these university programs vanished or were replaced with other disciplines (e.g., conservation of biodiversity) after waterfowl professors retired, moved, or passed. Papers have been published asking "Who will mind the marsh?" to broadcast the need for new generations of waterfowl and wetlands professionals to study and steward these natural resources.

In 2000, I met Mr. James C. Kennedy, an Atlanta, Georgia, businessperson and philanthropist who remains deeply engaged in waterfowl and wetlands conservation in North America. Mr. Kennedy asked me what might be the fate of the waterfowl and wetlands program at MSU when I retired. Given how impressed he was with teaching, research, and outreach from our program, he funded and created an endowed chair at MSU in 2008, allowing the waterfowl and wetlands program there to persist in perpetuity. This James C. Kennedy Endowed Chair in Waterfowl and Wetlands Conservation was the first such endowed chair at a university at the time. Currently, there are eleven endowed university waterfowl programs (ten in the United States, one in Canada). Graciously, Mr. Kennedy has funded four of these endowments, including the second such endowment at CU.

I was fortunate to serve as the Kennedy Chair at MSU until my retirement in early 2015. Mr. Kennedy was so impressed with our accomplishments at MSU that he inquired about establishing a similar endowed program in his home state of South Carolina. Because CU hosts an internationally respected Wildlife Science and Management Department and degree programs, I suggested that Mr. Kennedy consider CU, especially given the importance of South Carolina to North American waterfowl and CU lack of expertise in waterfowl ecology and management at that time. Thus, CU was invited to submit a proposal to Mr. Kennedy in 2014. He gifted the university $3.3 million to establish the James C. Kennedy Waterfowl and Wetlands Conservation Center. Because of South Carolina's wealth of wetlands and waterfowl in the Lowcountry and the existence of CU's Belle W. Baruch Institute of Coastal Ecology and Forest Science in Georgetown, South Carolina, the Kennedy Center was headquartered at the Baruch Institute on the 16,000-acre Hobcaw Barony, bequeathed by the Baruch family to South Carolina universities.

What a unique, exciting, and privileged opportunity to become the inaugural director of CU's James C. Kennedy Waterfowl and Wetland Conservation Center, especially after also serving as the Kennedy Chair at MSU. Dr. James T. Anderson succeeded me as director of the Kennedy Center in August 2021. Dr. Anderson is continuing past programs and has launched new initiatives for the center with several graduate students.

I can't begin to tell all that we do at these Kennedy Centers. The CU's Kennedy Center was established in 2015; all of its annual reports can be read or downloaded by clicking on them in the lower left corner of the center's home page.

In conclusion, everyone may not need ducks, but we all need wetlands to provide us with clean air and water and their other myriad ecosystem services. If these wetlands are naturally functional and do provide clean air and water, they will also provide habitats for ducks and other animals and plants, all of which are bioindicators of healthy natural environments. I needed ducks in my life; that need has allowed me to teach, research, and serve two outstanding land-grant institutions and the people of Mississippi, South Carolina, and North America. Indeed, ducks are important to me but not most important in my life. To quote a dear friend and colleague, Dr. Guy Baldassarre, "Family is first; there is no second."

TILTED ARC

Donald L. Collins
College of Architecture
1972–2005

American artist Richard Serra's controversial sculpture titled *Tilted Arc* came to my attention in the mid-1980s when I read an article about it in *TIME Magazine*. The eighty-foot-long piece, made of Corten steel, had recently been removed from the plaza in front of the Jacob Javits Federal Building in Lower Manhattan. On reading the article, I had a brainstorm: I knew just the place where *Tilted Arc* should be reinstalled. But first, a little background on the controversy surrounding the piece and, more specifically, where it was installed and why it was removed.

Tilted Arc was commissioned by the U.S. General Services Administration (GSA) as part of its "Art-in-Architecture" program. People were used to seeing statues of generals on horseback or statues of Greek gods or goddesses. *Tilted Arc* was created not to beautify the public space but to prompt passers-by to experience the sculpture in a physical way. Critics decried the installation as big and ugly and wanted it removed. Supporters of Serra claimed that removing the sculpture would infringe on his First Amendment right to free speech.

Eventually, the GSA appointed a panel to hold public hearings and, at the conclusion of these hearings, voted to relocate *Tilted Arc*. Serra countered that the sculpture was site-specific and sued the GSA for violation of his contract and his First Amendment rights. He lost, and *Tilted Arc* was removed.

I knew nothing then about the artist's position on the piece—only that Clemson University could gain a great deal of publicity and notoriety if *Tilted Arc* were to be fittingly installed on campus. I was so bold as to believe that I knew the ideal place on campus: the open area between the Cooper Library and the Strom Thurman Institute. The tilt and arc of *Tilted Arc* would be a perfect metaphor for Senator Strom Thurman, who, in the long arc of his political career, had leaned over and switched political parties.

It was not my intention for Thurman's "tilt" to be the center point of my argument for bringing *Tilted Arch* to campus. Quite the opposite—the metaphor would be there, just unspoken. After all, Thurman was still alive at the time. My sales pitch was going to center on the notoriety that would accrue to Clemson University. I could even see people coming to the campus who might not have ever had a reason to visit, just to see *Tilted Arc*.

To advance my vision, I needed allies—or *an* ally. John Acorn, head of the Department of Art in what was then the College of Architecture, was the first person to come to mind. Acorn was a logical choice because he was also a sculptor. He would surely know of Richard Serra and the controversy surrounding the piece. Perhaps he could add insight to my strategy.

On hearing my idea, Professor Acorn told me that he would be in New York City in a few weeks for an art association conference where Serra was to be a keynote speaker. Acorn said that he would speak to him about my vision and see what Serra thought. It never happened. Acorn was in line, waiting to speak to Serra, when a person just ahead asked Serra about taking *Tilted Arc* out of GSA storage and installing it somewhere else. Serra was offended by the suggestion. He went off on a tirade about *Tilted Arc* being created for a specific location, vowing that he was never going to let it be installed anywhere else as long as he

Tilted Arc (With permission ....)

was alive. I think a few expletives were mixed in his speech as well. Acorn said that he shrugged his shoulders and walked away.

But I have not changed my mind. I still believe in my crazy brainstorm. *Tilted Arc* would be a fitting piece for the area between Cooper Library and Strom Thurman Institute. Maybe someone in the future will pick up on my brainstorm. Someday. Maybe.

Printed by Libri Plureos GmbH in Hamburg,
Germany